New York

Random House

Michael Stern

no innocence abroad

Second Printing

Copyright, 1947, 1948, 1950, 1951, 1952, 1953, by Michael Stern
All rights reserved under international and Pan-American
copyright conventions. Published in New York by Random House,
Inc., and simultaneously in Toronto, Canada, by Random House
of Canada, Limited.

Library of Congress Catalog Card Number: 52-5873

Manufactured in the United States of America
by H. Wolff, New York
Design: Marshall Lee

Picture credits: 1, Wide World; 2, AP Newsphoto; 3, photo
by the author; 4, photo by the author; 5, Acme; 7, Wide World;
8, Wide World; 9, True Magazine

preface

In making this collection of unusual portraits I leaned heavily on friends and enemies of the subjects, an admirable method for securing balanced results. To these friends and enemies, scattered in many corners of the world—indeed, to the subjects themselves for having "sat" for me—my thanks for their co-operation.

Because all these people were in such distant parts, the time and expense involved in running them down was considerable and so, to *True: The Man's Magazine* and to Ken Purdy, its very able editor, my heartiest thanks for having picked up most of the tab. My thanks, too, to Ralph Daigh, editorial director of the Fawcett

Publications, publishers of *True,* for allowing accuracy in reporting to be more important than expense.

My thanks, finally, to General Luigi Gallo, director of Linee Aeree Italiane (LAI) whose planes were the quickest and most comfortable means of getting both myself and the manuscript from Rome to the publisher's office in New York City.

Michael Stern
Villa Spiga
Rome, Italy
December 9, 1952

1 **Freddy McEvoy** | p. 3   2 **Luciano — Rome, 1951** | p. 27

3 **Giuliano** | p. 63

4   George John Dawson | p. 115

5   **Rossellini** | p. 157

6 Virginia Hill and friend | p. 183

7 Gulbenkian | p. 215

no innocence abroad

to Estelle

The McEvoy Story

The *Kangaroa* was a long, sleek yacht whose richly appointed cabins outshone the lush elegance of the finest Parisian pleasure palace. Her home berth was in Cannes harbor on the French Riviera. Her owner was Freddie McEvoy, unfailingly described by the international press as the Australian sportsman and millionaire playboy.

It was a description that erred only slightly, since Freddie was both an ardent sportsman and determined playboy. It was somewhat over-optimistic only in the matter of his finances. Freddie did not have a million. He did not even have a small fraction of it. This in nowise interfered with his expensive mode of existence, for Freddie had the kind of genius whereby, even on his flattened pocketbook, he was able to support the full-blown tastes of a millionaire. His success in bridging the gulf between means and desire lay in his great personal charm. A powerfully built athlete, he was a handsome, perennially tanned blond with a Douglas Fairbanks mustache. He wore his clothes, from a pair of Bikini bathing trunks to tails, with great flair. Just setting a yachtsman's cap at a jaunty angle on his head was enough to give the impression that here was an expert mariner. It goes without saying that the women who flocked to the Riviera found him irresistible. Freddie, for his part, could take them or leave them alone. Mostly, he took them; like a gentleman, of course, his friends hasten to add.

One of the women was Beatrice Benjamin Pratt Gibson Cartwright, a rather elderly person of considerable means who extended her string of names even further when she married Freddie in 1940. She had, in addition to a fabulous oil fortune, an age advantage of thirty years over her playboy husband. Freddie once said, speaking cautiously of the affair, "You could not say that it was love at first sight. Let me say that we were admirably suited to each other since each of us had what the other one wanted."

Reminiscing about it with George Dawson, the Cockney war surplus dealer who makes his home on the Riviera, Freddie said, "It was a wonderful arrangement. I was to get a yacht and a million in cash settled on me.

Don't get the idea that this was a cold business deal. With all that loot hanging from her, I loved her with a mad passion. Besides, we were to be together only nine months in each year with the other three months being a sort of marital vacation for me, during which time I was free to travel and do as I wished. On my first three months' liberty I headed for Palm Beach where I met a luscious blonde. While I promoted her at some real serious drinking in my favorite bar, I noticed that there was a young pleasant chap standing around who seemed very lonely. I bought him a couple of drinks and we became friends; such good friends that I fixed him up with the blonde's girl friend.

"I might never have thought much of this except for what happened. One night, during an electrical storm, I was in my hotel room with the blonde. There were rumblings of thunder and the lightning flashes were so bright the room was as clear as daylight. I remember remarking what a cozy place bed was at a time like this and I may even have made some uncomplimentary comparisons about my choice in bedmates. In any event, a few days later, before my three months' liberty had expired, mind you, I got a hurry-up call from Beatrice's solicitors. When I arrived on the other side Beatrice was there waiting for me. There was a terrific scene in their office. I've heard of people being compromised by photographs, but they had me with talking pictures. The little bastard I was buying drinks for was a private detective hired to keep an eye on me. I've got to give him credit, though. He did a helluva good job. He didn't miss a pose and his recording machine didn't miss a syllable of my conversation. Beatrice, poor soul, suffered a stroke and has been confined to a wheel chair."

Notwithstanding this episode, Freddie complained bitterly that it was highly unfair of Beatrice not to live up to that part of the agreement whereby he was to receive a million in cash. She did, however, give him his first yacht, the sixty-five-ton, slender, high-masted *Black Swan*. I boarded the ebony black beauty in Cannes recently with an intimate friend of Freddie's who told me, "Between ourselves we called it the 'Black Swine.' No real reflection, you understand, because we loved Freddie very much. In any event it wouldn't have offended him because you couldn't insult him, if you had money."

Freddie McEvoy's dearest friend and companion in amorous adventures was Errol Flynn. When the movie actor was defending himself in the celebrated teen-age rape case in Hollywood, Freddie lived with him. It was, incidentally, at the wild soirée celebrating Flynn's acquittal that Freddie ran into Irene Wrightsman, his second wife who, by no coincidence at all, was also the heiress to an oil fortune. Father Wrightsman was so angered by this marriage that he cut his daughter off without a cent, an act so offensive to sensitive Freddie that it fractured the romance. When Flynn was charged by a French teen-ager with rape a few summers ago, his first reaction was to dash off a telegram to Freddie, saying, "We are in trouble again." Freddie was Flynn's best man when he married Patrice Wymore, just as it was Errol who stood up for Freddie when he married his third wife.

During the preparation of this profile, Freddie McEvoy was lost at sea. The news of his demise, naturally, came as a great shock to the Hollywood actor. "Freddie was one of the great livers of life," Errol Flynn said. "He lived it the way he saw it and he didn't give a damn. The people who knew him knew that he was a brave and generous spirit. I feel as though a part of myself has left the world. When I first heard the news I didn't know whether to have a mass said for him or go out and get drunk, so I did both."

As friends tell it, Freddie's romance with the young, beautiful blonde who became his third and last wife was a touching affair in which the hardened roué fell madly in love with the poor little country girl. In spite of her poverty, Freddie marched her to the altar and promised to love, honor and obey, 'til death do us part. Claude Stephanie Filatre was twenty-four and Freddie forty years old when they met on the Riviera. She had been born of French parents in Algiers, where her father was a tobacco merchant in modest circumstances, and she had lived there much of her life. Claude's face had a quiet, undramatic beauty, her dark wide eyes giving it the look of the eternal innocent. Her figure, which can best be described as divine, was very much in evidence on the Riviera, for her favorite costume was two minute strips of cloth which go by the name of the Bikini bathing suit and which leave little to the imagination. Yet she carried herself with such unconscious grace that women did not resent it and wolves respected it.

At the time she met Freddie, Claude was the mistress of Maurice Anguenot, wealthy French watch manufacturer by whom she had a lovely child named Marie Caroline. Claude was poor when she met Monsieur Anguenot but, quite naturally, in the years during which their relationship blossomed, the good Monsieur settled on her a large block of stock in his wealthy corporation as well as jewels, valuable paintings and some blooded race horses. Therefore, it is not quite accurate to report that when Claude fell madly in love with the dashing playboy she was a girl, as the cliché has it, in reduced circumstances. When Freddie offered to marry her, she immediately accepted. Being a decent girl motivated by honorable intentions, she confessed her change of sentiment to M. Anguenot. The choleric Frenchman hit the ceiling. Didn't she know that McEvoy was nothing but a penniless adventurer? Yes, she knew that Freddie was poor, but love in this case was so strong that it had overcome her carefully nurtured regard for security. With Freddie she would be happy even if he were a pauper. Pauper, snorted M. Anguenot. How could he be a pauper when Claude's money—the money he had given her—would be supporting him in high style for the next ten years? This stung Claude, and she protested that Freddie was in love with her and was not marrying her for her money. The good Monsieur's rejoinder stung her even more.

Very well, said Claude, I will prove that Freddie is marrying me for love alone. Whereupon she returned the stock in the corporation, the paintings and the race horses, keeping for herself only the jewelry.

Freddie and Claude were married in the summer of 1949. Shortly after the ceremony Claude related the above incident to her husband. Freddie, who was rarely surprised by anything, seemed stunned by the recital. "You mean you gave it all back to him?" he asked incredulously. "I flung it at him," Claude said triumphantly. Freddie hit her a short right to the mouth, dropping her like an ox. A friend who witnessed this incident said, later, "Even when he beat his wife, Freddie did it with a flair. He was always the gentleman, you know, the kind who removes his glove before striking a lady. Really, I don't think it was the loss of the money that bothered him as much as the bourgeois morality she displayed."

George Dawson was, next to Errol Flynn, Freddie's best friend. He told me recently, "Freddie wanted a bit of understanding. He'd do almost anything, for anybody, to get his hands on money. Yet it didn't mean too much to him once he got it. For example, when I bought my yacht, the *Mimosan*, from Alberto Dodero, it was Freddie who acted as broker in the sale and who later fitted out the ship for me. He nicked me for forty thousand dollars, a very steep price, yet I was glad for Freddie that he could get it. The money only lasted ten days. He dropped it all in the casino at Cannes. Even though Claude turned out to be a poor girl, after all,

Freddie continued to love her—in his own fashion, of course. I remember one night, Olga, Claude, Freddie and I went to a night club in Paris. Freddie was in his cups. He thought he heard a man at the next table pass slighting remarks about his wife, so he got up, walked over to this fellow who was about a head shorter than he, and swung a right haymaker. The fellow must have been a boxing champ for quick as lightning he blocked the punch, swung a short left to the stomach and crossed a right to the chin that knocked every bit of belligerency out of Freddie. He left the place, sulking. I paid the bill and the three of us followed. Freddie, still sulking, was waiting for us. Without a word he swung at Claude and knocked her down. Why did he do it? I don't even think Freddie knows. He was like that—unpredictable."

Freddie was the kind who rarely bore a grudge. For example, he quickly forgave Claude the night-club fracas. He was less magnanimous in his feelings toward Prince Igor Troubetskoy. The root of this uncharitable attitude was money. It seems that Freddie, who didn't care any more for money than did Polly Adler, met Barbara Hutton, the dime-store heiress, and was so fascinated by her charming company that he dated her steadily. This was a most unfruitful arrangement since Freddie happened to be married, while Barbara found herself between husbands at the time. Whereupon the playboy introduced her to Prince Troubetskoy, an eligible bachelor. It was a meeting from which stemmed their later marriage. According to Freddie, the Russian prince committed the unforgivable sin of forgetting to send him a proper expression of gratitude. This was not entirely fair to Prince Troubetskoy, since he gave Freddie the use of his Riviera villa and yacht, which Freddie used or rented to others, keeping the proceeds for himself.

Cards furnished Freddie with a source of income almost as important as women. An American millionaire out on a spree on the Gold Coast could not be said to have arrived unless he was clipped by Freddie. For consolation Freddie would not only introduce him into the best circles, like the Aga and Ali Khan set, but could whip up the gayest parties with the prettiest and most willing girls. For this reason some unfriendly critics, undoubtedly jealous of his high station in society, have dismissed him with the epithet of gigolo. In truth, Freddie bore about as much relation to a gigolo as Madame du Barry to a two-thousand-franc streetwalker on the Champs Élysées. When friends asked him how he earned his livelihood, his favorite response was, "Pleasure is my business."

Freddie was born in Australia in 1908. His father was a landowner and sheep raiser who died when Freddie was ten. His mother brought him and his brother, Theodore, to England on the modest inheritance left her, and enrolled them in Stonyhurst, the swank Catholic school in Lancashire. Freddie was a natural athlete and in such sports as boxing and automobile racing he performed with dash and courage. He was an ace bobsledder who broke records at

St. Moritz, St. Antonien and Garmisch-Partenkirchen, and who captained the British Olympics Bobsled team to victory in the final Olympiad before the war, earning the nickname of Suicide Freddie in the process. When war broke out in 1939 he was on the Riviera. Although single, sound of limb and well within the draft age, Freddie saw no reason why he should go off on what he termed a sucker's venture. The quarrel between the states was no affair of his and he was determined to take no part in it. He didn't. He sat out the war on the Riviera until the Germans came, then in Mexico City, Palm Beach, Hollywood and New York. The British government felt no sympathy for his views and as a result Freddie was not permitted to represent the Commonwealth in future bobsledding contests.

After the war, Freddie pursued pleasure and the toil-free dollar with great single-mindedness. He helped Ely Pearson, the Houdini of finance who produced, almost from thin air, a multimillion-dollar bankroll, in a highly profitable diamond deal. Through the years he acted as middleman in the purchase or sale of anything negotiable.

Dawson told me that Freddie had ingeniously arranged for the disposal of eighteen hundred trucks which he, Dawson, owned and which were a drug on the market. If the deal had been completed the playboy would have received a quarter of a million dollars. Freddie consummated a provisional sale to Alberto Dodero, the Argentine millionaire, who in turn was to sell them to Evita Peron who wished to convert these vehicles into busses. During the negotiations Dodero died and the deal fell through.

Freddie's absorbing interest in yachts dated from his acquisition of the *Black Swan*. He used the proceeds from the sale of this vessel to buy the *Kangaroa,* a Dutch-built, two-masted 104-foot ketch with auxiliary motor that was owned by a Greek syndicate. He paid fifteen thousand dollars for her—a bargain price, because the ship was in very poor condition. He brought her from Athens to Cannes where he transformed her into one of the most elegant vessels on the Riviera. Originally, he named the vessel *Kangaroo,* but when this name already appeared in the Maritime Registry, he changed the final "o" to "a." When the *Kangaroa* wasn't rented, he and Claude made their home aboard her. Lately, however, there had been a decreasing demand for craft of this size and he put her up for sale. Friends reported to him that the market for large yachts in Nassau in the Bahama Islands happened to be a good one at the moment, and so, in the fall of 1951, Freddie made plans to sail the *Kangaroa* there. Anticipating the sale, he bought the *Échappe,* a twenty-ton, sixty-foot yacht that had been built in the shipyards at Great Yarmouth, and rented it to Gianni Agnelli, head of the giant Fiat automotive plant in Turin.

There were several other reasons, in addition to his desire for a profitable sale of the *Kangaroa,* that led him to plan on the long ocean cruise to Nassau. The Riviera is an exceedingly dull and deserted spot in the winter. Besides, many of the moneyed habitués would be in Nassau, since December was the beginning of the gay winter season in that vacation resort. And there were always a few commissions one could pick up that would pay the expenses of the trip and perhaps leave a slight profit. With this in view he loaded forty cases into the hold of the yacht. "Scotch," he told the newly recruited members of the crew. Checking back on this—for it later developed that Freddie had gathered about himself as mysterious a bunch of characters as can be found in the pages of fiction—I found a heavy-set German seaman, Bruno Hertel, who had served Freddie as chauffeur, valet, cook and captain. Hertel told me that he quit McEvoy's employ five days before the *Kangaroa* sailed on her fateful trip not because of the niggardly salary of eleven dollars a week, but because for the last five months it had not been paid at all. McEvoy had assured Hertel that he was going to earn a goodly piece of change on this trip and that all back salaries would be paid. Hertel refused to be convinced.

Freddie went into the dark back alleys of the tough section of Cannes harbor for his seamen. He came up with Walter Prexmarer, a former SS officer in the German army wanted for murder by two countries; Franz Krotil, an Austrian who had been expelled from France a few months earlier for smuggling cigarettes and who had made his way back clandestinely; Seaman Willy Gehring, who was supposed to be a master mariner (The German captain of George Dawson's *Mimosan* told me, "He came to me five days before the *Kangaroa* put to sea and said that McEvoy wanted him for captain and that he said he didn't know that much about seamanship, but that McEvoy had told him to study up on it and he asked me what book he could read. I loaned him my sea manual, but warned him that you don't learn seamanship from a book."); Toledo Martinez, a highly paid Spanish cook at the swank Carlton Hotel who for obscure reasons gave up a lucrative post to serve under the prevailing McEvoy wage scale; apprentice seaman Jean Buisson, twenty; and Robert Guillat, nineteen-year-old cabin boy.

In mid-October, a week before the *Kangaroa* hoisted anchor, Freddie was seen in the company of an American who was suspected by the French Sûreté of being involved in a diamond-smuggling ring. At the time this was not regarded as unusual, since Freddie was often seen in the company of queer people. In the past, Britain's Military Intelligence and French Special Branch men had heard reports about Freddie's having run arms. But Freddie's destination, Nassau, was a most innocent one and since there is no market for weapons there, no special control was placed on the cargo.

Freddie McEvoy, Claude, her personal maid and the crew, steamed out of Cannes harbor into the Mediterranean Sea. It was only at the last moment that good friend Dawson talked Freddie out of the notion of taking along his two daughters, both six and one-half years old—Stephanie, child by his marriage with

Irene Wrightsman, and Marie Caroline—both born, oddly enough, on exactly the same day and both of whom, at the moment, were attending boarding school at Gstad, Switzerland. They carried a single passenger, Jack Heaton, bobsledding pal of Freddie's.

The weather on the first leg of the western run through the Mediterranean was fair and the sails of the *Kangaroa* were filled by a brisk breeze. On the first day out Heaton received a radio message calling him back to Paris on business, and the yacht put into the island of Majorca off the Spanish coast where the passenger was put ashore, then took off once again for Gibraltar. About half a day's run from the narrow neck it was hit by a storm. Freddie steered the buffeted craft toward Tangier.

He spent a week in this city of glamor and intrigue, and as a result many rumors spread as to the clandestine nature of his business. While it is true that Tangier is an international center for adventurers and smugglers, there is a mistaken notion that contraband is smuggled into and out of this city. It is a free port, so goods enter and exit unmolested. It is, on the other hand, a convenient take-off point for such places as Spain, France, Italy and Iron Curtain countries for smugglers of cigarettes, precious gems and arms. Much of Freddie's time here was spent in the company of a Captain Welding, a local man of mystery, and a certain Jimmy Ward who advertises himself as a ship broker.

Freddie's brief brush with the storm in the Mediterranean, which was unimpressed by the jaunty tilt of his yachtsman's cap, made him doubtful of his ability to cope with the far more rigorous weather he would find in crossing the South Atlantic, so he set about hunting for a skipper, but there was none available. Throughout his stay in Tangier the weather remained gray and threatening. Unwilling to wait any longer for clearing skies or a competent captain, he put to sea on November 4th.

The *Kangaroa* headed into the Atlantic and crawled southward, hugging the African coast. Freddie kept in constant radio communication with Captain Welding. By mid-afternoon of the following day, about ninety miles south of Casablanca, the vessel was struck by a southwester driven by seventy-mile-an-hour winds. The *Kangaroa* bobbed like a cork as waves rolled over the sides. Water poured down the companionways, half-flooding the cabins. It was almost impossible to stay on deck and frightening to stay below. Robert Guillat, the cabin boy, was washed into the sea so suddenly that no one saw it happen. It wasn't until sometime later when Freddie shouted for him and received no response that it was discovered that he was missing. Freddie hauled in the sails, erring in his handling of the stabilizer sail. The weak engine, capable of propelling the yacht five and one-half knots an hour, edged the vessel close to shore. Although unfamiliar with this coastline, Freddie could see, as the seas raised and lowered, the saw-toothed tops of the reefs that ran parallel to the coast about two hundred yards from the shore. At dusk, with the vessel out of control and the storm growing worse, he ordered Prexmarer to strike out for land to seek help. The ex-SS officer made it, although he was half-dead when he crawled onto land.

The shore was deserted, so Prexmarer beat his way inland and after a while came across an Arab to whom he tried to explain their predicament. The Arab couldn't understand a word he was saying and, regarding the unclothed, drenched German seaman as a queer apparition, took the first opportunity to flee. Prexmarer headed in the direction of what he believed to be the town of Safi.

Night closed in quickly, with darkness making the danger even more acute. The winds and the sea tore at the small craft with ever-increasing fury. Freddie tried to maneuver the half-wrecked vessel toward what he believed to be Safi harbor. As he rounded a spit of land called Cap Canten, the *Kangaroa* rode up on a reef with a tremor that was like the last spasm of a dying person. The mountainous swells raised the hull and, as they ebbed, dropped her back on the rocks with a sickening thud. The panic-stricken cook could stand the strain no longer. With an anguished scream that sounded even more weird in the roar of the storm, he threw himself over the side and was swallowed by the sea. His body was never recovered.

Claude kept her nerve, principally because she had absolute confidence in the ability of Freddie to get her out of it. Her maid, however, went to pieces and had to be tied to the mast.

There wasn't a trace of excitement in the manner in which Freddie went about his duties. It was as though battling storms of this intensity was old stuff to him. He who showed a natural contempt for living had the same contempt for death. About midnight Freddie saw the headlights of an automobile moving along the coast road and, when it didn't stop, he ordered Gehring to make for shore. When another three hours passed without any report from him, Freddie decided to head for shore himself. He reassured his wife that this time help would be forthcoming. He got into a pair of bathing trunks which he strapped about his middle with a broad black belt, and dived over the side. Although powerfully built and a strong swimmer, he had been much weakened by an ulcer operation the year before. His exertions aboard the yacht and the perilous half-hour swim in the rough sea sapped much of his strength. He made it to shore and crawled weakly onto the beach. He found himself on a deserted strip of African coast that would have been desolate in the sunshine. In the driving rain and howling wind it looked like the end of the world. He headed inland until he came to a road that girds the coast and trotted along it for a while without seeing a soul. It struck him then that even if he found some poverty-stricken Arabs, there was probably nothing that they could do to help. Besides, the *Kangaroa* was rapidly coming apart at the seams, and Claude's predicament became more dangerous by the minute. He swung around and raced back to the beach. He threw himself into the sea, and swam back toward the *Kangaroa*, the lanterns of which could be dimly seen through the lashing rain. He was breathing with difficulty when he climbed over the side. In his absence the young seaman Buisson and the maid had been washed away. Only Krotil and Claude remained.

Freddie gave the order to abandon ship. He put a cork life ring about Claude and together they jumped into the sea, followed by Krotil. Although his powers of endurance had been badly sapped, Freddie might have made it alone. With his wife it was impossible. Krotil waited for them on shore, but when an hour passed, he set out for Safi.

The storm continued unabated for three days. Prexmarer, Krotil and Gehring, the only three survivors, had made their way to the town of Safi and had notified the local French authorities, but there was little these officials could do while the tempest blew. From shore they could see the wreck with the heavy seas breaking over it.

At eight o'clock on the morning of November 9th, three Moroccan fishermen, walking along the shore at Oulaidia, came across the body of Freddie McEvoy. The head was unrecognizable and the body had already begun the process of saponification. Preliminary identification was made from his bathing trunks and black belt. The fishermen quickly advised the Sheik of Oulaidia who is the civil controller of the territory of Zedadra, and the Sheik ordered his tribes-men to move the body to the morgue in the little town of Mazagan. The following morning three more bodies, all nude and battered beyond recognition, were found by a fisherman. They were the bodies of two women and one man. The survivors identified them as Claude McEvoy, her maid, and Jean Buisson. The bodies were placed in caskets in the Mazagan morgue and pre-pared for burial.

Up to this point it was a rather ordinary, though tragic, story of the cruelty of the sea that was not rare in this distant corner of the world. The publicity given the survivors tipped off the international police that Walter Prexmarer, a man they had sought assiduously through the years, was to be found in Safi. Immedi-ately warrants for his arrest and extradition were sent on to the colonial French police. The wanted man's real name was Manfred Lendner. The German police charged him with having, in complicity with a young Czechoslovakian, killed Lisbeth Hofer in Berlin in 1945. The Czechoslovakian had been arrested and hanged, but Lendner escaped to Vienna. Here he was arrested on a charge of homicide and theft committed in the Austrian capital and was jailed to await trial. He escaped from prison and fled to Italy, where he fell in with a fellow German named Walter Prexmarer. Together they decided to fill out immigration papers for admittance to Canada. While these papers were being drawn up, Lendner stole Prexmarer's passport

21

and identity card and escaped to France, where he took unto himself the name of his friend.

Prexmarer-Lendner had also figured in a yacht murder—though somewhat more innocently—which had occurred exactly three years before the death of McEvoy. A rather low international adventurer named Habela had plotted the perfect crime. One night while the Countess Marga Dendurand was aboard her yacht in Tangier harbor, Habela slipped up behind her, killed her and disposed of the body in the sea in such a manner that it was never found. He discovered to his everlasting regret that the Spanish police in Tangier can proceed quite promptly in cases of homicide even when the corpus delicti is missing, and he was quickly convicted and sentenced to serve life imprisonment. In the course of official police interrogations of a more or less vigorous nature, Habela was prevailed upon to confess not only to the murder but to the fact that he had a certain Austrian friend named Lendner who was trying to secure a set of false papers for the pair of them to go to the British colonies.

The presence of Prexmarer aboard the *Kangaroa* naturally gave rise to all sorts of suspicions, one of them being that he had mutinied and killed off Freddie McEvoy, his wife and the missing members of the crew. French colonial officials poured in from all parts of Morocco. Drs. Cecaldi and Megen performed autopsies. Monsieur Georges of the Mazagan police took fingerprints and made positive identification. Judge Advocate Parrandin and Assistant Prosecutor Slambach came down from Casablanca to interrogate the prisoner who was lodged in the lock-up at Marrakesh.

By the time I reached Safi, this police suspicion had dissipated. Prexmarer-Lendner had already been transferred to jail at Rabat to await extradition to Austria. Gehring and Krotil were to be seen daily in the Café du Port in Safi. They were under orders to report to the local police chief each morning and night until they were cleared for repatriation. Out on the beach where the *Kangaroa* had foundered, the Mozagene, a team of Arab border watchers, had pitched a tent and were keeping guard over the wreck. The wreckage that had washed ashore had been collected into a pile near the tent. The wreck itself was clearly visible. The waters were calm and it was obvious, even to a landlubber, that it would not be a considerable task for anyone to go out to the *Kangaroa* to search through it, an act which, eight months after the mishap, had still not been performed. As I stood there I couldn't help wondering about the roundabout route taken by Freddie to reach Nassau. It reminded me of an assignment in which I covered a story in Milwaukee by going from New York by way of Miami Beach. An impelling reason for Freddie's having taken this circuitous route with forty cases of Scotch—if indeed it was liquor that filled these cases—could have been the acute need brought on by the heavy influx of highly paid American workers employed in the construction of Moroccan air bases. A single bottle brought twenty dollars, so that the forty cases would have given Freddie a four-thousand-dollar profit.

But there was another commodity that would bring an even higher price—one that had reached astronomical proportions because of the great determination with which France has tried to keep it out. This was arms. Morocco was almost the last French colony in which an uprising had not yet taken place. It was known that Abd-el-Krim, the legendary Riff leader who led the Moroccan revolt three decades ago, was plotting a new revolution from his place of asylum in Cairo. Aside from the awakening spirit of nationalism in the Arabs, the local populace had real reason for discontent, in small part, at least, stemming from American practices there. For example, the American corporation building the five mammoth air bases in this colony paid as high as four hundred dollars a week to skilled U.S. laborers; as high as two hundred dollars a week to a fifteen-year-old American boy. Second highest in the wage scale were the French. Still another rung down the ladder in wages came the local Jews and last, far beneath all of them, and barely earning enough to live on, came the Arabs.

Did the forty cases, then, contain arms? Ridiculous, snorts Freddie's surviving brother, Theodore. "You can rest assured that the cases contained liquor. Freddie needed it for his own personal use. You see, he was a heavy drinker."

The strangest fact in the McEvoy mystery is that the solution lies only two hundred yards off shore. Yet none of the parties who has an obvious interest in the affair seems very anxious to solve it. The French had announced that they were going to send down a diver but that this was impossible during winter when the seas are rough. In the summer the excuse evaporated, revealing their true attitude which was that no one be permitted to rummage through the hulk of the *Kangaroa*. Even the McEvoy heirs are determined to keep out of the affair, despite the knowledge that Claude had all her jewels and a $12,000 mink coat locked in the safe. The forty cases, whatever they contain, are a veritable collection of Pandora boxes, and no one wants them opened for fear of the evil that will fly out.

There is a moral somewhere in Freddie McEvoy's demise. The attempt to save his wife's life was a brave and decent act, though completely out of character. As long as he was selfish and self-centered all went well. His first attempt at nobility killed him.

Lucky Luciano

On a January afternoon not long ago I had occasion
to pay a professional call on a gentleman I had not
seen since a day in 1936 when he had stood before an
unfriendly judge in the Supreme Court of New York
and had been sentenced to serve a thirty- to fifty-year
term of imprisonment. At that time, the presiding
judge, the prosecutor and the assembled press agreed
unanimously that he was so grave a menace that the
security of the metropolis, if not the nation, depended
on his being locked behind bars for the rest of his
natural life.

Although far less than half a century had elapsed

since then, the place I was going to see him was not the state prison but a comfortable hotel on the Via Nazionale in Rome. The name of the gentleman upon whom I was calling was Salvatore Lucania, better known under his *nom de gang* as Lucky Luciano.

It was about four when I entered the Hotel Quirinale, which connects by a rear passage directly with the Royal Opera House, a fact which in nowise influenced his choice of residence.

"Where," I asked the *portiere*, "will I find Signor Luciano?"

The uniformed figure with the crossed keys on his lapels regarded me suspiciously. Who was it that sought Signor Luciano? he countered. Never mind who's looking for him, I said in Italian. Just tell me where he is. Did I have any business with the Signor? he insisted. My reply was a rude one. The flunky became apologetic. He meant no offense, it was just that the good Signor was a celebrity and he was protecting him from autograph hunters. At this very moment, he said stiffly, I would find him sitting in the salon.

I walked to the large, square lobby in the rear and looked around. In the far corner, his chair backed against the wall, sat Lucky Luciano, last living member of Murder, Inc. Seated around him were several swarthy individuals who, judging from the Mulberry Street cut of their clothes, had been exposed to the advantages of an American sojourn. In order to reach the group it was necessary for me to pass between a pair of gentlemen seated in overstuffed leather chairs which were strategically placed on either side of the doorway. The suspicious bulges inside their jacket pockets, I presumed, were not salami sandwiches. These delicate niceties in gang behavior, incidentally, so basic in the manners of a mobster who hopes to achieve a ripe age, are without point in Italy, since this strangely backward land has never adopted that bit of American culture known as the mob murder.

The conversation ceased as I approached the group. "Hello, Charlie," I said. He looked up through a professorial pair of glasses that partly covered the sinister droop of his right eye. Except for the gray in his hair and the stoop to his shoulders, there was little change in him. "What do you want?" he said coldly.

I explained that we were running a piece about his life in new surroundings, but before I could finish he cut me off violently. "Why don't you get the hell out of here? You ain't gonna get no interview with me. You guys have written enough about me."

I told him that I found both his manner and language most offensive. Furthermore, this encounter was more painful for me than it was for him. It was only my sense of fairness that caused me to make this trek to his headquarters and give him an opportunity to tell his side of the story.

"Are you going to say anything good about me?" he asked.

"No," I said.

"There, ya see. You're nothing but a pack of liars, all of you. Did you ever write a good word about me?"

I admitted that I hadn't. "Of course not," he sneered. "You're all prejudiced against me."

The reason I hadn't written anything good about him, I pointed out, was because I didn't know anything good about him.

"You mean that if I tell you something favorable to me, you'd print it?"

I assured him that I would.

"All right, then write that this business about me running a dope empire from Italy is full of baloney. There ain't a word of truth in it."

I carefully wrote that Lucky denies any connection with the narcotics traffic, adding the observation that the denial would have been far more forceful if it had not been made in the presence of three swarthy gentlemen whose names, reading from left to right, were John Schillacci, alias Frank Lanza, Serafino Mancuso, and John Pellegrino; all of whom, in common with their powerful friend, had done time in American prisons for violation of the Narcotics Act and had, thereafter, been deported to their native country. Of these three, Mancuso is particularly interesting. Before the war, Serafino Mancuso came to Italy for a visit, picked up eight kilograms of heroin and managed to make "a meet" with a French seaman in Genoa. The French sailor smuggled the contraband into the United States. Instead of turning it over to Mancuso, he went out peddling it on his own. This was terribly incorrect and Serafino, along with his two brothers, Salvatore and Giuseppe, ran down the Frenchman in New York, kidnapped him and tortured him for days in an effort to make him reveal where the heroin was hidden. The FBI arrested the brothers and they were quickly indicted and convicted on the crimes of kidnapping and smuggling. They were sentenced to serve forty years in federal prison. Immediately after the war the three brothers were deported to Italy as undesirables. In the spring of this year Serafino was picked up by Italian police and in his possession six kilograms of heroin were found. Brother Giuseppe, believed to have been in on this deal, is now being actively sought by Italian authorities, but he is in hiding. The third brother, Salvatore, was needed as a witness against still another figure who assisted them in the kidnapping and torture of the French seaman and the FBI asked the Italian government to issue a passport to him so that he could be brought back to the United States to serve as a government witness. Salvatore co-operated with the Federal authorities for a couple of weeks and then quietly disappeared. He is somewhere in the United States today, being actively sought by the Immigration, the FBI and the Federal Narcotics Bureau.

This was, for Lucky, added proof of my unfairness. "Are you going to blame a guy all his life for one mistake?" he asked with an attempt at sincerity. "Why, even I did time on a narcotics rap. Does that make me a dope peddler today?" I indicated that I was willing to listen to more, so Charlie Lucky brushed off his ex-American friends and the pair of us held a three-hour conversation. Occasionally a person would try to approach us, but the two gentlemen in the ill-fitting jackets were on the job and they saw to it that we weren't disturbed.

There have been so many charges, denials and countercharges flying around the head of the luckless Lucky that the truth about him lies half-drowned in a sea of printer's ink. Stories about him spring up as fast as weeds around a cesspool. As a result people still don't know why, for example, Governor Dewey, once the implacable foe of the racketeer, gave him his freedom. There have been many explanations of this, none of them wholly satisfying. I add my own to the list, with the notation that it has the merit of having been double-checked by Lucky who has, after all, a first-hand knowledge of the affair.

I listened patiently to his bitter complaints about exaggerations and untruths being written about him. There were articles accusing him of running an international white-slave ring; of trying to buy the Tibertina Island in the Tiber River where he supposedly wanted to erect a fashionable gambling joint. An article in the September, 1951, issue of *Reader's Digest* reported that "Lucky has not changed. Only a few weeks ago, a young New York businessman ran headlong into his European organization. Ken Rogers decided to introduce launderette washing machines in Italy. He was approached one evening in his Rome hotel by two hard-eyed gentlemen with Brooklyn accents. They were very polite. They simply wanted to bring Mr. Rogers' attention to the fact that any launderette operation south of

Naples would have to have the approval of one Mr. Luciano. Otherwise there might be difficulties. Mr. Luciano would, of course, expect to share in the profits of the venture, in exchange for his 'services and protection.'"

This is sheer fantasy. For one thing, the protection racket is an American nicety that has not taken root in Italy, and it is to be doubted that even Luciano, for all his admitted talents in mob business, could possibly make it work there. For another, any businessman who proposes to make money out of launderettes in the south of Italy belongs on a psychiatrist's couch. Trying to sell razors to the House of David or going after the champagne concession for the Mills Hotels would be comparatively shrewd.

Despite these obvious divergences from actuality, I don't seem to be able to work up much of a sweat over poor Lucky. This lack of sympathy doesn't conceal the real need for the truth about him, however.

Sight has been lost of the fact that Lucky, from his new headquarters in the Albergo Turistico in Naples, is as grave a menace to the American people as he was when he operated out of a tower suite in the Waldorf Astoria. Take it from Commissioner Harry Anslinger, head of the United States Treasury Department's Bureau of Narcotics, Lucky is the largest single figure in the traffic in this contraband in America today. The reason he directs all dope shipments from Italy to the United States has nothing to do with nostalgia. It is based on the fact that it is the country that pays the highest price for illicit drugs.

And so, as an expert on the subject of Luciano, having covered him in both the United States and Europe, I shall haul him out of the inky sea and apply artificial respiration.

In Italy, Lucky developed a sudden sensitivity to the things people say about him. It came as a surprise to see that an unfavorable press—which is all he had in the United States—could still upset him. To make sure that he doesn't miss any of these upsetting articles he subscribes to a British clipping service and reads about himself in all languages, including Chinese. From these he has discovered that there is a division of opinion about him. Whereas the American press writes bluntly that he is the vice king, a racketeer and killer, European newspapers take a far more charitable view. According to some of the early articles written about him he lives a simple, almost priestly life. He is extremely jealous of his reputation for rigid honesty. Even in America, where there has been a conspiracy to blacken his name, nobody has ever accused him of picking a pocket in a crowded street car.

Shortly before this interview I visited the town of Montelepre in Sicily, near the birthplace of Luciano. I had luncheon with Maria Giuliano, the sultry Sicilian beauty who is the sister of the island's late bandit king. She asked me if I knew Luciano and I explained that professionally I knew him very well indeed, having covered his trial in the Special Term of the Supreme

Court in New York. Maria asked what trial, and I explained that Luciano had been charged with the crime of compulsory prostitution, that a jury had found him guilty of the crime and that conviction carried with it a lengthy term of imprisonment.

"But that can't be true," she said. "Luciano is a lieutenant in the United States Navy. He was decorated for bravery during the war."

"Who told you that?" I asked.

"Luciano did," she replied.

The average Italian has only the haziest idea of what a racketeer is and so he is inclined to view his new compatriot as a sharp businessman who got into difficulties with the authorities but who more than paid for these indiscretions with the vital aid he furnished the Allied powers during the war. This picture of a retired war hero living out his declining days in peace is very much to Lucky Luciano's liking, and he considers it a most unfriendly act for anyone to upset it. He was assisted in foisting this image on the public by the ex-press agent for General John C. H. Lee, onetime commander of United States troops in Italy.

Strangely enough, the crime for which Lucky is most noted is the one of which he was least guilty. Newspapers have handed him the crown of vice czar and Lucky wears it with poor grace. The mere mention of the girlie business is enough to fill him with impotent rage, for he swears, like the thousands who fill prison cells, that he is innocent of the charge. With one slight difference. Lucky, this time, is close to telling the truth. But after a lifetime of lying nobody will believe him.

Lucky Luciano had safely reached the age of forty, was a leader in the criminal profession with three million dollars in liquid assets stashed away in safe places when Special Prosecutor Thomas E. Dewey, the much-publicized racket buster who is now Governor of New York, indicted and convicted him on the charge of compulsory prostitution, a felony under the laws of the State of New York. The testimony tended to show that Lucky had organized vice so that it was a centralized business paying enormous tribute to him.

I was a meticulous practitioner of the crime-reporting profession covering the local scene during this era. I covered this particular story by going out with vice cops on their investigations and helped them tap telephone wires of madams, bookies, prostitutes and doctors. On several occasions when the cops wandered off for a coffee, I would monitor the tapped wires alone. The result is that I can adjudicate with authority the rival claims of Dewey and Luciano.

The truth is that the closest vice came to being organized in New York was in the early thirties, when a big-time pimp named Nick Montana introduced the white-ticket system into houses of ill-fame. Montana was able to get about one hundred madams and four hundred girls to avail themselves of his services simply because he assured the houses a weekly turnover of talent, an attorney and a central bonding agency in case of arrest. For accounting purposes the girls were given a white cafeteria ticket so that the total number of punches—each madam, like a train conductor, had her own distinctive punch—registered the number of men served while the final figure represented the total earnings. A truly great prosecutor, Charles Pilatsky, whose misfortune it was to serve under Tammany district attorneys, convicted Montana and sent him away for a long term of imprisonment. This left the lush field of prostitution, or that part of it that Montana served, wide open for a lover of the fast buck, as Luciano notoriously is. The gang leader's chief lieutenant, a hardened murderer named Little Davey Betillo, on his boss's instructions, decided to look into the situation with a view to bringing it under the control of the Luciano mob.

At Luciano's trial, an underworld punk, testifying for the State, stated that he asked Betillo, "Is Charlie Lucky in back of all this?" and that Betillo answered, "It's all right for us to use his name, but anyone else who does gets his head knocked off."

The weakness in the case against Lucky Luciano resulted from the absence of a direct link connecting him with the vice racket. The reason, of course, was that Lucky was grabbed before he could get started.

The racket buster's minions, however, overcame this difficulty when they came up with a reluctant prostitute named Cokey Flo. Cokey Flo testified to the fact that Lucky had come to her door one day and had said, in effect, that he was taking over the racket and that she would have to pay tribute to him. Now there was never any doubt in the minds of many of us working on the story as to the accuracy of this bit of intelligence. It credited Lucky with a criminal carelessness in regard to his own safety that even his severest critics will admit doesn't jibe with his character. Staying free in the home of the brave was a ruling passion in his life. It means that Lucky, having ordered his chief lieutenants on pain of death to keep his name out of the set-up, blithely paid a call on a soiled dove and blurted out to her what he had warned the others to keep quiet about. Besides, anyone who knows anything about the facts of underworld life knows that protocol there is more rigid than in society's Four Hundred. It was tantamount to Mr. DuPont personally trying to get an order for cellophane from a stationery store in Hell, Michigan, or Mr. Swift trying to sell a ham to the general store in Millinocket, Maine. It was Frank Costello accepting a two-dollar bet over the telephone. For Lucky to have visited someone so far beneath him in the social scale of the underworld would have been a public act of degradation.

Somewhere along the line Cokey Flo gave evidence of faltering in her decision to testify. By coincidence the late Fulton Oursler, an editor who discovered in the twilight of life that religious articles were more profitable than sexy ones, offered Cokey $5,000 for her story. Obviously, she would have no story unless she were a witness. As the Chinese laundryman said, "No tickee, no shirtee." Cokey testified. Part of the money was used to pay for the upkeep on the house in New

Rochelle where, as a material witness, she was being kept.

As I say, the case against Lucky Luciano was an extremely weak one, and it hung on the nebulous testimony of this pair of soiled doves. The jury, aided by a strong charge from the presiding justice, found it sufficient, however, to convict the racketeer, and the judge sentenced him to serve up to a half-century behind the bars of grim Dannemora penitentiary. There was precedent for what happened to Luciano. Al Capone was handed a stiff prison sentence for violation of the income-tax laws when, in reality, the punishment was for a lifetime of violent crime. Death House Mike Alex, who beat the rap for a foul murder he did commit, died in Sing Sing's electric chair for a murder he did not commit.

Speaking to me about the terrible injustice done him, Lucky, by way of nailing down the ridiculous nature of the charge, cried out, "Why should I want to take dough from the whores when my men were already taking it away from the pimps?"

He is extremely bitter because no one will listen to his protestations of innocence. In fact, in order to get his point across, he has written a screen play. The scenario deals with a famous American gang leader whose life is ruined by an over-zealous prosecutor who frames the innocent racketeer in order to further his political ambitions. As a result of this unjust conviction the racketeer is deported to Italy where, through philanthropy and other good deeds, he earns the love of the native population. All this so touches the heart of the country which has done him wrong that it apologizes for its unjust treatment, and he returns in triumph to the place where, presumably, he is to be free once more to practice his brand of pure-hearted racketeering.

So anxious is Lucky to get this message broadcast that he put up seventy-five thousand dollars, an amount which covered the complete shooting cost. He offered the package deal—script, money and blonde mistress for the feminine lead—to Paul Tamburella, Italian movie producer whose reputation is based on such realistic Italian pictures as the Oscar-winning *Shoeshine*. Mr. Tamburella declined.

When I first read the news of Lucky's early release from imprisonment, I wondered what could have possessed racket-buster Dewey to have commuted the sentence of the man he had repeatedly denounced as the very worst type of criminal. It was an act that sliced more than forty years from Luciano's maximum sentence and gave him the necessary freedom to return to the dope racket which is the one he has practiced longest. I thought that perhaps Dewey's conscience had finally started bothering him over the manner in which he had convicted Lucky and that this had made him susceptible to the suggestion that a parole would be an act of justice.

When Lucky was freed, Dewey issued a public statement to the effect that the generous act was taken on the request of American military authorities who were anxious to reward the racketeer for having assisted our intelligence services during the war, and that this assistance was of such importance that it helped save the lives of American soldiers in the invasion of Sicily. It so happens that there is not a word of truth in the statement. Any GI who fought in the Mediterranean theater of war can tell you how phony the excuse is. Even the uninitiated would find it obvious that a gangster who has been absent from his native Sicily since the age of ten and who has spent the five years preceding the war locked up in an inaccessible penitentiary would hardly be able to speak about that distant island with any degree of credibility.

Since this statement was issued, both the Army and the Navy have declared that they know of no usable information that was passed over to them by the imprisoned racketeer and have flatly denied that they issued any request in favor of rewarding Luciano. Dewey could not really have been convinced of Luciano's wartime contribution because in the official public papers of Governor Dewey the following appears: "Upon entry into the war, Luciano's aid was sought by the Armed Services in inducing others to provide information concerning possible enemy attack. It appears that he co-operated in such effort although the actual value of the information procured is not clear."

Lucky told me during the interview that before trying the war-hero gag, which was successful in gaining him his release, he tried to make a deal with Dewey. He offered to give the governor the names of the murderers of Carlo Tresca, editor of an anti-fascist paper in the United States, who was murdered in New York in the early nineteen-forties. Lucky claimed that the murderers were professional killers from Italy and that he could identify them. Dewey did not go for this.

Later, when embarrassing questions were being asked, it was stated by the governor's office that Dewey acted on the advice of his Parole Board. Columnist Robert Ruark of the Scripps-Howard newspapers, something of a Luciano specialist himself, telephoned Dewey's office and in a monitored conversation asked what precise information it was that Lucky furnished the United States military authorities that caused the governor to take so unprecedented a step. Dewey's office replied that Lucky had organized Sicilian fishermen into an anti-submarine patrol off Nova Scotia, an excuse that will rouse belly-laughs from our navy.

As far as I know, the exact story of what actually happened has never been told. Here it is. Lucky found life very difficult in Dannemora, which is known as the Siberia of New York penal institutions. The guards were tough, discipline severe, and the distance from New York City made it difficult for friends and relatives to visit him. His dissatisfaction with what should have been his last earthly place of abode developed in him, at the start of the war, a patriotic feeling. He wished to do his bit for what he presumed to be his country, especially if it meant transfer to a milder institution. With this in view, friends of his approached an ex-politician named Haffenden, at the time a lieutenant commander of naval intelligence working in the

New York office, and told him that the racketeer was anxious to help the war effort. Haffenden interviewed Lucky Luciano in Dannemora and, following the interview, requested that the prisoner be transferred to an institution closer to the metropolis. Lucky was sent to Great Meadows, known as the country club among New York's prisons. Luciano's attorney went before Judge McCook, the judge who had sentenced Luciano, and pointed out that his client was on his way to becoming a war hero and would the judge please relent and ease the sentence. McCook denied the request, pointing out that the only recourse would be an appeal to Governor Dewey for executive clemency. After the war Luciano's lawyer, Moses Polakoff, a noted Republican, asked Haffenden, by this time a private citizen in politics again, to write a letter to Dewey's office telling of the great value of Lucky's secret contribution to the war effort. This was written on May 18, 1945. Dewey asked the Parole Board to investigate. They did, and, although they eventually approved the application, they were skeptical of the war-service claim. Nevertheless, Dewey commuted the sentence. In subsequent investigations, the value of Lucky's war services appeared even more dubious.

Chairman Frederick A. Moran's term of office on the Parole Board had already expired before the Luciano matter was being considered. Oddly, throughout the entire *Affaire Luciano,* Moran's continuance on the Board remained uncertain until March 1947, when Dewey renominated him to a new term.

After General William Donovan, head of the wartime OSS, said flatly that "the convicted panderer's alleged aid during the war was nothing but cheap talk from irresponsible persons and completely without foundation," Dewey's spokesman stated that Lucky's war aid was not the compelling reason for the executive act that permitted forty years to be cut from his maximum prison sentence.

During my interview with Lucky Luciano, while he was still in a confiding mood, I tried to get him to speak about the legal fees and expenses involved in handling this lengthy case, and while he spoke of certain specific expenditures, he refused to say what the entire cost was.

Lucky's life has followed the classic pattern of the gangsters of his time. He was born in the peasant village of Lercari Fridi in the Palermo province of Sicily on November 24, 1897. His father was a hard-working carpenter who emigrated to the United States when Lucky was ten years old. The family lived in a cold-water flat in Little Italy on Manhattan's Lower East Side. It was in this teeming tenement district that his education in crime began. He joined the neighborhood gang in their pushcart pilferings. By the time he was fourteen, still struggling manfully with the problems of the fifth grade, he felt that learning was all rhubarb anyway, and dispensed with it. He considered himself so thoroughly Americanized that he never bothered going through the formalities in later life of taking out citizenship papers, a miscalculation which was to make possible his later deportation.

Lucky's first job was with the Goodman Hat Company where he was paid five dollars a week. After two years of hard work, he was raised to seven dollars, most of which went home to help support the family. On one occasion Lucky used his week's salary to invest in a floating crap game in the neighborhood. This encounter with Lady Luck brought him $244 in winnings, an amount he never forgot because it represented an undreamed-of sum. Never again was honest toil to hamper his rise to fame and fortune. In June, 1916, Lucky—his nickname stemmed from that one game— had a streak of losses and found himself heavily in debt to the six-for-five Shylocks, a low set of usurious gentry who loan five dollars for a week's time at an interest rate of one dollar a week. This can be something of a nerve-racking experience, because some East Side moneylenders have a nasty habit when they are not paid of sending guerillas whose efforts at collection sometimes have fatal consequences. Lucky claims that it was necessity that forced him to throw in with George Scanlon, a shifty-eyed margin man working between the wholesaler and peddler. Scanlon taught him how to make a fast buck by retailing morphine, taught him also how to buy milk sugar at the local drug store and dilute the drug by as much as ninety percent. The margin of profit was astronomical, and Lucky was able to pay off his debts.

But the risks were great, too, and shortly after Lucky

went into this new business, he was caught and sentenced to an eight-month stretch at New Hampton Farms. During the First World War, Lucky served as armed protector for neighborhood crap games. He was called up by the draft but was rejected because he had syphilis. The coming of prohibition gave him a chance to show that he had brains as well as muscle. He set up a phony company called the Downtown Realty Corporation as a blind, gave it legitimate-looking offices in Manhattan's financial district, and set to work as a distributor for hijacked alcohol. At the same time he had practically every bathtub on Mulberry Street actively engaged in manufacturing Lucky's special brand of Scotch. His goon squads proved to be remarkably efficient salesmen, and what the product lacked in quality the salesmen made up in persuasiveness.

Despite his rise in affluence under prohibition, he never lost sight of the profits to be made in narcotics traffic. He became, by his own admission, a banker in the industry. He made this confession to the federal agents who arrested him for violation of the Narcotics Act. No amount of verbal persuasion could have gotten him to talk, but the narcotics men had caught him in the act, and they dangled a heavy sentence as a second offender over his head. Lucky, in outraged innocence, told this story. He had loaned money to a dope peddler named Charles Lagaipa who was unable to repay it because competition had moved into the East Twenties which was his territory. To protect the investment, Lucky and a few of his boys went out and began beating up the rivals. He had the misfortune to perform one of these strong-arm acts in the presence of the officers. This explanation, truthful as it may have been, in nowise softened the hearts of the arresting officers. The case was placed before the Grand Jury and Lucky was indicted, whereupon he came up with an even more potent argument. He would tip off the agents to a cache of morphine valued at one million dollars if they would quash the indictment. On the basis of the information he furnished, new arrests were effected and, very quietly, the indictment against him was nol-prossed.

Throughout the roaring twenties his rise in rackets was steady, and he became the dominant figure on the East Side in all bootlegging, gambling and dope-peddling activities. He also established a reputation for cunning and cruelty that was a byword in the profession. He dressed well, drove flashy cars and was a noted night-club figure. Although his interest in women was never great, something possessed him one night to make unwelcome advances toward a pretty Italian girl, the daughter of a New York City detective. The girl, her clothes torn by Lucky, fled in tears to her father. On the night of October 16, 1929, the detective took Lucky for a ride to a lonely spot in Staten Island and beat him with murderous fury. Lucky was stabbed in half a dozen places, one slash severing the muscle of the right eye and accounting for its sinister droop. The gangster was left bleeding and unconscious by the roadside where he was found the following morning. Lucky refused to name his assailant.

All through the thirties, Lucky managed to strengthen his grip on the profitable rackets. As his friends and former bosses were hastened along their abbreviated earthly courses, the abbreviation being punctuated by the bullets from Lucky's mob, he stepped into their places. With the repeal of prohibition, he moved into the profitable field of labor unions. Fifteen years ago in a series of articles on New York's racket kings, I broke the story of Lucky's being on the payroll of the Amalgamated Clothing Workers' Union, a large and wealthy labor group at that time headed by Sidney Hillman, confidant of President Roosevelt. Lucky's salary was $75,000 a year and the payroll was carried to him by a hoodlum bearing the unlikely name of Joe Strawberry. The temper of the times was such that neither Franklin Delano Roosevelt nor Thomas E. Dewey paid any attention to it, and the story crashed with the force of a feather alighting on the rocks in Central Park. The exact nature of the services which Luciano performed for the labor union for this princely stipend has never been explained by either Lucky or the union. This was not Lucky's only source of union income. The fabulously wealthy garment industry and its allied lines like trucking, contracting, dyeing and so on, was divided between him and Louis "Lepke" Buchalter. Lucky and Lepke were big business. They even used the labor-saving devices of big business to maintain control over their union rackets. Instead of supporting separate goon squads, they used, on a contract basis, an organization with the descriptive name of Murder, Inc. The exact number of homicides performed by this highly efficient group will probably never be known, although some of the lethal exponents of the corporation have confessed to more than forty. Lepke was eventually convicted on a charge of murder and sentenced to death. To the very end, Lepke believed that the State would never dare electrocute him. He was hustled to the electric chair, surrounded by a conspiracy of silence. Only two other men, Lucky Luciano and Frank Costello, are so big in politics, labor and crime that almost every shade of political opinion fears their confessions.

There were many enterprises to which Lucky turned his hand. He was in the loan-shark business and used Murder, Inc., as his collection agency. He was a heavy contributor to Tammany Hall which is the ruling body of Manhattan's Democratic Party, and for this financial aid was permitted to bring slot machines into the city without hindrance from the police. He ran the one-armed bandits with enormous profit until Fiorello La Guardia became Mayor. La Guardia, whom he calls a "fruit salad," ran the machines out of the city. But no matter how many profitable holds Lucky secured on illegitimate enterprises in his steady upward climb —and they netted him more than three million dollars —he always had big-time narcotics men in his entourage.

It is entirely likely that Dewey was convinced that

Lucky had been rehabilitated by his abbreviated term of imprisonment. If this is so, then Lucky let the governor down resoundingly. Because when he got to Italy, Lucky, who doesn't care for money any more than he does for his right eye, went back to work at the job for which his American training had best fitted him. Of course, the nature of the new terrain forced certain changes in his manner of operation. For example, protection in the Chicago sense of the word is foreign to the Italian mentality and it would have proved too expensive an expedient to try to educate his new fellow countrymen. Labor unions in Italy are likewise immune to strong-arm tactics, unless the rough stuff is coupled with a brand of politics called communism. In America a gang leader must see to it that his men are gainfully employed in some legitimate line of endeavor between jobs for the boss. Lucky's henchmen were to be found working in labor unions, restaurants, night clubs, dress factories and so on.

In Italy, Lucky, until recently, had no such preoccupation because the legitimate payroll for his boys was taken care of by the United States. This is not to suggest that Washington had gone into partnership with him. It is merely that the Luciano mob here was composed mainly of ex-draftees who were enrolled at various institutes of learning in Rome and who drew regular monthly checks under the GI Bill of Rights. This was a source of keen embarrassment to the Veterans' Affairs Section of the United States Embassy, especially since some of the students in the halls of higher education were like Dick LaRose, an intimate of Lucky Luciano whose criminal record has eleven entries, including two murder charges. What made him *persona non grata* in the States and brought on his deportation as an undesirable alien was a conviction on a dope-smuggling charge. The Federal Narcotics Bureau warned the Italian police to keep a close check on LaRose because he "is a notorious and dangerous character who is deported to Italy because of traffic in narcotics and who works with big narcotics smugglers." As soon as he hit the Italian shore, LaRose, known also under a long string of aliases, joined Luciano.

The Italian police have not, in the past, been particularly concerned with Luciano's activities. They are annoyed at the bad publicity he brings them, and they say that if they hadn't lost the war they would never have allowed him into the country. "After all the good America has done us," a high-ranking official told me recently, "you send us Luciano. He sets the Marshall Plan back two years."

It is Federal Narcotics Commissioner Anslinger, greatest living authority on international dope smuggling, who flatly names Luciano as the leader in the largest ring extant today. He bases his charge on the information collected by his world-wide organization of investigators and informants. According to him, the enormous rise in smuggling between Italy and the United States following Luciano's deportation was not a coincidence. Anslinger's investigations showed that in the early days of Luciano's Roman residence the contraband was being gathered in the Middle East, India and China by independent operators and shipped by freighter to the port of Genoa as goods in transit. For this reason there was no customs inspection on entry and departure, making it an easy jump-off point. From here it took only a financier and a front man; the first to put up the cash to swing the deal and the second to find a seaman who would do the actual smuggling.

Soon after Luciano arrived in Rome, a special agent of the Narcotics Bureau learned that a front man was on his way to Italy from New York. This individual, an American citizen of Italian extraction, had no previous criminal record. The ostensible reason for the trip was that he represented a Wall Street shipping and trading firm which, upon investigation, proved to be nonexistent. The man visited Lucky in Rome before departing for Genoa. This fact was known because Commissioner Anslinger had detailed George White, one of his best agents, to shadow the man. Rather than tip his hand, Agent White worked as a lone wolf. While he covered the suspect, he was shadowed by the Italian police. When I checked Italian police files, in gathering material for this article, I found that the dossier on Agent White was bulging while that of the suspected dope smuggler was blank.

In recent years narcotics smuggling between Italy and the United States has become so intense that it is a cause for real concern. So much of the contraband has been finding its way into the retail market that it has become easier for the addict to buy it. Experts in these matters say that there is a connection between the increased number of teen-age users of narcotics and the accelerated activity from Italy. Because of this the Treasury Department has sent a squad of narcotics officials, headed by Charles Siragusa, to Rome on a full-time basis. The latter, after a lengthy investigation in Italy, Greece and Turkey, returned to Washington to report to the Senate Crime Investigating Commission that Luciano still ruled the narcotics traffic in the United States. Agent Siragusa named Joe Pici, also a deported New York gangster, as Luciano's chief lieutenant in the narcotics trade in Italy. One operation by Pici, which Siragusa was able to verify, was the purchase in Italy of fifteen kilograms of heroin for which he paid $22,500, and which he sold in Chicago for $150,000, resulting in a quick profit of $127,500 on a single transaction.

In April of 1951, a notorious member of the 107th Street mob named Frank Calace was sent to Italy to pick up some heroin. At the time Calace applied to the State Department for a passport, there was on file the urgent request from Anslinger to the effect that passports be denied to known racketeers. Calace's first stop was Palermo where he picked up his uncle, an American deportee of the same name. Together they went to Rome where they met Pici and with him flew to Milan where the latter delivered three kilograms of heroin. Pici said good-bye to the Calaces, who flew back to Rome on the first leg of a return trip to New

York. At Ciampino airport they were picked up by the Italian police. The heroin was found in the younger Calace's suitcase.

Lucky's largest single source of heroin has been an Italian corporation called S.A.C.E. which is located in Milan and owned by Egidio Calascibetta. This latter organization deals in legal narcotics. In other words, they receive huge amounts of heroin which are to be sold to the medical and pharmaceutical professions. However, through a trick of bookkeeping, they were able to divert 500 kilograms of heroin—that is half a ton—into the illegal wholesale market. To get an idea of how much this amounted to, a single kilogram of smuggled heroin pure on the wholesale market brings $70,000. It will be noted that the price of the illegal drug, delivered in the U.S., has increased tenfold since the nineteen-forties. A single kilogram of heroin pure makes fifty kilograms of heroin cut, with each diluted kilogram selling for $10,000 each. This means that the United States wholesaler will pay $35,000,000 for the half-ton whereas on the retail market it will bring in $250,-000,000. It took an okay from Lucky for the American mob to do business there. When Giuseppe Biondo, called a "left fielder" by United States narcotics officials, which means the big, silent guy who pulls the strings—he is a friend and business associate of Frank Costello and is known as a sinister power in labor affairs—came to Italy last spring, his first stop was to see Lucky and both of them went to Milan where Lucky introduced the visitor to Calascibetta. At this point, the Italian police, tipped off by United States narcotics officials, moved in and picked up Biondo for questioning. The latter stated that he had met Calascibetta only for the purpose of buying acetic acid, a very strange request since this product is far more abundant and cheaper in the United States. Biondo said that he represented several large United States firms, but when these were questioned none of them had ever heard of Biondo. Lucky was picked up, too, and questioned. He admitted bringing Biondo to Calascibetta but stated that it was for the purpose of helping Biondo to buy acetic acid. When Calascibetta's niece was married she and her husband spent their honeymoon on Capri as Lucky's guests. The books of S.A.C.E. were seized by the Italian police and when the phony records were uncovered, Calascibetta was indicted.

Shortly after his arrival in Italy, Lucky secured an Italian passport and traveled to Havana where he set up offices. One day, quite by accident, Robert Ruark ran across him. So surprised was the columnist that he didn't trust his senses and spent the following two days searching for a Luciano acquaintance who would make positive identification. Finally he came up with Connie Immerman, once proprietor of the noted Connie's Inn and at that time working as a stickman in a gambling joint. The news that Luciano was in Havana caused the United States Government to clap an immediate embargo on all legal dope shipments to Cuba and this embargo was maintained until Luciano was unceremoniously placed on a Turkish vessel headed for Naples.

Luciano had another sad encounter with the press shortly thereafter. An article of mine perpetuated what he claims to be the fiction of his connection with the narcotics traffic and this stung Roman officials into arresting him and giving him a *foglio di via obligatorio,* which is a police order forbidding him to enter Rome. The reason for this was not that it might hamper him in his illicit activities as much as it would keep him away from newspapermen. On the whole, however, Italian police have treated Lucky mildly. They say that the reason for this is that they can't catch him doing anything wrong. Senator Kefauver, working in Washington, was, perhaps, more fortunate. He was able to piece together several statements made to his investigators by the deported gangster and come up with the information that the ex-convict had illegally imported at least $57,000 into Italy. He passed the information on to the proper authorities. For this Lucky had his wrist slapped lightly with a $4,000 fine.

This writer, too, can assist the police who can find nothing wrong with Lucky's Italian sojourn by pointing out that he has illegally imported a green Oldsmobile sedan which still bears 1948 New Jersey license plates number RU 37X. The car was delivered to him by Pasquale Matranga, who says he is a Brooklyn businessman. Lucky says that Matranga gave the car to him as a gift, but Matranga denies this, saying that he was only delivering it. Actually, the car was a gift from Willie Moretti, the New Jersey racketeer who was killed last year following testimony before the Kefauver committee.

On the surface Luciano's life is quiet, even sedate. Before he was barred from Rome he lived in a flat on the Via Lima which he had purchased for $21,000 and which he resold in April of 1952. Since his ejection from the capital he's been living in Naples, first in the Hotel Turistico, and now in the penthouse of an apartment house in the Vomero, high on the hill in the swank part of the city overlooking Vesuvius and the beautiful Bay of Naples. The penthouse is at the top of a ten-family house, and Lucky owns the entire building. He paid $150,000 for it. He has also started construction on a villa at Santa Marinella, a lovely seaside resort just north of Rome on the Tyrrhenian Sea. His summer home will make him a close neighbor of the Roberto Rossellinis.

Lucky has a regular schedule. He rises at nine sharp every morning. At 9:05 A.M., just about the time he has finished brushing his teeth, Johnny DiPietro, a hoodlum from Houston and Mulberry Streets and a confirmed opium smoker who is Lucky's fixed bodyguard, puts in his appearance. It was Agent Siragusa who arrested DiPietro in the United States before the war. He found ten toys of opium on DiPietro which the latter was trying to sell in Chinatown. Immediately after the war DiPietro was deported to Italy as an undesirable alien. At 9:15, Lucky and DiPietro—Igea Lissoni, Lucky's girl friend, stays behind in bed because she is a late riser—go down to the café for coffee and brioche, which is the

57   **Lucky Luciano**

extent of their breakfast. From there they go to a barber shop where DiPietro sits near the doorway while his boss is shaved. It's always the same barber, who opens up even on Monday, the day most barber shops in Italy remain closed, just to shave Lucky. From then until lunch there is never a fixed program. If business acquaintances come in from the United States Luciano takes them to a café where they can talk, with the ever-present DiPietro keeping the curious out of earshot.

Lunch is a ritual. Lucky eats it every afternoon in the same place, a restaurant called Giacomino. Since he is a big tipper waiters hover around the doorway waiting for him to put in his appearance, very much as sparrows hover about a horse. During the last two years it has become a daily event for United States Navy personnel to line up in front of his table for autographs. This Lucky loves. In Giacomino's he is a real celebrity. Lunch lasts from about a quarter to two until about 4:30. During the racing season he goes to the track every day. On days when there is no track meeting, especially during the warm weather, he returns to his home for a siesta. After the siesta he sits around a café—he has no favorite —and then from 8:30 to 9:00 he goes to Zi Teresa, a restaurant on the Naples waterfront. He stays there until about 11:00 P.M. when he goes home to bed. He has no night life whatever. His routine is very tranquil and he wants it that way because he thinks he has heart trouble.

Lucky has about thirty suits, all of them made by Italian tailors, who are among the finest in the world.

Although he was known as a flashy dresser in America—
you may recall that it was the sharp distinction between
Lucky's splendor in dress and the cheap, unstylish dress
of the detectives who pinched him that led to Mayor
La Guardia's issuing the famous muss-'em-up order—
Lucky's taste in clothes today has become simple and
Italian. The average cost of each suit is about $80, cus-
tom made. He has about twenty pairs of shoes.

Lucky seldom gambles except on the horses, even
though in Italy there are many opportunities for legal
gambling. His attitude toward gambling is more or less
that of a certain small garment manufacturer toward insurance. An insurance agent sold the manufacturer a
policy on fire, accident, and several other forms of insurance, and finally got down to hurricane insurance. This
the little manufacturer refused to accept. The agent
pointed out that it cost only fifty cents a year. The
manufacturer was adamant. "After all," he said, "how
could I possibly start a hurricane?" If the betting has no
edge in his favor, it is not interesting for Lucky. Even
at that he doesn't always win. On one occasion he fixed
the jockeys in a horse race, only to have them sell him
out to the bookies. He dropped $6,000 on that deal. On
another occasion, though, when an American friend
went to the track with the mobster, Charlie Lucky
handed the friend a "sure thing" in a six-horse race. The
friend bet a cautious 10,000 lire on the nose. The nags
took off in a cloud of dust with Charlie Lucky's selec-
tion far in the rear, a position he maintained until the
closing 200 yards. Then, as the friend recalls it, a sight

smote his eyes, eclipsing anything he had seen in years of devoted horse following. The five opposing horses almost slithered to a stop as their jockeys pulled on the bits. One of them was pulled up so sharply he almost backed up. The Charlie horse came through a winner.

The Italian sojourn has brought one change in Lucky. There is in him a deep yearning for respectability, a feeling that was totally absent during his forty years of American residence. This has led him to invest in legitimate enterprises, which was most uneconomical since he has had absolutely no training in that direction. He dropped twelve thousand dollars in a spaghetti factory which he started in Sicily. Another was a Chinese restaurant in Rome which was run by a pair of personable Italo-American New Yorkers who, in their spare time, were also drawing monthly checks under the GI Bill of Rights. Somewhat less respectable were his investments in such clubs as the Colibri, the Columbia and the Grotta delle Piccione. These are girlie joints as frank and open as the Montana joints in New York.

If these places tried to get along on their poor entertainment and worse liquor they would go broke very quickly. Luciano's interests in these enterprises are handled by Ralph Liguori, who was also convicted of compulsory prostitution and deported to Italy. Ralph feels that whatever popularity the clubs enjoy stems more from his sparkling personality than from the easy moral sentiments of his undraped employees. He points with pride to the fact that two touring United States senators have availed themselves of the hospitality of the Colibri and uses this as proof of the high tone of his establishments. There are two kinds of girls employed in the club, the B girl who does not differ from her American sister, and the *artiste*. The B girl, of course, gets a percentage on what she can induce a customer to buy and keeps for herself her after-club-hour earnings. The undraped *artiste* puts on what passes for a floor show. When her number is finished she must circulate among the customers. Since her salary as dancer or singer, plus percentage, is not enough to keep her decently clad in G strings she, too, must depend on after-hour earnings for a livelihood.

A few years ago, Lucky went into a Neapolitan waterfront dive called the Trocadero, looked over the crop of B girls, most of whom were saggy bags, and chose Igea Lissoni, a fresh-looking bosomy blonde of twenty-four. From the start the couple hit it off nicely. Lucky set her up on the Via Lima in Rome, but when the police threw him out of town, he took Igea down to Naples with him.

Igea Lissoni looks upon Luciano as some kind of American god; a combination Gregory Peck, Robin Hood and J. P. Morgan. A girl in her station of life, meaning one who has played the Italian night-club circuit as an *artiste*-B-girl is precluded from respectable marriage, and the very best she can hope for is to meet a man with money who will keep her. If he keeps her a year, it is great fortune. If he gives her furs and jewels and shows every indication of keeping her permanently, it is beyond her wildest dreams. She loves and reveres Lucky. His every whim is her command.

The Italian cinema continues to interest Lucky despite the initial rebuff. Recently he tried to buy the North American distribution rights to a pair of films called *Chastity Belt* and *Vespro Siciliano*. His original idea was to open each picture with a brief scene showing him seated at a desk. He would say to the audience: "Ladies and gentlemen, perhaps you have been told that I do nothing in Italy. This is not true. I work like all the others, from dawn to sunset, in the film studios. I now present one of my films. I hope you like it." The producers were attracted by the generous cash offer, but when they heard the original manner in which Lucky intended putting the films across, they fled.

Today Lucky Luciano has his movements restricted to such plebeian places as the Isle of Capri, the Naples and Milan race tracks, Lake Como and Venice. This may be all right for American society folk, but not for Lucky. He wants out. Back to the U.S.A., preferably, and he almost made it when he hit Havana. Recently he applied for a visa to Germany and it had already been granted when the United States narcotics officials in Rome learned about it and nixed the deal. Lucky complained to me that it was another example of persecution.

As our interview terminated and I started to leave, Signor Lucky said, "Remember to say that I am only a retired businessman and that all I want is for everybody to leave me alone." I promised him that I would quote him.

62

Giuliano

3

Once upon a time, many, many years ago, there lived
in the lush green woods of Sherwood Forest a bandit
named Robin Hood. Once upon a time, though much
more recently, there lived in the gray mountains of
Sicily another Robin Hood who, like his rugged British cousin, is already legendary.

Quite naturally there were differences between
them, for the Britisher was a myth, the Sicilian a man.
While the former interests mainly children, the latter
was a hot subject for discussion amongst grown-ups,
and because he was a bandit with social significance,
the Communist, Socialist and Christian Democratic

Parties have become involved in bitter debates about him.

I first heard of the modern Robin Hood in the fall of 1946. At that time he was an obscure outlaw who commanded little sympathy from the few outlanders who had ever heard of him. I went down to Sicily where I interviewed and photographed him, and the resultant articles, reprinted in almost every known language, made him an international figure. My first visit to Sicily on this story in the winter of 1946-1947 was at a time when the Truman Doctrine was being heatedly attacked by communists everywhere. I found, when I got there, that the doctrine had arrived before me. In the desolate mountains of this feudal, semi-autonomous island, it had found its firmest supporter in Salvatore Giuliano, a picaresque bandit who was a synthesis of Robin Hood, Pancho Villa and Dillinger.

The rural gang leader, aided by his advisers on foreign policy, had studied the doctrine, which was addressed to freedom-loving people throughout Europe, and felt its message was aimed directly at him. Giuliano's reasoning ran this way: The doctrine is a bald promise of aid to those who resist communism. In Sicily, where the communist forces hold a majority of the seats in the regional assembly and therefore might give Russia a cheap foothold in the Mediterranean, my guerilla army is the only military force opposing their domination.

Why, then, asked the anti-communist bandit, should it be unreasonable to ask for the type of aid needed—

anti-tank guns of small caliber, mortars and bazookas— in order to implement the Truman Doctrine?

The logic of his position established, the gang leader took pen in hand and laboriously wrote a letter to President Harry S. Truman, The White House, Washington, D. C., asking for military supplies and promising in return to stamp out the Red menace and deliver Sicily to the United States as the forty-ninth state in the Union. Enclosed in the letter was a cartoon, drawn by the bandit, to illustrate how he hoped to accomplish this. It showed Giuliano cutting the chains that bound Sicily to Italy, while a confederate in the United States pulled Sicily across the South Atlantic toward us. In one corner of the cartoon was written: *"A morte I sbirri succhiatori del popolo Siciliano e perche sono I principali radici Fascisti. Viva Il Separatismo della Liberta,"* which, in poor Italian, means "Death to the blood-sucking police of the Sicilian people, because they are the principal roots of fascism. Long live separation and liberty."

There may be critics to whom the support of an outlaw will appear the reduction to absurdity of the Truman Doctrine. Giuliano brushed these critics brusquely aside. "Too much talk about putting down communism and not enough action," he said.

To show what he meant by action, Giuliano made a simultaneous attack on Communist Party headquarters in six towns. Using tommy guns, hand grenades and pamphlets for the assault, he wiped out offices in Partinico, Carini, San Giuseppe Jato, Cinisi, Borghetto, and Monreale.

Even in Italy, where politicians are inclined to be incendiary, Giuliano was regarded as a scorcher. Before he turned politico, he was a killer, kidnapper, racketeer, poet, artist and commanding general of a hard-riding, tough-shooting army. The local press called him a modern Robin Hood because he robbed the rich and gave freely to the poor. If, in transit, some of it stuck to his fingers, his many beneficiaries have never complained.

No one has ever figured the exact amount of his criminal take, but it has been estimated as well over a billion lire. While this is a modest $1,600,000 at the official rate of exchange, it becomes, when geographically weighted, a figure so enormous that a local economist with a sense of humor has pointed out that feudal Sicily, for the first time in centuries, was experiencing a redistribution of wealth.

Giuliano's charity, while freely distributed, was done on a personal basis and quite naturally won for him the affection of the superstitious peasants. An old woman, dying because she could not afford an operation, woke to find fifty thousand lire under her pillow. Families facing starvation found that money had been left mysteriously behind their doors during the night. When a town had its spaghetti ration cut off, he hijacked two truckloads of government supplies and distributed them free of charge in the public piazza. That the Italian authorities did not look kindly on his operations is the mildest sort of understatement, especially since Giuliano, in the course of his philanthropy, had taken the lives of some two hundred persons, including one hundred and eight police officers.

The Minister of Interior once printed notices offering eight hundred thousand lire for Giuliano's capture dead or alive. Giuliano countered with an offer of a million and a half lire for the capture of the Minister of Interior. When this minister, who is chief of all Italian police forces, spoke disparagingly of the bandit, Giuliano challenged him to a duel to the death. He suggested that the minister have at his side the entire Italian cabinet, making ten against one. The one who remained alive would rule Italy.

The existence of a Giuliano is easily explained. He was produced by a combination of wartime and geography. The Allied invasion of Sicily left the island a physical and economic wreck. It pried loose Mussolini's heavy hand and replaced it with a political freedom that bred self-seeking political parties and grafting politicians.

Liberty is only a word, but bitter poverty and hunger are grim realities to the shepherds of Busambra, isolated in the squalid loneliness of the *latifondo,* and to the sulphur miners who eat no more than broad beans and their skins.

Most politicians believe they have overcome this problem once they have lined their own pockets. The underpaid policeman, receiving as little as five dollars a month, is depended upon to keep law and order. He takes as naturally to grafting as his superiors. There is, also, the matter of geography. Villages are situated atop isolated mountains and are untouched by outside influences. The peasants retain the customs and beliefs of their forefathers, and for centuries the state has been to them a hostile force which came periodically to collect army recruits and taxes. It was likened to a plague of locusts. Therefore, it is little wonder that they supported an outlaw who combatted this foreign power successfully.

The peasants also supported him in his self-appointed job as dispenser of justice. It was not the justice of the courts of Rome, but the justice of the mountain people. Guiliano took unto himself the role of judge, jury, prosecutor, jailer and executioner.

Such was the case in the barrel-head court that convicted Joe Terranova, owner of a general store in the village of Montelepre. Joe sold flour, shoes, soap and so forth to the people of the town, extending credit to them at usurious rates. Giuliano took him into the piazza, read the execution order, gave him time to pray and shot him. The mountain folk considered this, eminently just.

Another citizen, Leonardo Gritti, stole a cow by the simple expedient of telling the victim he had been sent by Giuliano. Leonardo was stood against a stone wall and executed. The bandit leader—he always spoke of himself in the third person—left a note on the victim's chest. It read: "Giuliano does not rob from the poor." Nothing more.

Another man, accused of squeezing his townspeople and condemned to death for it, was Salvatore Abate, postmaster of Montelepre. It was his habit to hold out on postal money orders which, he felt, the ignorant peasant would know nothing about. One of the victims was Giuliano's sister-in-law. This lack of professional courtesy on the part of Abate was, of course, fatal.

The police did not look very kindly on these proceedings. They called it murder. But the peasants looked upon the author of these acts as a saint and asked God to grant him health. And my favorite news weekly's boudoir correspondent, remarking on the bandit's hold on the public imagination, reported in an article in *Time* Magazine that a Roman matron overheard her young son's evening prayer. "God bless mother and father," recited the tot, adding on his own, "and save Giuliano from the police."

Giuliano the Great was one of the few who had become a legend while still alive. Like all legendary figures, no two stories told about him were alike. In the reams of copy Italian newspapers have devoted to his exploits, they have noted that he was the son of a general, a naval lieutenant with a record for bravery, a brilliant attorney who gave up the practice of defending criminals to become one himself and an undercover agent for the Allied army.

It had even been reported that Giuliano the Great was a disguise adopted by Lucky Luciano so he could continue his operations in Sicily. This latter view gained some currency because Giuliano's headquarters in Montelepre was just a few miles east of Lercari Fridi, where Lucky was born. The weakness in this theory was that, while Lucky was an acknowledged expert in amassing illegal wealth, he has never been accused of giving any of it to the poor.

Giuliano's love life, too, has been widely commented upon in some very lush prose. Beautiful baronesses bared their bosoms and swooned at his touch. Countesses ran away from home to spend the night at his lair. "He can have his choice of any woman he wants," one writer smirked lasciviously, in a pamphlet entitled "The Secret Loves of Giuliano." This same writer reported that even Signora Michael Stern, the mature woman who represents an American journalistic trust, when she interviewed Giuliano, told friends that she was very much attracted to him although he had made no improper advances toward her. If the pamphlet furnished a true picture then Giuliano must have been so busy with his love life that it left him few free moments in which to squeeze in his regular job as *bandito*.

Actually, the pamphleteer's picture of the bandit was not very accurate. Nor was the one I found in *Time*. In an interview evidently conducted by telepathy, it quotes Giuliano on the new land reform: "If it comes about, I will have to capture hundreds of peasants when I need money. Now all I need to do is capture a single baron and get all I want."

The facts about the Sicilian Robin Hood are simple. He was born Salvatore Giuliano in the mountain village of Montelepre, Palermo Province, on November

16, 1922. His birth almost reversed a trend which has seen Sicily exporting its surplus gangsters to America. He was conceived in New York City, where his father was an immigrant hod carrier living on East 74th Street. In a town where education is not too highly regarded, Giuliano was noted for his application to studies. After passing through the fifth grade of grammar school with flying colors, he went into the fields to help the family share-crop. Montelepre's priest told me that Giuliano was ambitious, extremely intelligent and, all told, a fine son of whom any father could be proud. Even in devoutly Catholic Montelepre, the youth's devotion to his church commended him to his spiritual advisers. This religious strain is visible in the poetry which, with fine Sicilian fervor, poured from him.

His first contact with the law occurred while he was carrying a donkey-load of wheat to the black market. He was challenged at a police check post, where he murdered one of the challenging officers. A wanted killer with a price on his head, Giuliano fled to the impenetrable mountains.

For one whose first attempt at crime was so clumsily handled, he developed a surprising flair for the illegal profession. Gradually a mob, consisting at first of outlaws banded together for their mutual protection, built itself around him. Giuliano was a natural leader, and soon all orders emanated from him. He decreed that only the rich would be robbed and that a part of the proceeds would be divided among the poor. There were cynics who said that the decision to rob the rich arose less from social conscience than from a fine sense of double-entry bookkeeping.

Giuliano's reputation as a gentleman bandit came from the exaggerated courtesy and deference he accorded to some of his victims. This was discernible in his encounter with the Duchess of Pratomeno, reported in the Italian press. Giuliano invaded the ancient castle of the regal duchess, kissed her hand in greeting and joined her at tea. It was his way of observing the social amenities while his men rifled the castle from dungeon to tower.

Only once did the Duchess complain. That was when the bandit pointed to a large diamond ring she was wearing. "Please don't take it," she begged. "It is the engagement ring given me by my husband. It is a reminder of my youth, of my first and only love."

Giuliano bowed courteously. "Knowing the story behind the ring will make me treasure it the more," he said, relieving her of it.

As he was leaving the castle he saw an Italian translation of *In Dubious Battle* by John Steinbeck and asked for permission to borrow it, explaining that Steinbeck was his favorite author.

A few weeks later the book was returned with a note which read: "My Dear Duchess, I am returning to you the copy of Steinbeck's *In Dubious Battle*. I do not know how a reactionary like yourself could possibly have appreciated it, therefore I was tempted not to return it. But since Giuliano gave his word, he keeps it."

Perhaps the largest single source of Giuliano's income was kidnapping. No accurate count has ever been made of the number of victims, because many of them preferred paying and saying nothing.

Luigi Agnello, Palermo's largest mill owner, and Giovanni Battista, the city's wealthiest industrialist, both of whom partook of Giuliano's "hospitality," paid the regular fee of twenty-five million lire, at the present rate of exchange about forty thousand dollars, for the privilege. They described their host as an extremely polite, handsome young man.

The band soon broke out of the narrow confines of the mountains surrounding Montelepre and spread throughout the province of Palermo, and it began functioning along business lines. The peasant families who shared in the profits were principally the families of his mobsters. Gangsters went to prison without talking because they knew that their families would be on Giuliano's payroll as long as the organization existed. At the height of his power there were about sixty of his cohorts behind bars, with their families drawing regular pensions. The rest of his funds were plowed back into the business, which meant that he used them for the purchase of armaments for use against the police. So far as protection in the American sense of the word was concerned, he never paid any. At first the village *carabinieri* made a determined effort to capture him, but the death rate amongst them rose so sharply that these efforts ceased and there was between them a sort of unwritten agreement. They let him alone and he permitted them to go freely about all other business.

In spite of the local policy of *laissez-faire,* Inspector Ettore Messana, the stocky, bald chief of the public security forces in Sicily at that time, did make a determined effort to bring Giuliano to book for crimes which filled a closely printed, six-page folder. The majority of these were murder, attempted murder and kidnapping. Inspector Messana, an unsentimental realist, looked at Giuliano's philanthropy and found that it left him cold. "It is easy to be generous with someone else's money," he sneered.

Inspector Messana's first attack in force on the stronghold of Giuliano took place on the night of December 23, 1945, when eighty *carabinieri* suddenly descended on Montelepre. Thirteen of Giuliano's cohorts, along with a large haul of armaments, were seized and transported to the police barracks. That night Giuliano counterattacked, killing the *commandante* and several of his men. The bandits captured the barracks, released all the prisoners and carted off not only their own weapons but the entire police arsenal.

Force having proved costly and futile, guile was tried. An attempt was made to starve out his adherents in Montelepre. The *carabinieri* persuaded the *Istituto Mezzogiorno d'Italia,* the corporate landowner for whom most of the inhabitants are sharecroppers, to get new tenants for the land. This was tantamount to starvation for the Montelepre peasants.

Giuliano's reaction was to visit the director of the organization and push an automatic into his ribs. The bandit said that although there were moral reasons for asking the Institute to alter its decision, he hadn't sufficient time to dwell on them. Instead he was limiting himself to the fourteen unbeatable arguments that were in the clip of his automatic. The Institute, struck by the force of this logic, reversed the order.

For a time Inspector Messana tried to use the old police standby of the stool-pigeon, but no sooner did an operative bring in usable information than his body would be found on a lonely Sicilian road. Usually a note would be pinned to his chest, reading, "So end those who spy on Giuliano." Messana's final effort was a complicated one in which the informers were armed with five high-powered police rifles which were to be used to assassinate the bandit. Somehow, during the subsequent maneuvers, the weapons found their way into Giuliano's hands and he used them to execute the informers. In the end, Messana, too, was forced to sue for peace. The police chief and the bandit met secretly on several occasions and at these meetings worked out a modus vivendi. The police would cease their persecutions of the family of Giuliano in return for which the bandit would not attack the forces of public order, except in self-defense.

Perhaps the most nearly effective attempt to catch Giuliano was that employed by Cardinal Ruffini, who went unattended to Montelepre and, from the pulpit, asked Giuliano to give himself up. Giuliano is a devout Catholic, and the word of a Prince of the Church could not be lightly regarded.

Giuliano finally wrote to the Cardinal. He stated that he was forced to decline the invitation because the law which was to adjudicate his own guilt made no provision for establishing the responsibility of the police. He added that it might be better for the Church to use its persuasive preaching on the *carabinieri,* who were in greater need of spiritual and moral healing.

Giuliano became firmly established as the un-crowned bandit king of the mountains. His gang numbered about three hundred and fifty, with an inner circle of thirty relatives and close friends forming his personal bodyguard. Members known to the police lived in the hills with their leader, changing their residence each night. The others tended crops at home until called into action. Stores of war material left by the retreating Germans and advancing Americans found their way into his hands. He also secured a mass of technical equipment, including radio transmitters, which became part of an elaborate warning system.

Part of the income of the gang derived from a tax placed on wealthy landowners by Giuliano. In making collections Giuliano jealously guarded what he considered a reputation for honesty and fair play.

A prince near the town of Riberra on one occasion sent five hundred thousand lire as an advance payment for his extensive olive orchards. Giuliano returned the sum with a note stating he was sorry he could not accept it, as he already had promised the yield to the poor of the town of Riberra. The crop was to be harvested by them under the protection of his army.

When the European war ended, Giuliano changed from the criminal to the political phase of his career. As he wrote in his letter to President Truman, he always hoped for a Sicily that would be independent from Italy. Now, as a power in the community, he had decided to do something about it.

There was at the time a Palermo politician named Finocchiaro Aprile, who headed the Separatists in a movement called MIS (*Movimento Indipendenza Siciliano*). Giuliano joined it. He learned that the aid required of him was more military than political. He added to his original band and brought into existence an army called EVIS which stands for *Esercito Volontario Indipendenza Siciliano* (Voluntary Army for an Independent Sicily.)

Best available figures show that the army's strength was about five thousand, consisting mostly of peasants and students. These men, though they fought in the subsequent battles against government forces, took no part in the purely criminal acts of their leader nor did they receive any pay for their services. They were eager political novices, imbued with an ideal and following a romantic leader.

The army was divided into two groups. One was concentrated in Palermo Province, with headquarters in Montelepre, and was commanded by Giuliano. The second group covered Catania Province, with headquarters in San Mauro Caltagirone, and was headed by a man named Gallo.

Since these were revolutionary forces, the Italian army launched full-scale attacks against them. An armored division attacked San Mauro Caltagirone and captured Gallo and many of his men. While in prison, Gallo ran for the *Costituente* and was elected. As a member of the Italian Congress he became immune from arrest and was released.

The thought that Giuliano might follow Gallo's lead and go from lawbreaker to lawmaker—a sort of Al Capone for senator—sent cold shivers down the spines of the police, and they quickly brought him to trial in absentia and just as quickly convicted him of a felony, thus effectively blocking him from candidacy for public office.

The victorious armored column, flushed with its triumph over Gallo, launched an attack on Giuliano's army, but the *bandito's* generalship was too good. He not only beat off the assaults, but launched a counteroffensive. His men roared in on the police barracks at Grisi, Bellolampo, Borghetto, Montelepre, Pian dell' Occhio and elsewhere. As many as three establishments were hit in a single night.

Dozens of police officers and soldiers were killed during this phase of the war. In one of the skirmishes in which four officers were killed and one wounded, Giuliano carried the wounded man into the hills, where he was treated by the gang's doctor and turned free.

Giuliano pointed to this incident as proof of his contention that he killed only when he was forced into it.

The Italian government took cognizance of the strong separatist feeling and granted Sicily regional autonomy. This was highly effective in limiting Giuliano's political following. When a slate of candidates for the new local assembly was prepared, Giuliano tried to convince Signor Aprile that the Separatists could not, in spite of his technical ineligibility, find a stronger candidate than Giuliano. The bandit stated later that in spite of promises made to him by Sicily's leading politicians, his name was omitted and this brought about a break between him and his political associates. Giuliano and his army remained neutral in the elections.

When the votes were tabulated it was found that Sicily, which only a year before had voted overwhelmingly to retain the monarchy, had now given a majority of its votes to the Communist Party. Giuliano felt that this was a terrible thing for the island for which he professed so much love, and he determined to do something about it. In hamlets, villages and cities, offices of an anti-Bolshevist front sprang up. Although the members were law-abiding citizens, many of them being persons of considerable substance, the guiding hand behind the movement was that of *il bandito*.

His personal response was violent. He led a group of masked horsemen across a ridge near the town of Pian Del Greco, where a communist May Day celebration was being held. His men opened fire with machine guns and, when the smoke lifted, eight townspeople lay dead, with thirty-three wounded. Labor unions called a general strike which paralyzed the country and almost overthrew the De Gasperi government. The Minister of Interior raised the price on Giuliano's head to three million lire. It had no effect on Giuliano. A few weeks later he struck again, and Communist Party headquarters in half a dozen more towns were blasted out of existence.

The communist leaders blamed these acts of violence on me. In a free-swinging, four-column attack on me in *L'Unita,* the Italian daily newspaper that is the official organ of the Communist Party in Italy, I was unmasked as an American spy. I quote the article * verbatim:

"Stern was one of the animators of this pogrom. He promised and sent arms. About a month after the meeting between Stern and Giuliano, the headquarters of the Communist Party and of the workers' committee of Carini, Partinico, Monreale and of other villages in the zone of Montelepre were taken by assault by the Giuliano band. Numerous workers were massacred.

"But the force and the prestige of the parties of the people and those of the democratic Sicilian movement supported by the great and moving in-

* The articles in *L'Unita* furnished the basis for a criminal libel suit brought by the author against the newpaper's director and the two authors of the articles. The case was tried in June, 1952, in the Twelfth Section of the Criminal Court in Rome. The Communist editor and writers were convicted.

dignation of the entire country were able to break this criminal combination; the very crime that should have extended his [Stern's] power in all the provinces of Palermo, helped kill it. In the houses of the members of the Mafia of Alcamano, a few days after the assault of the 22nd of June, the dynamite and bombs needed to blow up Communist Party headquarters of that town were in readiness. At the last moment, however, the Mafia members renounced the attempt. The same defections took place in the towns of Camporeale and other centers. Little by little there were even greater defections from the front of the provocateurs.

"It was like this that the mission of Stern, certainly not because of the vigilance of Minister Scelba, whose functionaries had helped point out the road to the American spy, finished miserably. The special agent of the American Friends of Sicily returned to America, where he was consoled in his failure by writing the romantic history of the king of Montelepre. With him went the brother-in-law of Giuliano, Pasquale Sciortino,* with the credentials as ambassador of the outlaws to Washington. Sciortino maintains contact between the emissaries of Stern and the Giuliano band."

I had no idea, when I first set out to interview Giuliano, that it would have such repercussions. At the time

* Sciortino was arrested in the United States in September, 1952. His disguise was a near-perfect one. He had enlisted in the United States Air Force.

it appeared to be the simple sort of assignment that the late Bill Williams, the two-fisted drinking man who had been *True's* editor, would toss off in a more or less off-hand manner. Go down and see Giuliano, he had cabled, and live with him long enough to get the whole story; with photographs of yourself interviewing him, so that there will be no question as to the authenticity of the report. Of course, there was that little matter of staying alive long enough to get the story down on paper, but that was a small detail he was sure that I would consider. This was like telling a stateside reporter, "Dillinger just broke jail. The whole FBI is looking for him, but don't let that worry you. Find him and watch him pull his next job. Remember, exclusively for us."

The editor of a feature syndicate for whom I had written, very briefly, during the war, was particularly fond of assignments of this sort. When I suggested that I could parachute behind the German lines into Yugoslavia and there join forces with Tito, he cabled back that it was a fair suggestion, but to make it a really smashing one, we would have to run interviews with Tito and Mihailovitch side by side. The fact that Mihailovitch was living with the German southeastern command was a little detail he would let me worry about. The day Rome fell he cabled: "Exclusive interview Pope urgentest."

That's the dangerous part of having a reputation. Editors spend their spare moments thinking up tough ones with which to stump you. One of these dealt with the Greek civil war. All I had to do was join forces with Markos, the Greek guerilla leader. I spent three months battling Greek red tape in trying to procure a visa. Finally, through the good offices of Jean Ghikas, their press attaché in Rome, I was able to get one. In the meantime, George Polk, a radio correspondent covering the Middle East, set off on the same assignment. It was his last one. A group of Markos' partisans took him, blindfolded, aboard a rowboat in Salonika Bay, bound his hands behind his back with thin wire and pumped some bullets into his head. The body washed ashore a few days later.

I lost the race to reach Markos first because Homer Bigart, the New York *Herald Tribune's* excellent correspondent, had already traveled down through Yugoslavia and sneaked across the border into the northern mountains of Greece where he established contact. On his way back from Greece, Homer stopped in Rome to telephone me. My wife, who answered, asked who was calling and he said, grandly, "This is the man who saved your husband's life."

I didn't give any special importance to the Giuliano story. It was the coverage of the Mt. Etna eruption, which I was doing on the same trip, that was uppermost in my mind. I drove from Rome by jeep. The trip took a week because I stopped in so many villages in Puglia and Calabria. Rarely in any part of the civilized world had I seen such awful poverty. People were actually wasting away from hunger. When rain made it impossible for a peasant family to work the fields, they stayed in bed because in that way they didn't become so hungry. As an American who believes strongly in the aid we are sending Italy, it was all the more appalling to me to see how little of it was reaching the very poor. The contrast made it even worse for as a long-time resident of Rome, I had seen the results of American aid in the capital city. There were more flashy automobiles, more luxury goods in the shops, more prosperous high-fashion houses and a very swank night club built with the aid of an ECA loan.

There was an even division of opinion on the mainland as to whether or not Giuliano was a figment of the imagination. On the island of Sicily there were no such doubts. To the rich he was an awful reality. To the poor he was a popular hero.

In Palermo, I stopped at police headquarters and spoke with Inspector General Messana. He, if Giuliano was Robin Hood, was the Sheriff of Nottingham and a most unlikely looking sheriff he made, too, for he was short, stout and bald as an egg. The Inspector furnished me with a complete list of crimes with which Giuliano was charged. Just copying it took a full day. While I was working in the Italian version of a squad room, special agents would furnish me their names and ask me to make some sort of favorable mention of their work because they had a brother-in-law in Cleveland, an uncle in Chicago and an aunt in Brooklyn. The only lead I had on the whereabouts of the bandit was that the center of his power was the town of Montelepre.

The next morning, bright and early, I climbed into

my jeep and set out across the Palermo plain toward the almost sheer, forbidding gray cliffs that marked the boundary of Giuliano's empire. The mountain road was a series of difficult hairpin turns, with the road doubling back on itself until it reached the top. Although Montelepre is only twenty-five miles from Palermo, it took almost two hours to reach it. It was a typical poverty-ridden town, a gray stone mass of low houses clustered around a high church. I stopped in the main square opposite the statue of a mustachioed figure of a judge who, until then, had been the only citizen of Montelepre to have made good. There were some people idling about and I asked them where Giuliano lived. They stared at me in surprise for a moment, then turned on their heels and fled.

I spoke to a group of filthy *ragazzi* who had stopped their play to examine the jeep. Did they know where the family Giuliano live? The answer was a who-knows shrug of the shoulders. First I tried persuasion, pointing out that Giuliano was, after all, a very famous figure, and it would be impossible to keep from me the address of his parents. When this failed I tried guile, but it, too, was getting me nowhere very fast when an old man, his back stooped with age and his knuckles deformed with arthritis, came up to the jeep. The first words he spoke were unintelligible and it took me a while to figure out that the language he was trying to speak was English. His entire vocabulary did not exceed ten words, and he added to these words in Sicilian dialect which sounded like a mixture of Greek and

Albanian. I convinced him that it would be better to speak his native Italian and succeeded in achieving a means of communication between us.

"Where does the family Giuliano live?" I asked, after having carefully explained why I wanted this information.

"Which Giuliano are you looking for?" he countered.

"Salvatore Giuliano," I replied patiently.

"It is a very common name in these parts."

"The famous bandit."

"Oh, him," he said, as though it was a matter of surprise. He thought for a moment, then laboriously climbed into the back of the jeep and told me to drive straight ahead. We went through the town and stopped at the stone house which marked its outer limit. This was the bandit's home. I went in and met the Giuliano family: Mama Maria, short, squat, gray, toil-worn, shrewd, already convinced that the three greatest figures in history were Churchill, Roosevelt and Giuliano; sister Marianina, flashing-eyed, raven-haired, the favorite of *il bandito;* and Giuseppina, fat, matronly, stolid, to whom all this excitement over her kid brother was somewhat incomprehensible. The only member of the family not present was an older brother who was doing time in a mainland prison for having aided and abetted Giuliano. I didn't meet him until three weeks before writing this chapter, when he came into my office in Rome with a movie script that had been authored by the sorry remnants of the once merry band.

Throughout my conversations with the various

members of the family, the old man who had led me there stuck closer to me than a mustard plaster. This bothered me because I felt that I was doing very well except for his annoying interruptions. I told him that I was very grateful for his assistance, but now that he had completed the chore, I had no further need of him. He didn't take the hint, so I put it more bluntly. Would he not favor me by going back to whatever work he had been doing when my original request for information interrupted him? The old man, hurt by this suggestion, drew himself up and said, with a show of pride, "I am the father of Giuliano."

I spent the remainder of the afternoon with the family, reaching the point where I secured their complete confidence and promise of co-operation. I cannot reveal the exact steps that were taken thereafter to bring about my meeting with the bandit for it would bring police displeasure to those who helped me, and this, in most European countries, can be most disagreeable. At any rate, on a warm, sunny morning, a short time afterward, I stood on a corner of Via Libertà in Palermo. A jeep pulled alongside me and I climbed in beside the driver. In the rear seat sat Giuliano's father.

We traveled quickly through the crowded part of downtown Palermo, then headed west. We rolled past the police check post at thirty miles an hour. I waved to the musket-laden *carabinieri*, and they waved back in a friendly manner. A few miles past the police post the fertile valley that surrounds Palermo ended abruptly in a sheer wall of rocky, gray mountains. We climbed the initial rise and, where the road doubles back in a U-turn, pulled to a halt.

We sat for twenty minutes in the broiling sun, not speaking. Then I heard the clop, clop of hoofs. A moment later a gray-haired farmer, leading a tired donkey, clambered out of the rocky draw and continued up the road. He ignored us, and we ignored him.

"Is he part of the gang?" I whispered.

Papa nodded.

Ten minutes later, two roughly dressed men on horseback walked their mounts toward us. As they drew abreast, Papa pulled the visor of his cap down twice and said: *"Buon giorno."*

The men scrutinized me carefully, returned the *"Buon giorno"* and went down the rocky draw.

When there was no visible traffic on the road, a man came hurrying down the mountainside. He was a thin, swarthy individual with a finely trimmed mustache. I learned later that this was Gaspare Pisciotta, Giuliano's second-in-command, and the only member of the gang who had pledged his fidelity in blood. This is performed by slicing a finger and, as it bleeds, placing it against a similar bleeding digit of the commander and swearing eternal allegiance. As his open gray jacket tailed out behind him I could see a United States Army .45 caliber Colt automatic strapped to his hip. He said "hello" to us, and Papa told him everything was okay. Whereupon he climbed into the back seat and told the driver to swing the jeep about and go back down the road.

We drove to within two hundred yards of the police before turning left into a small lane. The vehicle picked its way between the ruts, turned off into an unkempt wheat field, bumped across it and stopped in front of a farmhouse that had been wrecked by a direct shell hit. We climbed out of the jeep and walked toward a small olive grove where three men stood. Two of them held machine pistols in the crooks of their arms. Two paces in front of them stood a barrel-chested man, his head held high, his thumbs hooked behind his belt. There was leadership in his stance.

This was Giuliano.

As we shook hands he said he had been looking forward to meeting me, and he wanted me to understand that by his friendship for me he was extending his friendship to all the people of America.

My first impression of the man was that he was possessed of tremendous strength. His thigh muscles filled out the corduroy work pants. He had a swarthy face marked by more than a dozen small scars, level brown eyes and carefully groomed, curly black hair.

It was the frank, open face of a man you would call in to watch the baby while you went to the movies. He looked like Turridu, the rustic gentleman who is the hero in Pietro Mascagni's lovely Sicilian opera, *Cavalleria Rusticana*. A writer for a slick magazine describing Giuliano from the photographs I took of him on this occasion wrote, "Giuliano's was a dynamic face: proud, ambitious, with no look whatever of ordinary criminality, but gave appearance of the unreconciled, of a superior energy that cannot help rising out of a context unfit for it. The best known of the pictures reminds one of certain faces in the earliest Soviet movies, or of those young Israeli fighters who have been ennobling the rotogravure sections in recent years: shirt open at the neck, jaw round and hard-set, mouth full and firm, head raised with a somewhat posy vigor. Giuliano is seen in three-quarters view, to emphasize even more the look of staring high past all danger and personal concern to the Goal." Truthfully, he didn't quite strike me that way. My first impression was that it was Errol Flynn playing Pancho Villa—in technicolor.

Rumor had it that he dressed in the uniform of a general, but today he wore a G.I. sun-tan shirt, open at the throat, and a green corduroy hunting jacket. At his right side was a fourteen-shot Browning.

"I was particularly glad you were able to come today, because I have a matter of great importance to discuss with you," he said. "Here is a letter I have written to President Truman. I would appreciate it if you would read it."

We sat on the ground in the shade of an olive tree. Giuliano's machine gunners were deployed at a distance from us. One guard climbed to the top of a stone fence and trained his binoculars on the police check post which was just a few hundred yards away. Another man wigwagged signals toward the gray face of the sheer cliff behind us, presumably teeming with members of the band.

Once I had settled myself comfortably, I read the letter. It opened with a humble apology for disturbing a man in so august a position and went on to say that while he was certain that Truman had heard of him, he wasn't at all sure whether these reports were accurate, since most of the government-controlled press called him simply a bandit and assassin. He wanted it clearly understood by the American President that whereas he practiced banditry and had committed many homicides, these were usually done with a noble purpose in view. "Therefore," he noted, "permit me to introduce myself in correct guise. I am GIULIANO." While it was true that he was an outlaw, there were many law-abiding persons (meaning persons not yet under indictment) in his entourage so that if the President felt that it was undiplomatic for him to deal with a bandit, Giuliano would set up one of these legitimate characters as his front man. He then launched into an urgent plea for aid as a worthy recipient under the Truman Doctrine. With fine Sicilian pride he did not ask for this assistance as a hand-out. He was willing to make it an even swap by giving Truman Sicily as the forty-ninth state of the Union.

"What do you think of it?" he asked, when I had finished reading it.

"A remarkable document," I said carefully.

Then, in utter sincerity, "What reception do you think it will get in Washington?"

"Well, I think that you ought to know that the American President is an extremely busy man and that sometimes weeks go by before letters, even important ones, are placed before him by his secretaries. Also, there is a very delicate diplomatic question involved. The United States government has its regular ambassador at Rome and the Italian government maintains an embassy in Washington. For the President to answer you directly might be construed as encouragement of a revolutionary, and I do not think that he would risk giving offense to the Italian government. For that reason I think you should be prepared for, at the very least, a long delay before any answer reaches Montelepre."

I steered the conversation away from politics. I asked him how a Robin Hood goes into business.

"I became an outlaw on September 2, 1943," he said. "You remember how bad things were right after the Allies took Sicily from the Germans. We didn't have enough food to eat. I was taking one hundred pounds of wheat on my mule from Montelepre to town, and as I went through San Giuseppe Jato two *carabinieri* stopped me. Since it was against the law to transport wheat, they arrested me.

"I told them they could take my animal and the wheat. I begged them to let me go, but they insisted on making me a criminal.

"While we were arguing, a big truck and trailer loaded with wheat came by, and the driver handed a roll of bills to the police. Here were the big black marketeers doing their work without being stopped. The little fellow was being made to suffer. I lost my head and started running. One of the policemen fired his rifle at me. The bullet hit me in the back, and I went down. He fired a second shot while I was on the ground, and he hit me again. I had a little gun hidden in my sock, and I pulled it out. I shot once and killed the *carabiniere*. I wounded the second one and managed to get away."

Giuliano continued bitterly: "If I had had ten thousand lire to give those police, I would not be called a criminal today. I would be called an honest man. Since that day I have lived in the mountains. I knew I was an honest man, but the police called me a bandit. I said to myself, very well, I will use bandit methods to do good for the poor and oppressed people of my country.

"The police do worse things to line their own pockets. You tell me who is the greater bandit, the policeman who squeezes money out of the poor to put in his own pocket or I, who rob from the rich to give to the poor.

"Why, if I were interested in myself, I would put in my pockets the proceeds from a single kidnapping, and with it I could live like a gentleman for the rest of my life. Instead I use it all to do good."

Because this correspondent has often found it expedient in his labors to pause and give thought to the subject of an unperforated skin—his own—I felt that the moment had arrived where it would be to my interest to give the internationally minded bandit a lesson in one phase of world history. I told Giuliano that there was a recent precedent for him in the person of Pancho Villa.

"And who," Giuliano asked suspiciously, "is Pancho Villa?"

"You know, the bandit from Mexico. There was a wonderful motion picture made about him with Wallace Beery."

"Never heard of it," Giuliano said, still not satisfied with the explanation.

"He was just like you. He was called an assassin and kidnapper and it's true he did those things, but he did them in order to gain control of the country he loved. You know where Mexico is?"

Giuliano nodded.

"All right, then. Pancho Villa was hated by his government. He was loved by the common people and in spite of the murders he committed he won them over and was able to march on the capital of his country. He would have been the ruler of Mexico to this day except for one small mistake that he made. He killed an American citizen. It wasn't even important to him, just an ordinary American. And what do you think happened? Why, the whole American army crossed the border and he couldn't fight against them. They caught him and hung him."

I let the words soak in and then continued the interview. I had read much, I told him, about what a hand he was with the ladies.

"I have read many of these stories," he said, "and I find them very interesting. I wish, too, that I was able to do all these things. Unfortunately, when you live the life of a bandit you cannot afford the luxury of a woman. It is the one sure way the police have of finally trapping you. I was in love only once. Her name was Mariuccia and she was a girl from my village. When I took to the hills I had to renounce her, for this is no life for a woman.

"About the murders the police have charged me with? Most of them I did commit, although the reasons given by them are not exact. Some crimes, however, were charged against me even though my men had no part in them. For example, there was a hold-up of a train near Messina in which all of the passengers were robbed. Most of the passengers were poor, so you see that this could not have been me."

His chief lieutenant, Pisciotta, said, "Tell him about the Misuracca brothers."

At first Giuliano objected, saying that I might think that he was boasting, but when I urged him on he grinned boyishly and launched into the recital.

"There were three brothers named Misuracca who joined my band. They had been members about two months when the police started a strangely accurate series of raids against us. I started checking back and found that two of the brothers had been arrested flagrante delicto during the commission of a burglary, yet the very next day they had been released. Now the police would never have done that unless a deal had been made between them, and the only thing they could offer the police was information about me. Did I go out and kill the brothers?"

"No," Pisciotta said admiringly. "You gave them a fair trial."

"I certainly did. About two o'clock in the morning we went to the house of one of the Misuraccas' friends and picked him up. Then we went to the Misuracca house and knocked on the door. One of the brothers asked, 'Who is there?' and I said, 'This is the *Maresciallo*. We have Giuliano trapped in the hills. Get dressed quickly and help us take him.' 'All right, *Maresciallo*, we'll be ready in a minute.' I knew then that they were spies. When the door was opened we went in and took all the brothers and the friend to the village square. I gave them a minute to say their prayers, but while they were praying one of them fled. We were able to kill only the friend and two of the brothers. I wrote a short poem about this and placed it on the chest of one of them so that the police would know who did it."

Translated into English, the poem has a forbidding lilt. It reads:

> "The unhappy souls of spies
> Do not go to paradise.
> Giuliano"

"The American magazines have been writing about a new miracle drug." Giuliano pulled out a notebook and showed me the name that he had written there.

It was aureomycin. "It is a good cure for tuberculosis, is it not?"

I said that the popular magazines were describing it as such. Why, I wondered, was he so interested in it?

"It's for Pisciotta. He suffers from tuberculosis."

Giuliano asked me how I thought his war against the police would end and I neatly side-stepped a direct answer. I did say that while I was not the expert he was on the Sicilian police, from my experience, however, as a police reporter in the United States, I would say that if he were captured or killed, it would be through betrayal or because of a woman. These words pleased him, because he pointed to Pisciotta and said, "Men like this are with me to the death."

We were stretched out under an olive tree, heads resting on our arms. Giuliano was anxious that I understand him; that I understand the motives which prompted his actions; that Americans should understand that he was not all black. On a sheet of foolscap he began slowly writing from memory a thirteen-stanza poem he had written about his life. It dealt with the tragedy of an idealistic young man whose great love was shattered by the idiocy and greed of the police and who then dedicated his life to battling them and righting their injustices.

Giuliano was particularly bitter about the treatment his family had received at the hands of the *carabinieri*. On one occasion, when his mother and younger sister, Maria, were imprisoned, an angry Giuliano wrote a sharp note to the chief of the security forces, giving him one week to effect their release. It ended with a threat that if it was not done by the police, it would be done by him. Both mother and daughter were released.

While behind bars, Maria wrote the marching song which became the anthem of Giuliano's army. It is entitled: "March on the Prison." It tells of gentlemen coming to arms and of prison guards whose hearts beat in terror as they wait for the triumphal arrival. One line reads: "Oh, mother, a lawyer can't help me. I need Giuliano to set me free."

In this mountain kingdom Giuliano feared no man, especially if that man was a *carabiniere*. "You must have *fegato* if you want to win," he said, indicating that it was a quality he possessed but which the police lacked. *Fegato*, translated literally, means liver, and it corresponds to the American guts.

"One afternoon I got into a gun fight with four *carabinieri*. I had just jumped to the road when a bullet hit me in the chest and knocked me to the ground. I tried to fire back, but my gun jammed. None of my men was around. I dug into my pocket, pulled out a hand grenade and threw it, but I was very weak, and it exploded near me, almost killing me. The *carabinieri* turned around and fled."

Inspector Messana's final plan had been to set up road blocks on all arteries running into Giuliano's kingdom and thus seal it off from the rest of the island. Then, from these points of control, he conducted forays into the mountains.

"I'll tell you how good that system is," Giuliano said. "With three of my men I drove into Palermo. We were stopped at the road and asked for our identification papers. I reached into my pocket and pulled out a few one-thousand-lire notes and let them fall to the ground. While the *carabinieri* scrambled for them we continued peacefully on our way."

The shadows had lengthened. Members of the gang coming in from the hills were introduced to me and then took off again.

"The hope of my poor oppressed people is in America. That is why I have written to President Truman. We have so much in common. We both hate communism and love democracy. I have explained to him that I need more machine guns and especially anti-tank guns. If Mr. President does not send them to me directly, I will understand. After all, he must not give offense to Italy."

It was late now. We shook hands and said goodbye. I took a backward look at the figure of the handsome, powerful, fearless, twenty-five-year-old man with the morals of Dillinger and the philanthropy of Rockefeller as he hurried toward his familiar mountains.

In his left pocket he carried hand grenades, in his right an order of the day, still unissued, setting up Sicily as an independent republic.

Robin Hood had turned politician.

Somehow the fact that I had interviewed Giuliano became known to certain newspapermen and two of them, figuring that the earliest date my article could hit the newsstands was still some weeks off, decided to beat me to the story. They were Sey Korman of the *Chicago Tribune,* an enterprising reporter of the old school, and a *New York Times* second-stringer named Cianfarra. I didn't find out about their project until an hour after they had actually flown out of Rome so that, if I wanted to head them off, I would have to act immediately. I hurried across the street from the Foreign Press building to the central post and telegraph building in the Piazza San Silvestro and sent off an urgent rate message addressed to the home of the bandit's parents. It stated that I had just come across information that the Italian Secret Police had dispatched two of their agents disguised as American correspondents, bearing foolproof sets of credentials. As a result, more than a year went by before Giuliano permitted a stranger to enter his camp. His visitor was a young, attractive Swedish tourist who spent several nights in his company.

The publication of my scoop created a storm in Italy. Many magazines reprinted the article, one of them stretching it to twelve installments. Newspapers ridiculed the police because one American newspaperman had been able to do what thousands of Italian police officers and soldiers couldn't. It was not a very fair comparison but it stung nevertheless. Mario Scelba, the Minister of Interior, angrily removed Inspector Messana from his post and replaced him with an official whose effectiveness proved to be on a par with that of his predecessor.

There was no more doubt in the minds of the Italians on the mainland as to the authenticity of Robin Hood. He was a very real personage, and something of a national hero, besides. For this sentiment Scelba held me responsible. He ordered the foreign section of his ministry to study my writings with great care to see if they could find in them any good reason for expelling me from the country. The Communist Party, too, took a firm stand in the matter of these articles because Palmiro Togliatti, Duce of the PCI (*Partito Comunista Italiano*) had fixed the party line which stated, in effect, that Robin Hood was a reactionary. Their feelings about me followed this peculiar logic: No journalist had been able to get to Giuliano. Stern got to him. Therefore Stern is no journalist. If he is no journalist, then what is he? Very simple, he must be a spy.

With that, Senator LiCausi, PCI leader in Sicily, declared in a speech before the upper house of the Italian legislature that I was an army major (this is quite a jump from the merely assimilated rank of captain that all war correspondents hold); that I was President Truman's secret agent in Italy and that it was my special task to furnish arms to the anti-communist elements. I suppose that I should be grateful to the good Italian Senator because his attacks proved helpful to me in my work. There were many spy-conscious Italians who believed him. On several occasions when I visited a government ministry where a half day's wait is not out of the ordinary, I was amazed to find that I was received almost immediately. They went to special pains not to offend me; if they did, I might tell Truman.

It wasn't until I broke the Major Holohan story and tied a communist leader to the crime by proving that he received six hundred tons of United States arms from the men who murdered the Major that the Red press really got rough. What they had written about me before was practically a compliment. The Italian-language *Pravda* called *L'Unita* took out after me with an article under the headline: AMERICAN SPY STERN FURNISHED GIULIANO WITH ARMS. The subhead read "Does Scelba Know of This Criminal Traffic?" I quote the entire article, not only for its interest in connnection with a story on Giuliano, but because it is an example of the immorality that Joseph Goebbels brought to journalism.

"The circle tightens around me. Light arms are not sufficient any more. I must have heavy arms." With this request Salvatore Giuliano concluded a dramatic letter to the 'journalist' Michael Stern in the Via della Mercede 53 [this is close—my address is 54], Rome. The missive was intercepted by the police who in the first days of June, 1947, captured the bearer of it, a minor member of Giuliano's band. The letter was consigned to Minister Scelba.

"Who was Michael Stern? This individual came to Italy in the legitimate official capacity of correspondent for several large newspapers. In reality his job was far less legitimate. Stern was really sent to Italy by 'The American Friends of Sicily,' an equivocal association, the direction of which was in the hands of politicians tied to major American trusts, amongst them being General Donovan and Senator Karl Mundt. The ends of this association, one of the many analogous ones that flower in America, favored and encouraged by the State Department, were many times solemnly made known in public meetings. Its adherents affirmed that war was inevitable and that Sicily, because of the strategic position that she would assume in any future conflict, would have, of necessity, to accept the protection of the United States.

"In that period, as we already know, public order in Sicily was in the hands of Inspector General of Public Security Ettore Messana, whose ties with the Mafia and the brigands have been sufficiently illustrated in the course of the trial at Viterbo. It is not any more a secret that all the important doings of Giuliano's band had been faithfully signaled to the Inspector of Public Security and that he knew about the encounter between Stern and Giuliano and what they said to each other.

"In this conversation, Stern told Giuliano the ambitious plan of 'The American Friends of Sicily,' astutely pointed out to him the possibility of improving his position by helping in the plan to annex Sicily to the United States. He promised Giuliano immunity and honors. These promises were the same that were made to Inspector Messana to whom the followers of separatism had assured the portfolio of Minister of Interior in a Sicily separated from Italy and under the scepter of Umberto II.

"Giuliano adhered with enthusiasm to the proposal of Stern, to whom he gave a rhetorical message addressed to President Truman. In this surprising appeal, the outlaw ingenuously revealed the nature of the pact stipulated between him and the American spy. He wrote, literally: 'The thing of which I have essential need is your great and powerful moral support'—as you see Giuliano appreciates also material support, asking arms that were regularly furnished him—'I will fight a double war, one secretly against the communists, making them slowly disappear from the political life in Sicily, the other openly, headed not by me, because that would give ammunition to the international critics who might be against an alliance with a bandit, but directed by free men maintained and strongly supported by me in all ways.'

"Does Scelba know of this meeting between Giuliano and Stern? The Inspector of Public Security in Sicily certainly must have known this through his stool-pigeons in the Giuliano band. Is it possible that he did not inform the Minister of Interior?

"Does the Minister of Interior know the reason for the visit of Stern to Giuliano? The letter that the brigand sent to Stern and that the police intercepted and consigned to the ministry revealed every detail. Why hasn't Scelba asked an accounting from the American Ambassador concerning the grave mission of the false journalist sent to Italy with the task of provoking and feeding mutiny and revolt? Is this the manner in which Scelba believes he can protect the integrity of the country and the unity of the nation?"

The entire proof for this article reposed in a photograph in which I was interviewing Giuliano. This picture was lifted from the pages of *True* where it illustrated my original article. *L'Unita* labeled it: "A rare photographic document." When I filed an immediate criminal libel charge against the director of the paper and the authors of the article, *L'Unita* reprinted the photograph under a scare head which read: "Let Stern deny this photograph, if he can!"

In August, 1949, Minister Scelba set up a special unit of thirteen hundred *carabinieri* called the special force for the suppression of banditry in Sicily, and placed at its head a fearless veteran of both world wars named Colonel Ugo Luca. Almost at the outset, Giuliano embarrassed the new commander by dropping a hand grenade into a troop carrier which killed four *carabinieri*. The bandit sent each of the widows a fat check and a letter of condolence. Luca's force made little headway at the start, although its antics received wide publicity. At one point they sent flame throwers against every cave in the mountains, a procedure that must have decimated a goodly amount of wild life, although somewhat useless in the fight against Giuliano since he always slept under a roof. There were newsreels of tanks roaring up and down the mountainside, though the noise of their approach would have frightened off even less cunning crooks. These antics were usually coupled with the announcement of the imminent capture of Robin Hood which, after the third or fourth time, left the public weary. During the summer, at the height of a police campaign against an abbreviated bathing suit, known as *lo slip,* a humorous weekly published a cartoon which convulsed the nation. It showed Colonel Luca reporting to Scelba. The caption read: "Let Giuliano wear *lo slip* just once and I'll throw him behind bars!"

When Luca stopped playing for the headlines, his work began bearing fruit. He concentrated on the families of the outlaws. Literally hundreds of fathers, mothers, brothers and sisters were thrown into prison under the vague charge of suspicion of aiding and abetting. Since the writ of habeas corpus and admittance to bail are practices found only in decadent democracies, these people stayed behind bars. If, after a year, Luca secured definite proof of their innocence, he would apologize to them. Although he didn't get close to Giuliano, he did manage to kill off some of the leader's most trusted men. Other members of the band fled to foreign countries. Still others were betrayed by stool-pigeons who were becoming increasingly bold, especially since Luca had raised the reward on Giuliano's head to an unprecedented fifty million lire.

It was a knock-down, drag-out fight with no quarter asked and none given. For once Giuliano faced an opponent who was as tough and ruthless as himself. Almost a year after Colonel Luca had begun his war against the bandit, an informer put the finger on a pair of Giuliano's men named Castrenze Madonia and Tito Vitale. The pair was quickly picked up and thrown behind bars. It was a very ordinary incident, one that had happened dozens of times before, yet it brought the war to a climax. Even the succeeding event followed the familiar pattern. Giuliano kidnapped the informer and took him off into the hills.

The wife of the informer hurried to Colonel Luca's headquarters and hysterically threw herself at his feet, begging him to save her husband's life. Colonel Luca's forces roared into the mountains, made house-to-house searches through all the villages in the area, arrested and threw into prison scores of people, but the informer remained in Giuliano's hands. Two days later, Luca received a note from the bandit. It gave him twenty-four hours to release Madonia and Vitale. If not, the informer's body would be shipped to him with the usual card pinned to its chest, reading: "Like this end all who spy against Giuliano."

It was at this point that events took a different turn. Several days later, much to Luca's amazement, the informer walked into the Colonel's office under his own power. The story he told was even more amazing. When the two prisoners had not been released, Giuliano turned the informer over to Pisciotta with instructions that justice be done. Pisciotta took the condemned man to the place of execution, but instead of shooting him, told him that he would spare his life on a single condition: the informer was to return to Colonel Luca and tell him that Pisciotta was most anxious to converse privately with him. Not with an assistant, or a substitute, but with the Colonel himself. Furthermore, the conversation was to be held at a place of Pisciotta's choosing to which the Colonel, dressed in civilian clothes, was to come alone and unarmed.

It posed a difficult problem for Luca. Being a man of great personal courage, he did not fear for his own life in meeting Pisciotta under the conditions outlined by the outlaw. He did fear walking into a trap in which he would be held as hostage for the release of the imprisoned members of Giuliano's band. But because the release of an informer was an event without precedent he decided to keep the appointment. Dressed as a simple workman, he went to the town of Monreale and, late at night, placed himself just inside the gateway. After a short wait, a peasant walked by and placed two fingers to the brim of his hat. Luca repeated the sign. The peasant nodded his head and walked through the town, the Colonel following. The guide led the way to a poorly kept stone house, then up a narrow, dark, foul-smelling stairway to a tiny, dimly lit room. As Luca entered, the guide ran off. For half an hour the police officer sat on a rickety chair, waiting. Then he heard the creak of footsteps on the stairway. The door opened and a swarthy, mustachioed figure entered.

It was Gaspare Pisciotta. Giuliano's blood brother and chief lieutenant came to the point immediately. For some time now there had been a difference of opinion which was dividing Robin Hood's merry men. The group headed by Giuliano wanted to continue the war against the Italian police. The other group, whose opinions Pisciotta favored, although he very carefully kept this viewpoint from his chief, was that the band take the funds they still had and flee to other countries, like Pasquale Sciortino, who managed to smuggle his way into the United States where he is living today. Now he, Pisciotta, was ready to break away from the leader and join forces with the police. Not as an informer, for his Sicilian sense of honor would not permit it, but as a full-fledged partner of the police. For this partnership he wanted the fifty million lire reward, a promise that he would not be prosecuted for any previous crimes and a safe conduct until he could emigrate to another country. Colonel Luca's promise that these things would be done was not sufficient. Pisciotta insisted on getting it in writing and signed by the Minister of Interior himself.

Colonel Luca drew up the papers requested by Pisciotta and signed the Minister's name to them.

In mid-July, 1950, Pisciotta arrived at the house of an attorney-at-law in the village of Castelvetrano where Giuliano was staying and brought him the reports from the various members of the band. For greater security, Giuliano had ruled that only Pisciotta was to know where he was hiding and all reports were to be channeled through his lieutenant. At three o'clock in the morning both men lay in the same double bed, Giuliano fast asleep, Pisciotta merely pretending. The blood brother of the outlaw chief slowly drew a revolver that lay under his pillow, held it against the back of his leader and squeezed twice on the trigger.

Pisciotta pocketed the gun, quickly left the house and hurried to the outskirts of town where Captain Antonio Perenze of Luca's forces, and a group of *carabinieri*, were waiting. "It is done," he announced simply, and disappeared in the darkness.

Captain Perenze slipped into the lawyer's home through the door left open by Pisciotta, entered the room where Giuliano lay dead. He leveled his submachine gun and fired a burst into the inert body. Then, with the help of two of his men, he dragged the body out of the house to the stone courtyard.

It was thus that the Sicilian Robin Hood ceased being a man and became, like his Sherwood Forest cousin, only a legend. It is entirely likely that the foregoing carefully documented story of his end will be ignored by history in favor of the far more colorful one that appeared in my favorite news weekly. *Time*

110

of July 17, 1950, covering the story in its usual breathless fashion, gave this fulsome report.

BANDIT'S END

"All day long the wrinkled mother screamed denials of her son's death. 'They'll never catch him,' she cried, 'never!' Next morning, when the *carabiniere* thrust her through the throng outside the morgue gates to view his body, Maria Giuliano broke down. 'My blood,' she croaked hoarsely, 'my own blood.' Then, turning fiercely toward a bank of news photographers, she spat out, 'It's you who've brought my son to hell.'

"Like Maria, few Sicilians could believe at first that Salvatore Giuliano was really dead. He had been as handsome as a schoolgirl's dream, as vain and indestructible as a god on Olympus. For seven years in the mountain fastnesses of Sicily he had been king of bandits in a land where every bandit is looked upon as king. . . . Like Robin Hood's men, his army would strike swiftly in small groups—kidnapping some purse-proud landlord here, killing a sheriff's man there—and fade elusively into mountain caves, vineyards and wheatfields. . . .

"Last year, Rome sent to Sicily hard-eyed Colonel Ugo Luca, a World War II Italian intelligence officer. With a special task force of two thousand picked men, mostly bachelors, Luca set about combing Sicily for his prey.

"Probing the hills and villages, Luca and his men identified one bandit after another, painstakingly weaned peasants away from their hero worship of Giuliano. Some of the bandits surrendered. When word got around that Luca treated them well, others followed, seventy-six in all. The *carabinieri* shot seven more in the hills and arrested one hundred and fifty-seven. So the band scattered, some of the leaders fled to other lands, but the bandit king himself remained in Sicily.

"Two months ago, Luca heard that Giuliano was moving down from the hills toward the vineyards of the south. The Colonel ordered all his men in the area out of uniform and let it be known that he himself was off to Rome. Then he baited a trap for Giuliano's vanity. He sent a troop of *carabinieri* into the wine district camouflaged as a moving-picture unit. They were ordered to spread the word that they were making a picture about bandits. The unit was told to drop strong hints that a leading role might be available for Giuliano. With no names mentioned, a series of return hints from Giuliano soon led the 'moviemakers' into the town of Castelvetrano.

"There one night last week they found their man. The *carabinieri* opened fire. Giuliano fled, firing over his shoulder as he went. For fifteen minutes the chase led on through labyrinths of twisted alleys and courtyards. Captain Antonio

Perenze, leader of the *carabinieri*, hid in a doorway. A stalking figure crept up, machine gun set.
Perenze blasted point-blank. The figure whirled,
tottered and fell face down, a dark red splotch
welling up under his white shirt.

"A few minutes later Salvatore Giuliano lay
dead, his upper body shattered by bullets. In his
pocket was a packet of mentholated cigarettes, a
small flashlight and a photograph of himself."

Sometime afterward Pisciotta was arrested by the
police and imprisoned. He was lumped together with
the surviving members of Giuliano's band and placed
on trial. In his defense he triumphantly produced the
official document issued to him by the Minister of Interior. General Luca—he had been promoted for his
work in suppressing banditry in Sicily—then stated
that the document was worthless and that he, Luca,
had forged the Minister's name. "In my war against
the bandit," General Luca testified blandly, "I employed deceit and forgery where I found it necessary.
In the end the forces of law and order were successful." Since this trial has not been concluded, it is impossible to say what end finally befell Robin Hood's
trusted blood brother * who suddenly found himself
without safe conduct, absolution or reward.

This trial, being held in Viterbo, has already run
ten months. The name of Salvatore Giuliano appears
as one of the defendants. A defense lawyer requested

* Convicted and sentenced to life imprisonment.

the court to strike it from the list and that evidence against him be ruled inadmissible. He based his request on the fact that there existed incontrovertible proof of his death.

The judge took the matter under advisement, then issued a Solomon-like ruling. "I will continue to receive evidence against Giuliano," he said, "but if he is convicted, I shall set aside the verdict."

George Dawson

4

George John Dawson is the only man in the world officially believed to have made $100,000,000 since the end of World War II. He made it in war surplus, and it wasn't easy—but it would have been much harder if he'd been choosy about his customers.

Twenty-five years ago in England there was a squat young Cockney who used to be up driving a truck by 4 A.M., a good deal earlier than most others, and who didn't come off the job until 11 P.M. His name was George John Dawson, and he worked for his father who was a poor and honest junk dealer.

As recently as seven years ago this same George

Dawson was still unknown and was still a junkie, buying and selling second-hand cars and trucks. But by then he was his own boss, had three kids and a childhood sweetheart for a wife. He lived modestly, but his honesty had begun to wear a little thin. Three times Scotland Yard had him. Once he was packed off to jail for eighteen months.

Today, as always, George Dawson is still a junkie and relatively unknown. Only now he has a variety of reasons for not wanting to be better known. He lives in a sparkling fifteen-room villa in Cannes on the French Riviera. By his own count he has eleven cars, five of them Cadillacs, and until recently had four private planes. At the dockside, simple millionaires stare jealously at his new yacht, the 250-ton *Mimosan*, which is more lavish than the one owned by Egypt's playboy ex-King Farouk. Along with a lot of other memories from the early grimy years, the childhood sweetheart has vanished. Now there is a second Mrs. Dawson, a handsome blonde of twenty-eight, whose fingers flick an emerald ring once worn by England's Duchess of Kent and whose pearls once graced the neck of the ex-Queen of Italy.

What has happened to George Dawson during the last seven years is simply that he has made more money than anybody else on earth. In fact, he has made, although he may not have kept, $100,000,000— repeat, one hundred million dollars—since the end of the war.

Dawson found his rainbow when Hitler shot himself and Germany surrendered. All over Europe and Africa supply depots bulged with tanks, guns, jeeps, trucks, engines and equipment, suddenly and sometimes mistakenly reclassified as "surplus." According to a U.S. congressional committee now investigating Dawson, the tireless, unknown Cockney got his hands on a billion dollars' worth of it, mostly American, for a modest 10 percent, or, if you prefer help in your arithmetic, a fabulous hundred-million-dollar profit.

Naturally, an ordinary man using ordinary business methods might find it hard to make this kind of money in seven years—and still be making it. But Dawson obviously is not an ordinary man and his methods of doing business, if the name even applies, are not precisely those favored by Better Business Bureaus. The financial shenanigans in which Dawson has been involved have left a murky mark all over the world, the White House not excluded.

Recently I paid an uninvited call on "Jolly George," as the British papers call him when they feel playful. Cannes at its best is one of the world's true garden spots. At its worst it is just a sunny place for shady people. The Villa La Saugette which Dawson rents is situated on a hill overlooking the Mediterranean. It is a sizeable although—for Cannes—not pretentious villa, considerably smaller than the Aga Khan's, a short distance down the road. As I entered the flagstone courtyard, a bored-looking chauffeur stood beside Dawson's silver-gray Cadillac convertible, one of the five. The chauffeur, a Frenchman who, I later learned, is also one of Dawson's bodyguards, ignored me, and I pushed through the front door. The second Mrs. Dawson, expensively dressed in good taste, was standing in the living room. Her bleached-blonde hair, high bosom, broad hips and neat ankles suggested that she might have been a chorus girl who had recently become acquainted with the better things in life. In her case, this was true. She was Olga, "Jolly George's" ex-chorus-girl wife.

She came toward me suspiciously and asked what I wanted. "My husband never grants interviews," she said testily in answer to my reply. I had just begun to argue when a high-pitched voice, indelibly Cockney, called downstairs and wanted to know who in the hell was there.

"It's an American who wants to interview you," Olga yelled back.

"Never give interviews," snapped Dawson.

Having nothing to lose, I began to do a little screeching myself. I shouted that I'd come all the way from America to see him, that I had with me the testimony of the congressional committee investigating his affairs, that I'd just been in Geneva, Switzerland, with ex-New York Governor Charles Poletti, "one of your bitterest enemies," and, finally, that "it's as important for you to see me as for me to see you."

There was a pause. Then Dawson called down, "I'm shaving. Why don't we meet at the Carlton in an hour?"

The Carlton Bar is the smartest meeting place on

the Riviera. An hour later to the dot Dawson marched in. He is uncommonly short, only 5 feet 4 or 5, with an exceptionally long torso and abbreviated legs. Perhaps because he has rarely been to sea, he was dressed like a musical-comedy admiral: a double-breasted blue jacket with pearl buttons, blue slacks, blue canvas shoes. A pair of small brown eyes looked straight at me.

Dawson started pitching first and threw over a couple of fast balls. How long had I been working on him? Six weeks. What sources had I covered? I told him American Intelligence files had been made available to me, together with the testimony of Congressman Bonner's subcommittee, and that I'd had frank talks with innumerable civil and military officials besides ex-business associates of his.

"I suppose you're going to crucify me," he snapped.

"Not at all," I said. Most of the people I'd talked with had passed on a mountain of uncomplimentary material about him, much of it dealing with the bribery of government officials and the sale by Dawson of surplus war material to communists. But I hoped, I told him, that he would now give me his explanations. For instance, how about his attempt to bribe one of the U.S. prosecuting attorneys in Frankfurt, Germany, with $40,000?

"Bribery, my foot," Dawson snorted. "This chappie was trying to shake me down for forty thousand. Wanted that to dismiss an indictment by your government against me. I wouldn't let him put the squeeze on me, so I said no. The most it was worth was five thousand—strictly for nuisance value, you understand."

I understood perfectly. It was outrageous for a public official to ask for a $40,000 bribe. But $5,000 would have been neither outrageous nor criminal. Simply sound business.

Still feeling him out, I asked about his dealings with a company called Mogurt. Mogurt is owned by the Hungarian communist government. It buys trucks and cars outside the Iron Curtain and ships them back inside. In recent years Dawson's business with Mogurt has been brisk.

In the summer of 1950 he had picked up 360 U.S. six-ton, six-by-six Army trucks parked in a motor pool in the U.S. Zone of Germany. Although brand-new, they had been classified by the American authorities as "surplus." Even more peculiar was the fact that they had been sold to Dawson for about $100 apiece. He had then resold them at an unknown but presumably killing profit to the Red Hungarians of Mogurt. But the most disturbing aspect of this deal was that these 360 trucks, vans loaded with spare parts, complete and ready for combat down to the entrenching tools strapped to their sides, were shipped out of the U.S. Zone to the Hungarian Commies on August 19, 1950, seven weeks after Korea, at a time when our own military command was hollering for trucks.

They were hauled by railroad to a small town on the Czech-German border where a Mogurt representative was waiting for them. Once across the border these trucks would either go to North Korea for use against Americans who had built and until recently had owned them, or they would be used by the Russians to replace other trucks sent to North Korea.

As the train bearing the first batch of 360 trucks chugged to a halt at the border, an American MP sergeant attached to a customs unit stepped forward to make a routine check of the shipping documents given him by the Mogurt man.

The documents were in perfect order, including an export permit signed by the U.S. High Commissioner in Germany, John J. McCloy. How was it possible for George Dawson to arrange all this? How, seven weeks after the fighting in Korea began, was it possible for Dawson, an English junkie with a prison record, to get permission to hand over 360 U.S. Army trucks to the Reds legally and with the okay of McCloy, a former head of the World Bank, a trusted friend of Presidents Roosevelt and Truman, a man widely regarded as a person of the highest integrity?

While such questions must necessarily worry you and me, they did not bother the lone MP sergeant that day at the Czech frontier. He told the Mogurt man to go jump. He pointed out that since the trucks still had U.S. Army insignia stenciled on them, they were still American property and he for one was not letting them through.

The Mogurt representative spluttered angrily. "These are U.S. Army surplus which we bought through regular channels and which we have the permission of your High Commissioner to take out."

"I don't care whose permission you've got," the MP told the exasperated Hungarian. "I'm referring this shipment to my captain. Until then, none of the freight cars go through."

The captain passed the buck to his major, and so on up. By the time the matter reached McCloy's office certain facts finally dawned on the top civilian brass. Hungary could not possibly absorb all the trucks and jeeps Dawson had been selling to them. The eventual destination of these vehicles was very much on the wrong side of the Korean firing line. McCloy countermanded his original approval. And then, because like most statesmen he is sensitive to criticism from the outside, he clucked, "No comment," and tried to sit on and hide the rotten egg that had turned up.

"It shows," said Dawson, jabbing a stubby finger into my midriff for emphasis, "a lamentable lack of discipline on the part of your troops. It's the first time I ever heard of an enlisted man flaunting the orders of his superiors. Terribly incorrect from a business standpoint, you know. I've already filed suit for damages against your government.

"When you get right down to it," he went on, still jabbing away, "it's hard to understand why you American chaps get so excited. I've done quite a bit of business with Mogurt and I've always found them highly correct. They pay the highest prices, and always in advance. If there was anything wrong with the sale of military trucks to them, why did the U.S. High Commissioner approve the many transactions I've had with them?"

That was a fair question. Very fair. Later I went up to Frankfurt. McCloy, the High Commissioner, couldn't see me. Benjamin J. Buttenwieser, his deputy and a one-time partner of the banking house of Kuhn, Loeb, wouldn't see me. Over the phone his answers, or lack of answers, were what the journalistic profession calls the "no comment" run-around.

By the time we had passed fifteen minutes together, Dawson fairly exuded good will. He was beaming and jovial, the eternal salesman, pounding me on the back and calling me by my first name. This was more in keeping with the press notices that call him "Jolly George, the Mysterious Millionaire." According to Dawson on the subject of Dawson, he is the super-mechanic who takes a worthless tube, adds it to a worthless crate and makes the whole come miraculously to life as a truck of great value. He is up-from-the-slums George, a diamond in the rough who sends his Rolls-Royce for fish and chips, which is like sending a liveried butler to a diner for beer and a hamburger.

He said that he and his wife would be happy to entertain me at luncheon. I accepted and spent the rest of the day with him at his villa. Until he drove me to the station in one of his Cadillacs that night, I spent eight hours with him in an exclusive interview.

From the villa at Cannes, which also serves as his office, though he keeps no office hours, Dawson makes the cable and telephone wires hum. His phone bills are fabulous. Telegrams twenty-five pages long are normal. He uses the phone as unthinkingly as he breathes. After I left him, he phoned me seven times. Once he phoned from Paris to Rome and couldn't even remember why he'd called. "Oh well," he said, "it was nice talking to you anyway."

Hobbies and sports have no place in Dawson's scheme of things because money takes up all his time. He is either making it or dreaming about more of it. His greatest wish is to make so much of it that through the sheer weight of his millions ordinary people will be forced to grant him respectability.

Though Dawson never reads a book and only glances at a paper to read about himself, his knowledge of the world is considerable. He travels widely through Europe and Africa, and twice has gotten to the U.S. Through his own agents and technical experts abroad and through representatives of foreign purchasing missions beating a track to his doors, Dawson keeps his business at his finger-tips. He knows what France has that Spain might use, or whether a certain type of surplus machine will find a better market in Portugal than in Brazil. To help him, besides the experts, he has his son, his son-in-law, and a Swiss attorney, Paul Hagenbach of Zurich, who is his second-in-command. Actually Dawson has no employees. As a friend puts it, only confederates.

Considering the gross improprieties of his business life, Dawson is a reasonably model citizen in private.

He doesn't throw wild parties and eats mostly at home with his wife and children. His mother-in-law lives with them, but Dawson has solved this proverbial problem by putting her in a separate wing. Her meals are served to her there.

When Dawson goes on the road, however, he puts on quite a show. His retinue often consists of fifty or more friends, attorneys, technical advisers, couriers, hopeful foreigners and general hangers-on. In America his simple living expenses were $1,000 a day. In Paris, which he visits periodically, he keeps a bodyguard in the person of an American ex-GI who waits there permanently for the boss to arrive. On arrival, Dawson and his wolf pack take over an entire floor of the Plaza Athénée Hotel, one of the city's best. At night there are likely to be a series of pretty flavorsome parties, attended by the Parisian sisters of the type of girl that Johnny Myers employed with such success in Washington and New York. But Dawson is not likely to be there. He is devoted to his wife and kids and has kept himself singularly free of gossip.

Except for the handmade monogrammed silk shirts from Sulka and the eleven cars, Dawson is a relatively subdued new merchant prince. His one really sumptuous showpiece is the yacht, and all it proves is that you can be rich as Croesus and have much less fun. Bought for $125,000 from the late Alberto Dodero, the Argentine shipping king, the 250-ton *Mimosan* was redecorated for Dawson by his friend, the late Riviera playboy, Freddie McEvoy, for an undisclosed sum. But the amount must have been breathtaking, because McEvoy used to boast of having cleared $40,000, and when the poor *Mimosan* lumbered out to sea, she was so top-heavy that she had to turn back. Neither the yacht nor Dawson has been out since.

It was while McEvoy was redecorating the interior of the yacht that he showed Dawson the $200 humidors that went into each guest cabin.

"What the hell are those?" the junkie demanded.

"Humidors," said McEvoy.

"Yeah. But what do we use them for?"

"That's where your guests keep the dollar cigars you give them."

The Dawson story is a rags-to-riches saga that Horatio Alger would have been the first to shun, for in his rise to wealth Dawson demonstrated a remarkable resistance to those homely virtues which that highly moral author insisted were the prerequisites for success. There was nothing new in Dawson's operations, for they followed a previously established example. At the close of the First World War, Europe was flooded with instruments of destruction that suddenly were of no further value to their owners. It was a situation made to order for that internationally minded man, Sir Basil Zaharoff. This suave Greek reasoned that while the major powers would stop beating out each other's brains for a while, there were many minor states which were willing to have a go at small-scale mayhem if they had the tools with which to fight. And so Sir Basil bought war surplus low and resold it high to war lords in China,

Arabs in the Middle East, Riff tribesmen in Africa and revolutionists in the banana republics of the Western Hemisphere. When Sir Basil died peacefully, nobody should have been surprised that he was one of the world's richest men.

At the close of the Second World War, the same situation prevailed. Europe was again flooded with instruments of destruction and a new group of merchants of death, led by Dawson, jumped in to help the new "minor league" states, like Poland, Red China, Yugoslavia, Greece, Israel and the Arab countries. But Dawson jumped first and Dawson has made the biggest splash.

Dawson's mania for money undoubtedly originated in his slum upbringing. The man whose yacht today outshines the King of Egypt's and whose wife wears the pearls that once graced an Italian royal neck was born forty-five years ago in a tenement in London. Until fifteen, young Dawson attended Saint Olav's School and then, at the end of a most undistinguished period of instruction, went to work stringing tennis rackets in a sporting-goods factory. He twisted catgut for a year and then left to join his father in the junk business.

At eighteen he married Florence Redford, a childhood sweetheart, now living quietly in England. They had two sons, the older of whom was killed in a plane accident. The younger one works for Dawson. Their daughter, Bubbles, married a man who is now associated with Dawson in business. Four years ago, Dawson's first wife divorced him so that he could marry a good-looking blonde of twenty-four, who had been kicking up her heels in Lupino Lane's *Me and My Girl.* Born Olga Mirinoff, the daughter of a Russian colonel and an English mother, she had a four-year-old daughter, Tanya, by a previous marriage. Since her marriage to "Jolly George," they have had two baby sons, François and Daniel, who live with them in the villa at Cannes.

Dawson has always possessed a drive and daring in business that must be admired. At twelve his family gave him a bike. Much as he would have liked pedaling it, instinct told him that he could make money by renting it to other poor boys. Presently, with the money earned in this manner, Dawson had three bikes. One to ride and two to hire.

When Dawson was twenty, he and a friend bought a truck and went into business as truckers. Dawson used to be up by 4 A.M., driving alone to the hop fields in Kent. He'd take a load of hops for delivery, drive back for another load, then—without stopping for lunch—drive to Aldershot with a load of asphalt, unload the stuff himself and drive home. He used to get home at 11 P.M. and fall into bed exhausted.

Gradually he acquired capital and more trucks, until he had other poor devils driving for him. By 1935 he had expanded and was reconditioning busses. Supposedly he could take a look at a truck and within thirty seconds estimate its worth. Now he was beginning to enjoy life for the first time. He had a Bentley

and went to night clubs. He learned to fly. Next he
started buying big trucks. "I cornered them all over
England," he recently boasted to *Empire News,* a British Sunday paper. He made business so tough for the
competition that they used to line up to buy the first
published copies of the trade magazine that carried
advertisements of the sales of big trucks so that they
would know about these sales before Dawson. Then
they hopped into racing cars waiting at the curb and
rushed off to the seller to buy the trucks before Dawson could arrive.

"But I was smarter. . . . I used to beat them every
time," Dawson told the newspaper. How was he
smarter? What did he do that the others didn't? As
usual, Dawson didn't quite explain. But some suggestion of the manner in which Dawson had begun to
operate in his scramble toward success is indicated by
the next deal in which he engaged.

In 1938, Dawson and a friend, Tony Ryman, who
owned the Assurance Finance Company, purchased a
large number of exceptionally heavy trucks. Ryman
put up the funds of his insurance company as a guar-
antee. But they made a mad miscalculation, especially
for men engaged in the transportation business. The
government passed a Traffic Act limiting the combined
weight of a truck and its load to twelve tons. This
meant that a truck of eight tons could only carry a load
of four, which was very uneconomical. As all the Daw-
son-Ryman trucks were heavy, the loads they were
now permitted to carry were unprofitable. Dawson and

George Dawson

Ryman were suddenly stuck with almost $2,500,000 worth of depreciated trucks.

But the most interesting part of this deal is that it was criminal from the start. The creditors howled and then it came to light that the money that had been put up for the trucks was the capital of an insurance (in England, assurance) company. The British don't go for that nonsense any more than we do. The incident reflected Dawson's growing inclination, soon to become a habit, of using other people's money for his own speculative use. Scotland Yard collared both young men and after a three weeks' trial, Dawson was sent to Wandsworth Prison for eighteen months. Ryman was also jailed and, when last heard from in 1948, had just been convicted for fraud, this time in the criminal court of Genoa, Italy.

Dawson was released from prison after the war started. He was promptly drafted and assigned to the engineers as a private. His military service, however, must have set a record for brevity. On his first day in uniform the side-leaf of a truck dropped on his head. He collapsed to the ground with a severe concussion. This terminated his period of active service with His Majesty's forces and after a siege in a hospital he was invalided out of the Army.

Dawson spent the remainder of the war in the trucking business and in and out of court. He black-marketed gas and fuel oil, and Scotland Yard caught up with him twice. In 1941 at Hendon he was fined 100 pounds or three montns for violating fuel rationing. He got off on appeal. On May 1, 1943, he was convicted at Hereford for having knowingly received a stolen truck. Again he won the appeal.

These minor setbacks seem only to have stimulated his itch for wealth. Like many other men, Dawson realized that as soon as the war ended in Europe and Africa the supply depots would be crammed with war matériel and equipment that would suddenly become "surplus." Came the great day. Hats in hand, businessmen jostled each other trying to push through the front door of the ministries in London to get permission to go to Germany to look over and bid on captured German equipment. But not Dawson. With his growing inclination to use the back door, he flew his private single-engined Proctor plane over to the British Zone of Occupation and landed, within hours of the surrender, without hat or permission.

This bold maneuver placed Dawson illegally, but placed him nevertheless, on the ground floor. Through methods which he has somehow never wanted to divulge, he set down a deposit and purchased 30,000 captured German trucks. Next he wangled his way through another back door and came out with all the German surplus stuff on Guernsey, the small island off the Cherbourg coast. Shortly thereafter, he walked through another back door and came out with most of the leftover Nazi equipment in Norway.

Dawson has always claimed that he resold these rich hauls to people in Sweden. Perhaps. But hard-working American Intelligence officers have never been able to locate these buyers in Sweden. All they know for certain is that the two largest buyers of surplus in the world at that time were Red China and Russia.

From Germany, Dawson flew to Africa. As usual, there is a deep division of opinion between Dawson and the Intelligence Services of America, Britain and France as to what Dawson did with the booty he bought on the Dark Continent. U.S. files contain some interesting information to the effect that Dawson bought captured equipment in Tripoli, including mortars and machine guns, and sold it to agents of Red China. The Reds, say these reports, paid in gold and plunked down the yellow stuff in advance. The material was then shipped on a Russian freighter and ended up in China via the USSR. Dawson, the files say, then took the gold to Tangier where he swapped it for diamonds. As a final coup, he took the diamonds to France, Belgium and England and sold them for cash.

Dawson's version is naturally different. When questioned awhile back by French police, he flatly stated that these shipments went, not to Red China, but to struggling Israel. To me he added, with a look of horror: "Mortars and machine guns! Utter rot. Never handled a gun in my life. Trucks, that's my business. People credit me with doing all kinds of things. Like the time I picked up 16,000 General Motors, Chevrolet and jeep engines. There were acres of the stuff, all mislabeled so you'd think it was worthless. Not my fault, old chap, if the officer in charge of the dump wants to make a private business on his own."

Money is the consuming passion in Dawson's life. He pursues it with an intensity and singleness of purpose which, were they directed toward religion, might have made him a saint. Money, he feels, can buy anything. When it fails, say in the attempted purchase of a public official, Dawson blames the failure on circumstance, never on the possibility that the office holder might be honest. In Dawson's limited view, honest officials don't exist. His habitual recourse to the back door when dealing with officials, rather than any technical judgment on his part, is the secret which has brought Dawson $100,000,000 in seven years.

"Dawson has the idea of pay-off on the brain," says one American official whom Back-door Dawson hasn't been able to reach. "Why, he would pay $5,000 under the table for what the ordinary guy could get for a drink or a cigar. He just doesn't know the way through the front door." Seen in this light, Dawson's success is based on the fact that his "Jolly George" handshake contains thousand-dollar bills.

He operates in a way that is pristine in its simplicity but costly to the American taxpayer. In 1947, American surplus permanent and semi-permanent electrical installing wire and cable were gathering dust on Trinidad. Dawson barely remembers this particular deal because his profit was only a miserly $240,000 and he himself did not have to put down a penny. But he recalls enough of it to enable it to serve as a guide to the way in which he swings his many multimillion-dollar deals.

After the war this electrical equipment, like similar

surplus throughout the world, was turned over in Washington to the Office of the Foreign Liquidation Commissioner which was to appraise surplus stock and then sell it to reputable bidders at the highest price. One logical buyer for such surplus on Trinidad would be the island's public utility, and, in fact, the utility wanted to make the purchase and pay a good price. However, so long as there are Dawsons—and so long as there are government officials who are not above a shake—a public utility on Trinidad is not likely to get even a crack at paying a fair price for the direct purchase of nearby equipment. That would be too logical, too efficient, and, worst sin of all, too honest.

As Dawson recalls it, an agent in the surplus-property field informed him that a friendly U.S. official had set a remarkably low price on an electric-generating plant and on some cables and wire. Dawson knows these facts for the disarmingly simple reason that the entire deal was consummated exactly as the agent outlined it.

Dawson told the man he was willing to buy at the suggested price—a reputed $60,000—but that he would first have to know to whom he could resell the equipment and at what price. As everyone who does business with Dawson knows, "Jolly George" rarely, if ever, buys before he has a purchaser. Several times he has waited until that purchaser has put down his money in advance.

In this case, as in most, Dawson had less trouble finding a buyer than most men have in selecting a necktie for the day. At the same time that the agent offered Dawson the equipment for $60,000, he told Dawson that the Trinidad public utility was prepared to pay, roughly, $300,000 for it. When it comes to a 500 percent profit, with no effort or risk, Dawson is every bit as bright as the next man. The utility was informed that Dawson was the middleman and that the utility's $300,000 should be deposited to his account. Once the money was placed, Dawson took $60,000 of it and paid the OFLC.

Thus, on the very same day that Dawson took legal title to the goods, he sold the title for five times more to the utility. Dawson never saw the equipment, never appraised its worth, never had to put down a dollar of his own. Yet for doing almost nothing he had a $240,-000 profit in one day. As he tells the story, a listener is forced to the conclusion that Dawson at the very least must have given the American official some token of gratitude.

This superlatively profitable sleight-of-hand is very easy for a man who knows his way to the back door and finds officials greedily waiting to welcome him. Dawson has been able to make huge profits with relatively little capital because he uses the eventual buyer's money to make his own initial purchase at a much lower price.

It is logical to ask, why don't the final users buy straight from the governments involved? The answer naturally is that they would like to, and the American taxpayer would benefit. But too often they can't. A dishonest official can't get his cut that way. It is easier and probably safer for a dishonest public servant to hold the higher-paying legitimate buyers at bay in the front office while he dickers for his own slice from Dawson, paying a lower price in the back room.

A few years ago the English junkie bought all the left-over U.S. supplies on Bermuda. A friendly American official named William E. Ryan, regional director for the OFLC had somehow set a price for the goods at 8½ percent of their total value. Immediately upon the signing of a binding contract between Mr. Dawson and Mr. Ryan (on behalf of the people of the U.S.) the latter went to work for Dawson. Ryan's resignation from his government job took effect June 1, 1948. He went on Dawson's payroll on June 1, 1948.

When Dawson got ready to do business in the United States it was only natural that he allied himself with another back-door specialist, John Maragon, the most publicized influence peddler in the nation's capital.

Maragon was a long-time Missouri friend of Harry S. Truman, a fact which he carefully advertised. Before Dawson came to the United States in January, 1948, for the meeting with Maragon, it was necessary for him to secure a visa. One of the requirements for the issuance of the visa was that Dawson sign an affidavit declaring that he had never been convicted of a felony. But this would have been perjury. So Dawson paid a $500 bribe to an official in the U.S. Consulate in London and secured the visa without going through the bothersome formality. On a second visit to the United States, Dawson was asked by the U.S. Consulate in Paris to state the reason for the trip. He carefully wrote: "To see General Harry Vaughan."

The first business deal put together by Maragon and Dawson dealt with the purchase of U.S. surplus generators. These were to be sold at what is laughingly called a public auction. Dawson and Maragon secured the services of Joseph Major, an official of the War Assets Board which was selling the property. Much to the surprise of nobody, Dawson's bid was accepted.

At a later date, Joe Major evinced surprise that anyone might consider his conduct irregular. "I would do the same for any customer," he said stiffly. Mr. Major comes from Missouri, is a graduate of the famous finishing school called Battery D and secured his job with this important agency solely on the strength of a recommendation by General Vaughan. He carried his passion for giving the customer personal service to extremes when he interceded for George Dawson in the matter of his request for an RFC loan.

Since these facts about Mr. Major had been made available to his superiors, I checked to see what action they had taken. The question was put to Jeff Larson, head of the important General Services Agency and the direct employer of Major. "Well," said Larson recently, "on the basis of his past actions, my investigation indicated that Mr. Major did not possess sufficient judgment to properly represent the government in such undertakings. I found, to my satisfaction, that the man was inherently honest and therefore I did not wish to punish him by separating him entirely from the government. But in all candor I must say that in my opinion Mr. Major does not possess the necessary ability to exercise the judgment that is required in carrying out responsibilities connected with procurement and disposal. But there are other things which he is doing and which he can do very well."

Dawson is a man of broad vision and undeniable courage. Some of the deals he has initiated are so vast they would have frightened ordinary millionaires. One of them in 1948 involved an attempt to acquire all the salable U.S. and captured enemy stocks that were left in Europe after the war. The sum total of these goods reached a staggering five billion dollars. What is more, he proposed to do all of this on an investment of a quarter of a million dollars.

Dawson's attorneys set up a company called Trans America Traders, incorporated in the state of Delaware. Associated with him in the venture were Allan Braithwaite, son of Sir Albert Braithwaite (fuel administrator in England during the last war) and John Maragon. Braithwaite, a partner in the enterprise, was useful because he had served in the U.S. Air Force and therefore could enter bids for surplus where veterans were given preference. Maragon's job was that of government contact man and he was to receive 25 percent of all profits. This was the most important function of all, since the success or failure of the combine depended on Maragon's ability to convince the U.S. official controlling this fortune in merchandise to give his group preferential treatment.

As a first step in his new job the Greek ex-bootblack went to General Vaughan and received from him a letter addressed to Major General Clyde L. Hyssong, the officer in charge of the disposal of all war surplus in Europe under U.S. Army control. Written on White House stationery, it read:

14 January 1948

My dear General Hyssong,

This will introduce my good friend John Maragon, who is representing George Dawson and Company, and who is interested in purchasing materials from the Foreign Liquidation Service.

Any assistance that you may be able to render to Mr. Maragon will be greatly appreciated by me.

Sincerely

Harry H. Vaughan

Major General, U.S. Army (Res.)

Military Aide to the President

In telling how he came by this letter, Maragon made this explanation recently: "I happened to be unemployed at the time, so I went to General Vaughan and told him that I had a job lined up with this guy Dawson and he said it's about time and I asked him if I could have some letters of introduction and he said to whom and I said I don't know, I don't know anything about war surplus. So then I found out the head man

139   **George Dawson**

was General Hyssong and that's how I happened to get the letter to him."

Although Maragon's assistance in securing surplus was something less than sensational, he was helpful to Dawson in a deal which, to characterize it as shady, is to place the most honest construction on it. In 1948 the French Ministry of Finance, in an effort to trap black marketeers and tax evaders, declared all 5,000-franc notes invalid. The decree was issued at 4 A.M. and the public could, between 8 A.M. and the close of the business day, change a modest number of the notes—I believe it was ten—without explanation. The mere attempt to change more would have subjected an individual to the intensive investigation of the fiscal authorities. This, in a country where tax evasion is a national pastime, meant that very few dared risk this latter procedure.

In Paris, where Maragon was staying as a guest on Dawson's floor of the Plaza Athénée Hotel, "Jolly George" handed Maragon a satchel full of the worthless paper, along with a letter on Trans America Traders stationery explaining that this was part of the company's regular operating capital. Now this in itself was far from proof that the money was honestly come by and that the taxes on it had been paid. On this exchange the French were really tough. When Maragon took the satchel around to the Bank of France, he passed sidewalk peddlers hawking the 5,000-franc notes, ordinarily worth $15, for as low as 5 cents. The line around the Bank of France extended for more than three blocks.

But Maragon was a White House big-shot who knew how to flash his White House pass at the right moments. Without delay he was ushered into the proper office and his worthless paper replaced with legal currency. Then it was Maragon's turn to perform a remarkable maneuver. Instead of returning the money to Dawson, he stuck it in his own pocket. As this is written, the lawsuit filed by George Dawson against John Maragon in the Washington, D.C., courts for the recovery of these funds is still pending.

Most of Dawson's business associates, like Maragon, have ended up by hating him bitterly. The feeling is not uncommon, even in the people still associated with him. Those who get along with him best realize that Dawson's promises are inclined to outstrip his performance, and they work with him on a payment-in-advance basis.

George Mitchell, an Argentine journalist turned businessman who holds Dawson's power of attorney for Continental Trust, a large Dawson enterprise, told a friend recently: "You have to know how to deal with George. If you should collect any money for him, take your end off the top before you pass it on. He'll yell, but that way you're sure you have been paid."

But even Mitchell, well as he knows the boss, is not immune. Not long ago Dawson said that he was anxious to get rid of his wife's special sports model Delahaye; that he'd let it go for one million francs. "It's too fast for her," Dawson explained. "I'm afraid she'll kill herself in it." Mitchell paid the million, about $2,850, only to find that there was a 900,000-franc mortgage that went with the car.

"He thought he was robbing me at that price," Dawson chuckled, "because he knows I paid three and a half million francs for it last year. But I had the last laugh."

The number of ex-associates willing to "tell all" about Dawson are legion. For example, there is an Armenian in Paris whose job it was to get the official purchase commissions of foreign governments to buy war goods in the names of their respective nations and, for a modest retainer, sell them to Dawson. He would resell them to countries who were on our black list. His principal customers at that time were the Chinese Communist Army and Yugoslavia. As a historical footnote, it is interesting to observe that Tito, at that time a member in good standing of the Cominform, was getting more arms from Dawson than from Stalin. Particularly helpful to Dawson in these operations were the purchasing agents for the Greek government.

Of all his ex-business associates, Maragon is the most bitter. The attempt to take over all U.S. surplus had failed only because the U.S. had turned the juiciest portion of the stocks over to the West German government in an effort to bolster its economy. Dawson blamed Maragon for the failure. When Maragon returned to Washington he told intimates that he didn't even cover expenses. He was so angry he filed a report with several Washington agencies in which he stated, among other things, that Dawson was dishonest; that he was surrounded by gangsters and thieves; that the British government was seeking him for tax evasion; that the French government wanted to question him about a shipment of forty tanks and several thousand trucks to the Chinese Communists; and that he was one of the leading suppliers of military equipment to countries behind the Iron Curtain. Maragon presented these facts to the OFLC with which Dawson had carried on an enormously profitable business.

A few months ago Representative Herbert C. Bonner (Democrat, North Carolina), of the House Expenditures Subcommittee, investigating U.S. Army surplus supplies, called in Travis L. Fletcher, the man who was the chief of investigations for the Office of the Foreign Liquidation Commissioner at the time of Dawson's operations. Fletcher is now chief of the Investigation Branch, Security Division, of the State Department. The committee wanted to know whether he had ever investigated Dawson or any of his affairs.

Congressman Bonner asked: "What I want to know is whether in your official position with the Office of the Foreign Liquidation Commissioner you were ever called upon to make any investigation of any kind concerning the activities of the Dawson syndicate?"

"No, I was not."

"There were some allegations made by Mr. Maragon that you received a consideration, a gift or a gratuity from members of the Dawson syndicate. Would you like to make a statement on your own concerning that allegation?"

"Yes, I think I should," Mr. Fletcher said. "I believe Mr. Maragon said that Mr. Braithwaite [the Dawson associate] had given me a set of Wedgwood china. Well, that is so far-fetched that it is ridiculous. I never have been offered a set of any kind of china by Braithwaite or Dawson, and I have not ever accepted any kind of presents from them."

The fact remains, however, that the only people investigated by Fletcher were business competitors of Dawson on complaints from Dawson. Dawson himself was never investigated.

Last year Maragon was called before a Senate investigating committee and asked, under oath, whether or not he had received any commission for the work he did for the Dawson syndicate. Maragon swore that he had not. For this and for other false responses made to material questions, he was convicted of perjury and sentenced to a term of imprisonment in a federal penitentiary. His prison job is teaching a class of convicts congressional procedure.

Officially, the U.S. frowns on Dawson's trading with Russian satellite countries and although most of Dawson's surplus property is located in the western zones of Germany which are under Allied control, U.S. officials have done little to control his trading with nations which are acting against our interests. The reason for this is that Dawson had always managed to secure the friendly co-operation of key governmental officials. He manages fairly well even when this co-operation is lacking.

There was, for example, a large shipment of half-tracks. These vehicles look like standard trucks except that the rear wheels are replaced by tank treads. Their use is strictly military. When I was in Germany recently, I ran down the means by which Dawson was able to get these vehicles into the hands of a very correct purchaser—meaning someone who was willing to pay an exaggerated price in advance—from behind the Iron Curtain. These vehicles were sold by Dawson to a French citizen who listed Israel as their eventual destination. The purchase papers were carefully documented and received the approval of the High Commissioner for Germany who issued an export permit for them. The vehicles were hauled by flatcar to the Antwerp Shipping and Trading Company in Belgium. Here they were placed aboard the *Mok III,* a vessel owned by the North Russian Railway Company. This took place more than a year ago. At this writing the *Mok III* has still not put in at any Israeli port. Trying to find the kindest explanation for Dawson, I can only guess that the Russian captain mistook Murmansk for Tel Aviv.

Dawson's disregard for what are considered the basic tenets of business ethics is best illustrated by his dealings with George deRandich, an ex-Czarist cavalry officer who in the postwar years worked as a commission man in the surplus-property field. DeRandich visited Dawson in Paris on July 15, 1949, and reported having uncovered 6,000 brand-new jeep motors that could be picked up cheaply. Dawson arranged for the purchase of these motors, but when the British government refused to approve a pound-sterling transfer of the purchase price, he backed out of the deal.

DeRandich therefore turned to a French company and put the deal across in the following manner. The German owners of the jeep motors received $48,360 or exactly $8.06 a motor. At the same time, deRandich sold these motors to the French Army for immediate shipment to the fighting front in Indo-China at $70 a motor or $420,000 for the lot, or a quick 768 percent profit.

There was only one slight hitch. DeRandich didn't have any money. So his French company went to a bank and secured the necessary cash on a short-term loan. After all, what was $48,000 when over $400,000 was being turned over in a week? With his fine nose for money, Dawson now stepped back into the picture. Flanked by a battery of expensive legal talent, he walked into the U.S. Attorney's office in Frankfurt and swore out a criminal complaint for fraud against deRandich. As the result of the complaint a warrant was issued for the arrest of the ex-Czarist officer and the 6,000 jeep motors were impounded pending the final settlement of the lawsuit growing out of Dawson's complaint.

DeRandich presented himself to the U.S. Attorney's office to answer the charges and was released in bond. Meanwhile the French Army refused to make payment

until the goods were cleared from legal entangle-
ments. The bank from which deRandich and the
French company received their loan began pressing
for immediate repayment and deRandich and the
company found themselves in desperate circumstances.
At this moment Dawson, who knew all about the ex-
orbitant price that the French Army was going to pay,
got in touch with deRandich and pointed out that
he was, after all, a man with a forgiving nature and
that if deRandich saw that $130,000 of the $420,000
payment to be made by the French Army was given to
him in cash, he would immediately lift all impediments
to what could be a very profitable deal for everyone.

DeRandich recognized the wisdom of Dawson's
proposal and paid the $130,000. It might be wise at
this point to note that the real victims in the entire
deal were the American taxpayers who in the final
analysis, through the various foreign-aid programs,
picked up the tab. What has gone unexplained is how
the U.S. Attorney in Frankfurt permitted his office to
be used as the lever by which Dawson separated de-
Randich from some of his unconscionably high profits.

DeRandich never forgave Dawson this affront to
his honor and pocket. As soon as the sale was consummated, and the criminal charges against himself lifted,
he prodded District Attorney W. Fred Johnson in
Frankfurt into making an investigation of Dawson's
phony complaint. It was as a result of this that Dawson was indicted in 1949 by the U.S. government for
perjury and fraud and a warrant issued for his arrest.

"It's a peculiar thing how intuition can sometimes help you," Dawson told me. "I had some business appointments in Frankfurt and I had my pilot fly me in the twin-motored Beechcraft to Germany. We put down at the civilian airport at Rhein Main. I felt that something was wrong, so instead of going right into town, as I usually would, I telephoned the office and Mitchell—he's my assistant—told me excitedly that I had been indicted and that the American police were looking for me. I climbed right back into the plane and flew to France. That was in 1949. I haven't been back to Germany since."

I ran into deRandich in Rome recently and he told me that he had read my piece about Dawson with great interest. "You weren't quite accurate when you said that I still hate him," he said. "I don't. When I went into business with him I knew that he had been a thief, that he was still a thief, and that he would always be a thief. So how can I complain if he afterwards robs me? The man I will hate for the rest of my life is Mitchell. I picked him out of the gutter and raised him like my son. I made him my secretary and took him to Germany with me. How did he repay me? First he stole my wife and then he sold me out to Dawson.

"I knew the way through the back door of STEG [of which more later]. Some friendly directors of theirs had a kind of understanding with me whereby I could buy any amount of goods and have a year's time in which to pay for it. It meant that I could pay them with what an eventual purchaser paid me. It was Mitchell,

148

working behind my back, who put Dawson in and froze me out. To keep me out they tried to kidnap me and dump me in the Russian Zone. As an ex-White Russian officer, I'd never have come out alive. When that failed they planted a package of opium in my wife's luggage and tipped off the customs agents that she was a smuggler. Luckily, she found the package in time."

The indictment has been an annoying thorn in Dawson's side. It kept him out of Germany at a time when his business interests there ran into the tens of millions of dollars. He made one determined effort to get the indictment lifted. An American attorney who practices law in Frankfurt visited him at his villa in Cannes and said flatly that for $50,000 he could square the rap. Present during this conversation were Dawson's bodyguard and a member of a French purchase mission whose relations with Dawson were so friendly that there was no apparent objection to his presence at the meeting. It was this latter person who was to become bitter over what he regarded as Dawson's betrayal in not paying a commission due him and who repeated the story to a member of U.S. Army Intelligence.

While in Frankfurt, I mentioned the incident to District Attorney Johnson and he said, "Oh, I know that attorney very well. Why, he came to my office one day and told me that I could make far more money working on the other side of the street. He said that he had one defendant who'd be willing to pay me $10,-000 to represent him. I laughed at him and he said the defendant would go as high as $20,000. I still thought he was joking so I kept laughing. Then he said, this defendant, Dawson, might be very rich but he wouldn't go higher than $40,000. It was then that I realized what he was trying to do, and I got to my feet and opened my jacket so that he could see the forty-five tucked behind the waistband of my trousers. I put my hand on the butt and yelled, 'Get out before I lose my temper.'"

Dawson has a set of standard responses to criticism. If the criticism is official, like the indictment in the U.S. Zone of Germany, he says that it is brought on by business rivals intent on forcing him out of profitable territory. "In Germany there is a French-American group who tricked the authorities into issuing a warrant for my arrest so that I would be barred from Germany. I stand ready to give evidence to support my innocence," he says. Despite this verbal readiness, Dawson has carefully avoided the criminal court in Frankfurt. Where the criticism is unofficial, he brushes it off as being made by parasites. "It's when you're a success that they begin gathering around. You don't find them shaking a rotten tree, do you?

"I find a tendency in you chaps to place all the blame on my shoulders. Take, for example, the American businessman to whom I sold a dumpful of rusting axles and gear assembles. He sand-blasted them clean, smeared them with cosmoline, and had them wrapped the same way that General Motors wraps new ones. He sold them off to your military as new replacement parts. Now the major part of this shipment was sent to

Korea. The only thing certain about its use is that it will break down. Suppose one of these axles is used on a truck hauling troops or badly needed ammunition. Suppose it breaks down and some of your soldiers are killed. When the fact that I was in any way connected with this equipment becomes known, an unholy holler will go up that it's George Dawson again. Rot, my dear man. I sold it to your very correct businessman as junk and what he does with it after I sell it to him is no affair of mine."

Dawson was referring to what is one of the biggest hushed-up supply scandals in Korea. This stock was shipped to the war zone with foreseen consequences. How many American lives were lost as a result is anybody's guess. Dawson says that if he is promised immunity while in America, he will come to Washington and tell the Bonner Subcommittee under oath who the American dealer was.

Probably the most fabulous surplus deal ever put across by a single individual is Dawson's purchase of STEG. The initials stand for Staatliche Erfassungs Gesellschaft. Future Germany historians will call it the greatest sellout since von Paulus. The background of the deal was as follows: In accordance with the American policy of promoting economic recovery in West Germany after the war, surplus army property representing about one billion dollars in original acquisition cost was turned over by the Army and the OFLC to STEG, a German quasi-governmental agency that was commissioned to handle this surplus stock. For accounting purposes the transfer was to be made at twenty-one cents per dollar of original cost. It was hoped that the billion dollars' worth of trucks, cars, automotive parts, steel and so forth would find its way into the civilian economy at low prices. Dawson's arrival single-handedly changed the entire structure.

Because this was an operation of great importance to the welfare of several nations, principally our own, it deserves to be examined in some detail. It is not only a fascinating study in postwar financial juggling, where Dawson is at his best, but it illustrates the great harm that can be done by misguided, or worse, American occupation authorities.

The agreement between STEG and the U.S. was a confidential one and the most stringent clause in it was that none of the goods that might be of military aid to Iron Curtain countries should be sold to them. In spite of this clear condition, it is almost impossible to get any high official in the High Commissioner's office to say why, in the case of Dawson, he was permitted to trade with the Communist states.

Dawson bought STEG—and his total cash outlay was only $30,000. The original contract called for him to take over all trucks, cars, half-tracks, jeep motors and automotive parts, in fact, everything dealing with transport. For the operation he set up a special company called Trucks and Spares Kraftfahrzeug G.m.b.h. which was incorporated in Lichtenstein, where all you need to get your papers is a bank account of a dollar and up, and which is regarded by European financiers very much in the same way as a Delaware corporation was regarded by American investors back in the days of rugged individualism.

He signed an agreement with the exceedingly friendly directors of STEG on February 28, 1950, the same day that Trucks and Spares received its articles of incorporation. Dawson was to pay $3,200,000 as a total price, 10 percent of which was to be deposited as evidence of good faith. Upon payment of an initial $30,000, Dawson took control of STEG. His first sale resulted in a $100,000 profit which he paid to STEG on March 21, 1950. On the next sale he plunked $150,000 down as a deposit on May 9, 1950. After the next deal he handed over a final $40,000, completing the deposit sum of $320,000, and was riding free from then on. He took over the STEG offices on Feldbergstrasse in Frankfurt; he even took over their telephone exchange. In the words of Colonel Jack E. Willis, a supply officer in Germany, "If you wanted to deal with STEG, you had to see Dawson."

In American Intelligence files it is noted that Dawson paid a million dollars in bribes. I spoke to Dawson at length about his dealings with STEG when he was in particularly confiding mood. "Wasn't a badly set up operation, that one," he said. "I only had to pay out three hundred thousand dollars. By the way, Olga, what was the name of the German fellow who got most of it?"

"Witzlaben, wasn't it?" Olga said.

"I guess that's the boy."

The publication of my Dawson story in *L'Europeo* brought an angry letter from Dr. Wolnik of STEG. It wasn't true about poor Witzlaben's having taken a bribe from Mr. Dawson. In fact, Dr. Wolnik called Witzlaben into his office and asked him point-blank whether or not it was true, and Witzlaben said that it was not. Dr. Wolnik's letter made no comment on the fact that three directors of STEG, having given the favored contract to Dawson, resigned from their jobs and became directors in Trucks and Spares.

Only once did the Army try to get to the root of the Dawson-STEG operations. Colonel John Flemming, a thoroughly honest and forthright officer, seized the books of both Dawson and STEG. While his auditors were scrutinizing them, the High Commissioner took over the case. The findings were shipped directly to the State Department in Washington where they were stamped Top Secret. The man who made the seizure was called up sharply and ordered to justify his actions in writing. The reason for this was that the High Commissioner's office for Germany at the time, had issued a direct order that no U.S. investigation into STEG be made.

Here was a situation made to order for an honest, unbiased investigator. But for some reason not readily apparent, Mr. Bonner suddenly lost interest in the matter.

Since a good part of the U.S. property sold by STEG has, through Dawson, gone to Russia and her satellites, it seemed curious that the High Commissioner should persist in his refusal to investigate thoroughly the Dawson-STEG deal. I asked Mr. Buttenwieser whether the maladministration of the German company represented a security threat and he refused to answer on the ground that the question presupposed that STEG was being wrongly administered. We do know that through STEG urgently needed equipment was moved from the United States Zone of Germany to behind-the-Iron-Curtain countries, not only by subterfuge, but openly, with the approval of the High Commissioner's office, so it was understandable why Messrs. Buttenwieser and McCloy should want to keep mum.

The existing situation finally became so notorious that in the end Secretary of the Army Frank Pace issued a freeze order on all STEG supplies. The order did block one deal. This was the sale by Dawson to Oakland Truck Sales of Pittsburgh of fifty junked half-tracks for $22 apiece. Former Assistant Secretary of Defense Paul Griffiths, representing the Pittsburgh company, filed a claim against the U.S. for $1,750 a vehicle—or eighty times as much as each half-track cost them. In other words, on an investment of $1,100, he is trying to collect $87,500.

Dawson feels very badly about the freeze because he still has some valuable property in STEG dumps and he is preparing a claim against U.S. occupation authorities for seven million dollars. Advisers pointed out to him that it would be easier for him to collect this money if he removed his name from the company rolls. In that way he could avoid suffering financial damage due to the odium in which his name is held. Dawson saw the wisdom of this advice and he transferred Trucks and Spares to a new company called Continental Motors. He gave his assistant, George Mitchell, a power of attorney to run the firm. The final paragraph in this transfer agreement reads: "Mr. Dawson has therefore no claim at all on the goods which were bought from STEG. The Continental Motor Trust is liable to pay Mr. Dawson a two percent commission . . ."

This paper transfer fooled nobody—except the High Commissioner, perhaps. A short time after the transfer was made, Dawson wrote a letter to an associate, Bill Davis, in which he said: "As you know, Hagenbach has started up the Continental Motor Trust for me and to which I am transferring the STEG contract. Have no worries about anyone else cutting in on me, because I own Continental lock, stock and barrel."

Roberto Rossellini

5

Stromboli is an active volcanic cone nosing out of the Tyrrhenian Sea and is about as desolate a piece of real estate as exists anywhere in the world. Not since the year it first erupted has it been in the news. Not, that is, until a few years ago. Since then it has lent its name to a motion picture which was a spectacular failure, a drink that packs a wallop, a love affair that packed an even greater one, and a bull-terrier pup owned by a Swedish actress named Ingrid Bergman.

The man who lifted the island out of centuries of obscurity is forty-six-year-old Roberto Rossellini, an Italian motion-picture director whose postwar works

157

—until *Stromboli*—were hailed by American critics as bearing the true stamp of genius. Because American newspapers have devoted even more space to his amorous activities, readers have become somewhat confused as to whether his is a genius for making pictures or for making love.

In Rossellini's mind, no such confusion exists: He is a genius in both.

This tremendous belief in himself has led detractors to say that he suffers from an over-inflated ego. Such opinions never bother Rossellini because he is thoroughly convinced that he is the greatest addition to motion-picture art since the introduction of the close-up. Once, when his chronic case of financial anemia was more acute than usual, he was offered a director's job in *Tale of Five Women*. Rossellini wouldn't accept unless he was given final supervisory powers over the entire production. When it was pointed out that his job involved directing only one of the five sequences and that the others were to be directed by four names equally as great as his, he said, quietly, "If God comes down to do a film with me, I still supervise."

Rossellini's claim to film fame in America stems from *Open City*, a brilliantly executed account of life in Rome during the German occupation. Movie-goers found that its honest realism was better entertainment than Hollywood's synthetic products, and critics coined a new phrase—the Rossellini touch.

The picture was produced immediately after the liberation of Rome, at a time when the Italian movie industry, its studios either destroyed or requisitioned, was stiff with rigor mortis. Hungry actresses had to seek out new employment entertaining handsome Fifth Army lieutenants who were rich in cigarettes—a unit of exchange that had replaced the lira. The male members of the industry, lacking the versatile talents of the actresses, found it a little tougher. Many became dealers in the *borsa nera*.

It was on one of Rossellini's forays into the market place, a girl friend's astrakhan coat over his arm, that he encountered Sergio Amidei, a brilliant film writer who would later author *Open City, Shoeshine, Paisan, Difficult Years* and *A Sunday in August,* but who at that moment was peddling wine to the boys in khaki. In this unlikely setting, Amidei recounted the idea for *Open City.* It dealt with a pair of unrelated incidents which Amidei had pieced together; his own escape over Roman rooftops while SS troops cordoned the street and the execution of a Catholic priest who had worked for the underground. Rossellini liked the idea, and the men shook hands on the deal.

To the surprise of everyone except himself, Rossellini separated Countess Carla Politi, an old ballerina who once had been the girl friend of King Fuad of Egypt, from seven thousand dollars and a promise that the rest of the money would be forthcoming when the American troops captured Milan where her cash was banked.

Rossellini wasted no time in getting to work. For a studio, he rented a bookie joint on the Via Avignonesi, next door to Rome's plushiest legal house of prostitution. On the floor above, a pair of soiled doves operated a modest, off-limits aviary which catered largely to the colored troops so that during the actual filming the realistic tramp of military boots was never absent. Aside from a camera and a few lights, there was little equipment. When the script called for a bedroom setting, the actress who played in the scene had to move the furniture in from her home.

American critics have raved about the effects that Rossellini got from the deep shadows on the sets. A production assistant, reading one of the reviews, said, "It wasn't artistry. It was just lack of electric current."

In spite of the countess and low production costs, money was Rossellini's principal worry. He ran through the original seven thousand before the Allied army could capture Milan. So he borrowed from *strozzini*, the Roman version of gangland's six-for-five Shylocks, in order to keep going. At the last instant, with typical luck, Rossellini found a cloth salesman who had just made a killing in the gray market. The salesman was persuaded to buy out the countess and advance the finishing money. But the salesman had misgivings from the start, and when he was offered a two-thousand-dollar profit, he sold out.

The picture, at this writing, has already grossed more than two million dollars in the U.S.A. Rossellini, who directed and produced it, made no more than eating money. Amidei, who wrote the script, received one hundred and thirty-five dollars. Anna Magnani, its fiery star, was paid seven hundred dollars.

Not since flamboyant Gabriele D'Annunzio, self-confessed genius in literature and love, has Italy had so colorful a double-threat man and, like D'Annunzio, Rossellini is far from looking the part of a romantic figure. He is middle-aged, slightly potbellied, and balding. But what he lacks in physique, he more than makes up for in hand-kissing and other manifestations of continental charm. Marilyn Buferd, Miss America of 1946, who was, until edged out by the Swedish actress, his great and good friend, said of the Italian director, "It's hard to put into words exactly what he has, but I can tell you this: Rossellini is more than a man; he is an act of God."

Some of the qualities that Marilyn found attractive in the Italian director were his warm sentiment and generosity. "Why, when I was leaving for America, he gave me a pair of clips and a bracelet of old design which had been in his family for years and which easily cost ten thousand dollars," she told a friend. Entering the United States, Marilyn neglected to declare the jewelry. The customs officials at La Guardia Airport lifted them from her and, being cold gents utterly devoid of sentiment, appraised the heirlooms at sixty dollars.

There was nothing in Rossellini's early life that suggested special qualities that would make for cinematic or amorous success. He was the son of wealthy parents and lived the ordinary, spoiled life of a well-to-do Roman. He had a passionate fondness for fast motor cars and his earliest ambition was to be a racer. Although he never finished in the money in the few races he tried, he managed to place the Rossellini imprint even on that sport. There was a blonde icicle in the stands during his final race who had hinted that she would be more apt to melt if Rossellini would, romantically, wave to her. Rossellini took the hint. Every time the car flashed by the stands, he enthusiastically lifted both hands from the wheel and shook them in the general direction of the spectators. At the conclusion of the race, Rossellini's mechanic, white and shaken, climbed out of the car and pulled himself together long enough to swing a haymaker at his chin. Rossellini is especially allergic to right hooks directed at him and he gave up racing as a competitive sport. His love for fast driving has continued, however, and while he was courting Bergman, the sight of his waspish red Cisitalia burning up Italian roads was a familiar one.

Today he has a fleet of five cars; a Cadillac, Chevrolet, Fiat, a Fiat station wagon, and a Ferrari 2000, the hottest thing in sports cars. He has infected Ingrid with a love for fancy motors and she has added a sixth car to the family garage—a six-thousand-dollar Lancia with sport body built by Farina.

Rossellini has always lived a Bohemian existence, which means that he is filled with the vagabond spirit, is a nonconformist, and is always short of money. He drifted into film making because it was a type of work that cut fewest inroads into his loose living arrangements.

Before scoring with *Open City,* he directed four films, all of which he would like to forget. These were, in the order in which they were produced, *The White Ship,* a frank propaganda film about fascist military hospitals; *The Victor Returns,* produced by Vittorio Mussolini, son of the Duce, and dealing with Italy's military victories in Africa; *Man on the Cross,* more propaganda about Italy's alliance with Germany in the war on the eastern front, starring Roswita Schmidt, a blonde German hoofer with a snap to her garter whose astrakhan coat later kept the wolf from their door; and *Desire,* a real stinker which has in its favor only the fact that the footage never left the can.

Rossellini's informal manner of making motion pictures never fails to delight his friends. Most of his films were shot without script. In directing *The Machine That Kills Evil-doers,* a film that was released in Italy in July, 1952, the genius worked in his usual unorthodox manner. The idea was written out on a single sheet of paper—all the script that existed—and was kicked around and lost after a few days. The story deals with a remarkable camera which has the power to kill any evil person it photographs. For location, Rossellini picked the little town of Maiori on the Sorrentine peninsula, simply because the mayor was his friend. The principal roles were the devil and a photographer. For the devil, he found an eighty-two year old tramp who was paid $1.60 a day. This sudden wealth upset the derelict's equilibrium. The fact that he would indulge in long drunks wasn't so bad; with native shrewdness, he would find a hiding place where he could wear off his stupor in bliss, and it would be days before he could be found.

Roberto Rossellini

The local carpenter was chosen to play the part of the photographer because he could also be useful in building sets. It wasn't until the superstitious towns-people refused to play in scenes opposite the carpenter-photographer that Rossellini discovered that his leading man's carpentry was limited to the making of coffins.

In the early days of the shooting, Rossellini took a trip to Paris and returned with Marilyn Buferd. He turned her over to his cousin, Renzo Avanzo, who was associated with him in the production, telling him to find a spot for her in the picture. Renzo protested that the story called for neither an American nor a beautiful girl. "Then change the story," Rossellini said airily.

Each time the director brought in a new protégé, the story was altered so that the final plot bore only a remote resemblance to the original.

Rossellini didn't mind running into debt. He just didn't want to run into creditors. These mad individuals appeared on the scene at the damnedest moments, and the director always had to turn on his dazzling charm. He would take them out for a big meal, get them drunk, bring in Marilyn for the smiles and send them home unsatisfied, but happy.

Anna Magnani, who is so wonderful in pictures because she always plays herself, was a regular week-end visitor. She was one of the women Rossellini, the lover, had set on fire. What brought her to Maiori, aside from a deep love for the director, was a suspicion that his interest in Marilyn Buferd was not entirely professional. During weekdays, Marilyn addressed the great director as Roberto, but on week-ends, when Magnani was present, she called him, with a great show of formality, Signor Rossellini. This bit of business finally got under Magnani's skin. One night, while the entire company sat around the table in a local *trattoria,* she turned bitter-sweetly on her younger rival. "Why don't you cut the act?" she said. "I was an old hand before you were born."

Another distraction was Rossellini's correspondence with Ingrid Bergman. It began with a rather silly fan letter the Swedish star wrote in which she said that she admired his work and that "If you should ever need an actress whose English is quite good, who has forgotten her German and whose only knowledge of Italian is *Io ti amo,*" not to hesitate to call on her. If this was an invitation to the dance, then Rossellini's answer started the soft music. Mail-order romance was something new, but he took it in stride. There was only the minor inconvenience of hiding Ingrid's letters in his aunt's house, lest the fiery Magnani find out about them.

In the midst of the shooting at Maiori, the genius developed a sudden love for swimming, with the result that his paunchy figure was seen more often in the water than on the set. This passion for aquatic sport annoyed Marilyn. "He's in training for Bergman," she told a friend. By the end of the summer, the film was still unfinished, but Rossellini had managed to shed fifteen pounds.

When the American producer, Rudolph Solmsen, took over *The Machine That Kills Evil-doers,* it was still unfinished. There were scenes in which the actor-photographer snapped, but no corresponding scenes to show at whom he was snapping. Marilyn waved happily, but there was nothing to show at whom she was waving. The producer, moved by the acclaim U.S. critics had heaped on Rossellini's *Germany—Year Zero,* an artistic and financial flop in Europe, said: "If I had the nerve, I'd show *Machine* as it is. Nobody would understand it, but that wouldn't matter. The highbrow critics would go crazy over Rossellini's new trend toward surrealism."

Eventually Solmsen sold his interest in the picture to Rossellini who has since tried, as best he could, to finish it—a very difficult job because the old tramp, shortly after his eighty-third birthday, died in a blissful alcoholic stupor. Fortunately for Rossellini, the picture opened and closed so quietly that the general public is unaware that he made it. When I saw it in its three-day run in Rome, there were seven people in the audience.

While critics have, especially since the release of the film, *Stromboli,* attacked Rossellini's genius as a director, his genius as a lover remains unchallenged. He freely admits that there are no secret means by which he achieved this overwhelming success. It's just that he is Rossellini. The ability to shuffle women like a deck of cards had made him a legendary lover even before the arrival of Bergman. The fact that he was married and had two children put no brakes on his extracurricular activities. While filming *Desire,* the entire company lived in a little village in the Abruzzi hills. His attractive brunette wife, Marcella—she was a twenty-year-old university student when he married her sixteen years ago—and the children lived in one hotel. Blonde Roswita Schmidt lived in the hotel across the street. With fine impartiality, Rossellini would spend a day with each of them. When Marilyn Buferd arrived in Rome, it was another blonde girl friend of the genius who met her at the station. When he corresponded with Ingrid, it was Marilyn who was his translator. When he took Ingrid to the Island of Stromboli for the realization of love's young idyll and, incidentally, a film, he borrowed Anna Magnani's personal maid to serve the Swedish star.

Only on rare occasions did any of the gals kick up a fuss when the shuffle was too fast. Anna Magnani was sitting in Nino's Restaurant in Rome one night when someone handed her an Italian news weekly. In it was a large picture of Roswita Schmidt talking to her friend, Marilyn Buferd, in Capri. "What's he doing, holding a convention of girl friends?" she screamed, and began smashing dishes.

When Anna Magnani turned up as the new queen of hearts, Roswita went into self-imposed exile on Capri. Magnani forbade Rossellini to set foot on the island as long as That Woman was there, and he heeded her warning. He did, that is, until the day several years later when he took Ingrid Bergman there. It was not reported whether Roswita, still in her self-imposed residence, came forward to greet the new member of the select sorority.

Roberto Rossellini

The still-lovely Roswita visited me in my office in the Foreign Press building in Rome recently, and our conversation, naturally, concerned the Italian director. Now an extra in Italian films and a bit-part player on the Italian radio, she had fallen, professionally, a long way since the day Rossellini threw her over. In spite of this she bears him no ill will. "Roberto has a big heart," she said. "People just don't understand him."

Rossellini's affair with Ingrid Bergman touched off more journalistic fireworks than any since Wally Simpson and the Duke of Windsor. Louella Parsons, in breaking her scoop about Ingrid awaiting the stork, wrote that few women in history have made such a sacrifice for love. She drew a parallel with Mary Queen of Scots who gave up her throne for the Earl of Bothwell and with Lady Hamilton who gave up her reign as society's queen to bear a child out of wedlock to Lord Nelson. None of them, Miss Parsons continued, gave up any more than did Ingrid, Queen of Hollywood. The fact that the scoop about Ingrid's pregnancy had been published three months earlier in *Giornale della Sera,* a Rome afternoon daily, in nowise bothered the imperturbable Miss Parsons.

Because Ingrid represented the paragon of married virtue to the American housewife, both the press and Congress took off angrily after Signor Rossellini. Senator Edwin C. Johnson of Colorado asked for the passage of a law for the licensing of actors, and this led Irving Hoffman, the columnist, to remark that because a Swedish actress went to bed with an Italian director, Ethel

Barrymore would have to stand in line to get a license to act.

Both Rossellini and Bergman feel that the facts about their romance have been distorted. Talking to a friend recently, Rossellini said: "It was about a week after our son Renato Roberto Giusto Giuseppe was born that I received a phone call from a Hearst reporter. It was the fiftieth phone call that day and so I said will you please get off the line, you people are driving me crazy. Would you believe it—the next day there was an eight-column headline in a Los Angeles newspaper reading: ROSSELLINI FEARS MENTAL HEALTH."

The momentous first meeting between Bergman and Rossellini was arranged by Ilya Lopert, theater owner and leading distributor of foreign films in the United States. It took place in the late afternoon of September 22, 1948, in Ingrid's suite in the George V Hotel in Paris. Rossellini had arrived two days late, and Ingrid, who was in Paris with her husband, Peter Lindstrom, almost didn't wait.

The name of the delay was Anna Magnani. She was kicking up a fuss about Roberto's going to Paris, and a Magnani fuss is only slightly less lethal, though as noisy, as a Kansas twister. It seemed that Rossellini had sold her on a United Life deal in which their union was not only physical but artistic as well. He, the greatest director, and she, the greatest actress, working as an indissoluble team—why, the entire movie world would revolve about them. Swell, said Anna, then why do you have to go running off to Paris? We don't need Bergman.

We already have a contract to start work on *Air of Rome*. Besides, what was that gossip I heard about letters passing between you and that woman?

Rossellini managed to square it with his suspicious girl friend, however, and hot-footed it to Paris. This is a blow-by-blow description of the meeting. Lopert introduced them. Rossellini kissed Ingrid's hand. Rossellini told the story of the proposed film, *Stromboli*, which, like *Open City*, was to be based on actuality. After he had outlined the film, Ingrid turned to her husband and, speaking in Swedish, said she thought that the story was good. Her husband said he didn't think too much of it nor, for that matter, was he impressed with Rossellini. Lopert coughed discreetly, and said, also in Swedish, that they had twenty-four hours to decide. Ingrid took Lindstrom aside, talked earnestly for awhile, and then said that she would accept if Rossellini personally brought a written draft of the story to America before January 15th. Everybody shook hands. Rossellini kissed Ingrid's hand.

Slipping past Magnani's guard for the trip to America was easy. The reason for the trip, Rossellini explained, was that he had to accept in person the New York Film Critics' award for *Paisan*. Once in the United States, he rushed with Lopert to Hollywood where the director was the house guest of the Lindstroms. Lopert signed Bergman and Rossellini and then sold his contract to Howard Hughes. Rossellini, who had been in training all summer for this occasion, must have given Ingrid a full treatment of his persuasive genius, because when she left to join him later in Rome, it was not for just a film.

Sergio Amidei, in trying to explain Rossellini's special charm, said: "He creates a dream atmosphere about himself. The women around him live in a dream world. He is very tender but at the same time can be brutal and vulgar. He is the true man of today. The rest of us are silly romanticists with foolish notions about how gently women should be treated."

Two days before Ingrid's arrival in Rome, he kissed Magnani good-bye and shipped her off to London to prepare the ground for the filming of their joint venture, *Air of Rome*, which was to go into production that week. She didn't find out about Rossellini walking out on the United Life until she read in the newspapers that the pair had left for Stromboli.

Ingrid's arrival in Italy was a field day for the press. Lest the newspapermen lose the full implication of her visit, Rossellini thoughtfully provided her with a suite in the Hotel Excelsior which was connected with his own by intercommunicating doors. And, unless this bit of subtlety be lost, he showed—only to his intimates, of course—a copy of the letter Ingrid had written to her husband in which she confessed that she had found a new soul mate. She was deliriously happy in Rome. Rossellini explained that he had already secured a divorce from his wife in Hungary, but that now it wasn't valid because the new communist regime had canceled the accord between the countries. But he was sure that he could solve the difficulty by having his docile wife secure it in Austria. Ingrid wrote to Lindstrom asking for a divorce, and the pair set the rest of their minds to work on picture making.

The island of Stromboli is one of the few active volcanoes in the world. As a place of habitation, it lacks the most primitive comforts. There are no horses, mules or cows, no electricity, gas, radio or telephone, no newspapers or movie houses. It did offer one attraction, though. There was plenty of solitude for a game of hearts. Ingrid found life on Stromboli a paradise.

Into this symphony of love intruded two sour notes. One was the press and the other Dr. Peter Lindstrom. When the doctor took the much-publicized trip from Hollywood to Sicily, Rossellini showed annoyance. He regarded Ingrid's husband as a churlish fellow who didn't take a sufficiently broad view of life, like his own wife, for example. The section of the press that Rossellini complained most loudly about was Robert Conway of the *New York Daily News* and myself, the first pair of American correspondents to reach Stromboli. It has taken me as little as fourteen hours aboard Linee Aerea Italiana's admirable DC-6 planes to traverse the distance between New York and Rome. The trip from Rome to Stromboli, a distance of about two hundred and fifty miles, took six days. The reason, aside from the lack of means of transport, was Rossellini. He didn't want us on Stromboli. Having heard that we were on our way, he quickly invited us, with some of the same generosity of which Marilyn Buferd complained, to make the trip aboard his three-masted schooner.

Conway and I took the day-long train ride from Rome to Messina, checked into the Albergo Reale and waited for the schooner. On the first day, Rossellini's assistant called on us to say that the ship was undergoing some repairs and there would be a few hours' delay. The second day the story was the same, and by this time we had missed the packet that makes the weekly round of the tiny Tyrrhenian islands.

Suspicious, we shopped the Messina waterfront for a private craft. In the late afternoon we found one to our liking and, tired but content, had a hearty dinner, went to a provincial girlie show and retired for the night. At 3 A.M. the door of our joint room flew open and two stalwart members of the *Pubblica Sicurezza* burst in and shouted something about arrest. While I gaped open-mouthed at them, Conway, in righteous wrath, roared in his best Italian that they were utterly lacking in good manners and that whatever their own habits might be, he personally was unaccustomed to receiving guests who were unannounced. With that he leaped out of bed, grabbed the minions of the law, threw them bodily out of the room, slammed the door and bolted it. During the remainder of the night I could hear the police officers carrying on a nervous conversation in the corridor. One of them complained, "He had no right to do that to us." His friend said, "He laid hands on us. It is an outrage against public order." "You're right," the first cop said. "You tell him." "No, you tell him," the other responded. They were still arguing when I dozed off.

At 7 A.M., we admitted them to the room to discover that it was Stern, not Conway, who was the person they sought. In the street one of the officers said, sullenly, that it had been a long night for them, especially since they had been on their feet all that time, and it would only be fair for me to hire some sort of public conveyance so that we didn't all have to walk to the *commissariato*. I hired an ancient fiacre that was tied to a drooping, miserable-looking beast and we took off.

It wasn't until noon that the *commissario* showed up and told me, apologetically, that I must not look upon this annoying procedure as a formal arrest. He was just interested in knowing what story I was covering. I told him, evenly, that it was none of his goddamn business. That was where I was mistaken, he pointed out. Certainly I must realize how embarrassing it was for the present administration, especially for the Ministry of Interior, for me to have found Giuliano, the bandit king of Sicily, to have interviewed him and to have broadcast the news around the world, at a time when fifteen thousand police officers and soldiers, engaged in the greatest man-hunt in Italy's history, couldn't find a trace of him. And was it not true that I had intentions of seeing him once more? I said that my assignments were matters that concerned only my editors and my conscience.

It wasn't until he had satisfied himself that the story I was on had nothing to do with Giuliano that I was released. Sometime afterward, I learned that it was

Rossellini, with a fine Machiavellian touch, who had tipped off the police that I was seeking to interview the bandit a second time.

News of the arrest didn't rate a line in any American newspaper. A reporter's arrest is newsworthy only when it happens on the other side of the Iron Curtain.

The trip was made in a thirty-foot boat owned by an ex-Brooklyn bootlegger who had returned to his native Sicily shortly after the First World War. We were about halfway to Stromboli when a sudden storm sent us scooting for safety to the prison island of Lipari. When we finally took off, the next day, the seas were still running high and the nauseating rhythm of the boat, as the prow aimed almost perpendicularly upward and then downward, had me in a constant state of anxiety and my drawn face must have shown it. For some reason Conway found this uproariously funny and he kept passing snide remarks about my condition. As we neared Stromboli, the laughter died on his face. His normal rosy hue was replaced by a sick black-green. He clutched the side of the boat and leaned far over the waters. I didn't start laughing until we had waded ashore on the island.

Rossellini's departure from the island had evidently been timed with our arrival. He saw us struggle ashore, greeted us with a cheery *ciao* and the advice that we make ourselves comfortable and that he would join us soon. As we struggled up the volcanic ash toward the peasant hut in which we were to bed down, Rossellini jumped into a boat and took off. He didn't return until we were safely on our way to the mainland again. Just for the record we took with us the first first-hand report on the romance and Ingrid's statement that her intentions toward her director were serious.

Rossellini's habits of work drove Howard Hughes's first company manager to distraction. The latter was replaced by Harold Lewis, a tough six-foot-four movie man with nerves to match his figure. When Lewis left, he wasn't walking too steadily. A sample day's work consisted of the crew, Ingrid and Rossellini climbing up the face of the volcanic cone where a single close-up of the star was shot. When Lewis pointed out that the same thing could have been done in the studio, with the same effect, in half an hour, Rossellini retorted that it wouldn't be realistic.

The fisherman whom Ingrid marries in the picture was a twenty-one-year-old fisherman named Mario Vitale, who was picked off the beach at Salerno and who received seventy-five dollars a week for playing the male lead. Commenting on Vitale's histrionic ability, one unkind critic said that he was overpaid. Even though the story calls for Ingrid to be pregnant, Rossellini rewrote the scenes so that his fisherman never kissed her. When the *Giornale della Sera* printed its story about Bergman actually being pregnant, the Italians, far more tolerant in such matters, said only that Rossellini was carrying his passion for realism a bit too far.

The natural disadvantages of filming on Stromboli, plus a love affair, domestic strife and the Rossellini touch resulted in the picture's being brought in eleven weeks over schedule and at an added cost of three hundred thousand dollars. Howard Hughes took a very poor view of this, holding that it was too high a price to pay for a simple game of hearts.

"That's the view of an American businessman," Rossellini said disdainfully. "My view is that of an artist." Whereupon he sent Hughes a bill for an added twenty-five thousand dollars on the ground that he had worked three months longer than his contract called for. This raised Hughes's blood pressure considerably. He waved contracts, called lawyers, and started suit.

Rossellini did nothing—nothing, that is, except hold out the last thousand feet of film so that the picture could not be completed. While a chorus of Hughes's lawyers yelled that it was an outrage, the head of RKO finally saw what is known as Rossellini logic. He quietly wrote out a check and sent it to the director.

Even the birth of the much-publicized Bergman baby had the famous Rossellini touch. It was on the night of the world première in Rome of *Vulcano,* Anna Magnani's starring film, that Ingrid hurried off to the Clinica Margherita and, during the second reel, gave birth to a seven-pound, eleven-and-one-fifth-ounce boy. The representatives of the world press, attending the première just a few streets away, deserted the theater in a body.

Magnani left the theater blazing. "He did it on purpose," she fumed.

Reminiscing with this writer recently, Rossellini gave his reason for having had the baby out of wedlock. "During the war, my family was never too far from starvation. Keeping my children alive was a day-to-day struggle. I even pawned my clothing. Then I made *Open City* and *Paisan*. I could afford to give my children things I only dreamed about before. I sent my son, Romano, to Spain to visit my mother and there, quite suddenly, he died.

"The bottom dropped out of my life. I didn't give a damn about anybody or anything. Not until I met Ingrid. When I learned that she was going to have a baby, I had to make a decision. It would have been very easy to do something about it. Remember, abortion doctors exist in our country, too. But if we did that, I would have felt as though Romano were dying a second time. Believe me, it took far more courage on our part to have the baby."

The same critics who hailed Rossellini as the great director of his day are now raising doubts as to his ability, principally on the basis of *Stromboli*.

Rossellini says: "Howard Hughes's people butchered the film in the cutting room. Here in Italy, the uncut version won for me the Rome Grand Prix."

During the height of this controversy, Rossellini told me that he intended inviting the ten leading film critics from the United States to come to Italy at his expense to view the original film. I told him that the idea was a good one in all but one respect. They might not like the original any better than the one they had seen, in which event, even though they had accepted his hospitality, they would show him no mercy. Rossellini thought about this a moment. Could I, he wondered, find the time to see the uncut version and give him my opinion on it?

Later that week I viewed the film at a private showing. When it was over, I told the director, "A very interesting film. Don't invite the critics." There was a discernible difference between the two versions. The uncut one was a half-hour more boring.

European critics say that whether his film is good or bad, Rossellini is one of the few directors who has something to say, and who doesn't let himself be bound by commercial considerations. This critique made a profound impression on him. For the motion picture to succeed *Stromboli,* he chose the non-commercial story of St. Francis of Assisi. The money for the production was furnished by Angelo Rizzoli, one of Italy's leading publishers. The film deals with a series of unconnected episodes in the life of the Saint. Most of the cast was non-professional, and their acting was about on a par with the graduating class of any American high school. Whatever message it was that he tried to get across in this picture was lost in the illiterate manner of its telling. It is Rossellini's worst film and that includes the unshowable *Desire.*

The failure of St. Francis—Joe Burstyn, the intrepid distributor of *Paisan, Open City* and *Bicycle Thief,* says that he is still going to show it to American audiences —put a serious dent in the Rossellini pocketbook. Worse than that, backers refused to put money into another Rossellini enterprise. Only when he packaged the deal by offering Ingrid as the star, were the funds forthcoming for *Europe, 1951.* Ingrid had already turned down one hundred and sixty thousand dollars to do an outside film. In this one, which was finished this spring, the package received one hundred thousand dollars.

The film deals with a woman (Ingrid Bergman) who loses her young son and tries to atone for it by work, the Biblical punishment, and then by a life of good deeds amongst the lower classes. For this she is eventually committed to the insane asylum by her family. The common folk disagree with this, saying that she is a saint. The question posed at the end of the film is, "Who's loony now?" with the probable response being the investors. *Europe, 1951* was unveiled at the Venice Film Festival this summer and Ugo Zatterin, erudite critic for the highly respected *Giornale D'Italia,* wrote, kindly, that it was a film filled with good intentions that remained in mid-air. Rossellini stated his problem in the first 1,500 feet of film and went so completely haywire in the next 10,000 feet that it was painful to watch the talented Bergman struggle to save the picture by sheer weight. It would have been far wiser, and perhaps more dramatic, for Rossellini to have resolved the problem of his protagonist by giving her a shot of hormones or by still another birth, preferably twins again.

The directors of the Festival handed one of the prizes to Rossellini for this picture and the director can now add it to the prizes he won for *Stromboli* and *St. Francis,* this latter holding, according to Signor Zatterin, the unawarded medal as *"primatista Italiano, forse mondiale, degli incassi mancati."* This tendency on the part of directors of the Venice Festival to make awards on the basis of back-room conversations instead of merit on the screen will do much to carry it down the road to suicide.

Rossellini's family life, now that Ingrid is his wife and they are, for the moment, working again—they were married in a proxy wedding performed in Mexico—is comparatively tranquil. Although money is scarce and they are still in debt—her funds are tied up in California —they spend at a furious rate. They have a modest five-room apartment on the Via Bruno Buozzi in Rome, but have purchased a one-hundred-thousand-dollar villa at Santa Marinella and a large schooner in which they hope to escape from Italy in the event of a Russian invasion.

"We'll probably wind up in the poorhouse," Ingrid told a friend recently. "But at least I will have been happy."

A life of domestic bliss is something new for the director, and it has amazed his Roman friends to see how he has taken to it. A producer, standing on Via Veneto conversing with Rossellini's cousin, saw Roberto and Ingrid drive by in a red sports car. The producer pointed out that Roberto seems, finally, to have settled down.

"It's time he grew up," the cousin snapped. "He's getting too old to play with dolls."

Virginia Hill

6

Because a somewhat notorious gentleman named Benjamin "Bugsy" Siegel, at one time highly regarded in Hollywood and Broadway sporting circles, was so inconsiderate as to have himself shot very dead in the sumptuous mansion of a volatile redhead, newspapers picked on the girl as an even bigger story than the murder.

Reporters concluded from the fact that since Bugsy had for some time shared the bedroom of the bosomy redhead he must be her lover, and this so wounded the girl's sensitive feelings that she will never again have faith in the American press.

183

"Now people keep saying nasty things about me—
that I was Ben's mistress and such stuff," she complained. This bit of girlish reticence was somewhat surprising.

The redhead is Virginia Hill, a thirty-six-year-old,
comfortably upholstered divorcée with sloe eyes and
full lips. Although she had for a decade assiduously applied herself in night clubs (in New York, Miami,
Mexico City and Hollywood) to the task of making herself a public character, it was not surprising to find that
when she did score solidly with the newsmen and make
the headlines from coast to coast, she no longer relished
the publicity. What is most unusual about one of the
decade's most publicized girls is that so little is known
about her. In the staggering volume of press copy devoted to her zany doings, facts have been inextricably
woven with fiction so that even the most discerning
newspaper reader finds it impossible to separate one
from the other.

What has most intrigued them are the reports of both
her fabulous spending and her apparently inexhaustible
income. They still talk about the La Conga party she
gave for Eddie Le Barron in New York and the giant
coming-out soirée thrown for her by a Hollywood man-
about-town at the Mocambo for which she lifted a
$7,500 tab. This writer found the latter affair chiefly
remarkable for a gents'-room conversation between a
Chicago columnist and his guest, an out-of-town newspaperman who, in common with most of those present,

knew none of the principals but who was impressed by the festivities.

"Who is the chump giving this?" asked the out-of-town newspaperman.

"I am," said a tall, handsome Latin at the adjoining urinal, trying vainly to keep looking like a man of distinction.

La Hill has done nothing to clear up the mystery surrounding her remarkable income. The few explanations that she vouchsafed to the televised Kefauver crime committee have been about as helpful as Robert Benchley's treasurer's report in double talk. This chapter is intended to separate the fact from Virginia's fancy and to give the answers to those questions that still make of her a mystery. It is, indeed, a modern-age American success story in which a poor little country girl takes on the city slickers in rather numerous numbers and beats them on their own home grounds. Those who place abiding faith in such homely virtues as truth, sobriety and respectability will find no solace in this recital. But others of more worldly bent may draw what inspiration they can from little Virginia's avoidance of those qualities which the story books tell us are necessary for woman's success.

The writer first ran across the then glamorous redhead in New York City in 1940 when she told the local reporters about a purported $60,000 investment she had just made in the Hurricane night club. She seemed slightly bored by the attentions of the press as she explained that her legal adviser had pointed out that, being the greatest party-giver since Diamond Jim Brady, she could, by spending it in a joint of her own, have the same fun and show a profit, too. From there she went on to talk about herself. She was born in Holland of an American mother and half-American-Indian father who returned to America and raised her in Georgia.

"Father struck it rich, you know," she explained. "Oil."

Broadway chroniclers found her the sort of sustaining dish that had enough screwball substance to nourish a hungry column. Dorothy Kilgallen wrote: "Virginia Hill, the Georgia heiress who's squandering so much coin around Broadway, flirting with her ex-husband. . . . John Carroll, who adores Virginia Hill, the heiress (and wants to marry her only she's never around) is consoling himself." And Ed Sullivan came up with the intelligence that "Virginia Hill and Miguelito Valdez split, but her valedictory gift to him was a $7,500 diamond watch and ring." His colleague, Danton Walker, followed with the flash that "Virginia Hill has been discovered by Gene Krupa—or vice versa. Miguelito Valdez is now apparently out of the pix." An anonymous writer pointed out that the incendiary redhead from Georgia was the gal who threw the egg in the Hollywood brawl that hit Errol Flynn in the eye, and for this a certain segment of her non-admirers applauded her zeal, aim and target selection.

The oil-heiress gag, which was all it was—the label was pinned on her for a rib by Nate Gross, noted

Chicago columnist in his daily Town Tattler in the *Herald-American* at a time when it had as much relevancy as naming Jimmy Durante social arbiter of New York's Four Hundred—began wearing thin, and Virginia propped it up with another beaut.

"You see, most of my money comes from George Rogers, my first husband," she told an inquiring reporter. "But he's dead, so let's not go into that. I was fifteen—no, I guess I was fourteen when we married. I'm no good at remembering dates. The marriage was annulled, but he settled a lot of money on me. I've got a friend in Chicago who is smart with stocks so the money has been doubled."

Dates aren't the only thing Virginia has difficulty remembering. Her memory is bad when it comes to husbands. Take Rogers, for example. There is no record of the marriage in the town in which she claims to have tied the knot. Nor has the most diligent search produced any record of an annulment. A similar search failed to reveal any will filed for probate in her favor. Even the name of the "husband" is in doubt. One of Virginia's sisters calls him George Brown while a federal investigating agency looked into the matter and claim that it was a man named George Randell who, in August of 1933, whizzed her away from her home town in a Model A Ford and carried her off to Chicago.

There is a record of a marriage to Ossie Griffith on January 13, 1939, but this was annulled six months later. Virginia refers to Ossie as her All-American fullback which, for Virginia, is reasonably close to the truth since Griffith played on the Bessemer, Alabama, high-school football team. She acquired a second—she counts him as number three—husband in Nuevo Laredo, Mexico, on January 20, 1940. He is a Mexican rumba dancer named Carlos Gonzales Valdez, and she aired him in New York just one year later.

Virginia's disregard for the truth added to the confusion surrounding the Hurricane, one of Broadway's plushier tourist traps. While she claimed that she had sunk sixty G's in the joint, her remittance man—that's the guy who foots the bills—told me that it was only $6,000 and that he ought to know. A check with the license bureau at police headquarters lists the officers of the Hurricane as Dave Wolper, Sylvia Wolper and Benjamin Schenkman and shows that these three were asked the following question:

"Has anyone except you three any financial interest in the club?"

"No," they responded.

Virginia has kept her secret, paradoxically, by talking too much. It is entirely possible that the fictionalized conception of herself has so merged with her real self that she fell victim to her own publicity. If so, then perhaps she was not prepared for the time when a snooping writer would cut through the baloney and come up with the facts. Here they are.

Virginia Hill was born on August 26, 1916, in the little town of Lipscomb, Alabama. She was one of ten children born to Margaret and W. M. Hill, a mule trader and livery-stable operator in modest circumstances. The family left Lipscomb and went to Bessemer where the mother operated a boarding house. Virginia, a skinny, plain-looking kid with mouse-colored hair, was called Tabby by her friends in the Roberts School where she completed eight grades of grammar school—which, so far as is known, was the extent of her education. One of the teachers remembers Tabby because she used to bring her a slice of pie instead of the traditional apple. She also recalls that Tabby was a sweet child, not too interested in her studies, but not any trouble in the classroom. One of Tabby's chums remembers that she always dreamed of going to the glamorous World's Fair then being staged in Chicago.

There is in each of us the very natural longing to succeed in the world and then come back to the old home town and parade down the main drag glittering as we walk. Virginia was no exception to the rule. They still talk about her triumphant home-coming. For gifts she bought a house for her mother, gave a convertible to each of two younger brothers and threw so lavish a party for the townsfolk that it stunned them. Her grade-school teachers didn't recognize the mink-clad, jewel-laden, titian-haired girl with the sexy eyes as the skinny Tabby they once knew. It was only natural that village eyebrows should be raised in surprise at all this splendor, and Virginia Hill didn't let them down. She had a ready, though somewhat thin, explanation.

"I took a beauty-school course in Chicago," she said demurely.

The attitude of the good burghers can best be summed up in a song Phil Regan has popularized in the supper clubs. It deals with a country lass who is driven from home because of bucolic dalliance in the woods with a bewhiskered figure that she claims was only Paddy McGinty's goat. She returns years later, with rings on her fingers and wearing a sable coat. The tag line is that "You can bet your hat she didn't get that from Paddy McGinty's goat."

Getting back to August, 1933, and pursuing the line of provable fact, a young gent, unknown to Virginia's friends—though quite evidently the Rogers-Brown-Randell she speaks of as her first husband—appeared on the scene and took her off in his lizzie. She arrived in Chicago in the midst of a sweltering summer and got herself a job on the Midway, first as a waitress and then as a shill, a girl who wiggles her scantily-clad wares to attract a crowd for a barker to work on. Friends who knew her during these days say that she was a pretty good kid who wasn't on the make. In fact, it has always been the boast of the men she favored that money never entered into their friendship. There's probably a moral in it somewhere. Virginia, who was the least grasping of those in her set, wound up with the most.

She got it from a man she met very casually at a quiet party given by a friend. It was a meeting that began a love affair that deserves to be ranked with the great ones of the ages, since the man continued to love

190

and support her through three marriages with other men, numerous love affairs, a murder and four suicide attempts. The measure of that love is that he is still supporting her. It isn't likely that any woman will dispute her outstanding qualifications to write on the topic "How to Hold Your Man." That he has been able to keep his name out of the news headlines proves him to be, in other respects, a sensible person.

He is Joe Epstein, a fifty-year-old Chicagoan of medium height, wide-mouthed and near-sighted. Joe is an accountant for and a part owner of a commission brokerage firm of Stern and Horvath. The commissions that this firm executes come from that section of the sporting rich which feels it can predict the outcome of a contest in which the speed of steeds is matched. Anyone so crass as to call it a bookie joint is completely out of touch with reality because this largest of national lay-off houses accepts no commissions from clients unless the size and frequency of orders is such as to justify putting in a special direct wire. It should be noted that the reputation of the firm in executing these commissions and in rewarding those clients who, surprisingly, sometimes guess correctly in this noble sport of kings, is excellent.

The income from such a calling is considerable, and Joe, a wealthy bachelor in love, and with no other claims on his money (except Uncle Sam who wants his cut even if the money comes from bank robbery) devoted himself to making a lady out of the Midway shimmy dancer.

The smart boys on the Loop said, "Joe bought himself a glamor girl." The year was 1934.

Many people have tried to figure out what it was that little Virginia had that made her stand out. Chicagoans who remember her at that time tell me that she was a short, dumpy girl with a big bosom and chestnut hair. Her face had an innocent, virginal look. The closest this writer can come to giving an answer is that Virginia was not a calculating female. She had a certain independence of spirit that asserted itself even when it was contrary to her pecuniary interests. She said what she felt without weighing the cost and this gave her a sincerity and openness of manner. Strongest of all was the fact that she was not for sale. She followed her heart rather than the dollar sign and, strangely enough, it was only in rare instances that the two did not coincide.

The first place Epstein set her up in was a pleasant, chintzy one-room-and-kitchenette affair on Chicago's lake front. A friend who attended a soirée at that place reports that Virginia was quite a party-giver even in those early days. The way the liquor flowed made it obvious that the man keeping her had taken the rubber band off the bank roll. The friend, happening to note that Joe Epstein was not there, asked Virginia what happened to him.

"He didn't come," Virginia said.

"Working late today?" the friend pressed.

"He wasn't invited," Virginia responded evenly.

Her independence expressed itself in choice of

escorts. Though Joe paid the bills, she still had other boy friends. One of them was Major Riddle, the Major being a first name rather than a military title, who inherited a trucking company and who was part of the triangle that made up a standing gag. Virginia, wearing a silver-fox cape and diamond pendant, would be accosted by a friend who would point to the cape.

"Epstein?" he inquires.

"No, Riddle."

He points to the pendant, "Riddle?"

"No, Epstein."

This was considered uproariously funny and both would double up with laughter. Riddle swears to intimates that he never paid any money to Virginia. Once he gave her a diamond bracelet and she became livid with rage. She screamed: "What kind of a girl do you think I am?" and flung the offending bauble into the toilet. There are some cynics who point out that Virginia could spot value in a stone at ten paces, but it would not appear that disappointment motivated this girlish outburst.

It is quite probable that her drab childhood had much to do with inclining her toward the tinseled life of the night clubs. A girl friend of the early Chicago days remembers Virginia's confiding bitterly, "Did you ever wake up in the middle of the night because of a bad dream? I have. And the dream was always the same. I was locked in a cell for a life term. Only with me it wasn't a dream. The town of Lipscomb, Alabama where I lived was my prison. There were ten kids in the family and no money. It's an unbeatable combination. To make it worse, my parents didn't get along too well and part of the time they were separated. My father worked in a livery stable as a horse-and-mule trader while my mother ran a boarding house. Why, even my grandmother who's past eighty and who lives in Kennesaw Mountain, Georgia, is still chopping cotton for a living. I swore that the same wouldn't happen to me.

"You know, Joe says I've got a lot of nerve. That's very funny because all my life I've been afraid. Maybe that's why I do so many crazy things—just to prove to myself that I'm not scared. I ran away from home to come to Chicago. That sure set my home town on its ear, wondering how a mousy kid like me ever got the nerve to do it. I was only seventeen years old. I knew that my father would go to the cops and that there would be an alarm out for me. Scared? Why, I was sure that every man I waited on in the restaurant—that was one of my jobs in Chicago—was a detective who was going to snap a pair of handcuffs over my wrists and drag me back home. I had a story all figured out in case they found me. I was going to tell them that I got married and if they asked to whom I would say to a man named George Rogers. And if they wanted to know where he was, I would tell them that we split up and had the wedding annulled. And if they wanted to know in what court all this took place, I would tell them to find out for themselves because I was under no legal obligation to tell them. I died a million deaths before I reached eighteen."

In Chicago, Virginia parlayed her friendship with Joe Epstein and her manner of living into what newspapers term a fabulous fortune. When she went out on dates with sporting gentry, she very naturally made favorable mention of the very respectable firm of Stern and Horvath with which her boy friend was connected. This direct advertising was highly effective. So great did the volume of business become that Joe Epstein rose from accountant to partner and eventual controller. A sizeable share of this enormously sizeable enterprise is turned over to Virginia regularly. She acts as though she has a vested interest in the firm. On one occasion she asked Joe for eight thousand dollars.

"Why do you want it?" Joe asked.

"What the hell do you care?" Virginia blazed. "It's my money."

"I know, honey. I just didn't want you to do anything foolish with it."

Some crass individuals have intimated that the wide financial latitude permitted Virginia by Epstein results from motives other than sentimental. They suggest that the sexy redhead with the sweetly demure face was nothing but a shill for the book and that a single customer steered in the right direction would not only pay for a year's wild spending but would show a profit for the principals. These crude and ungentlemanly opinions never fail to rouse the ire of the people involved.

After a few years, life in Chicago seemed dull and Virginia told Joe that life was passing her by and she wanted to hit the bright lights in New York and Hollywood before she got too old to enjoy it. That was when she took up with the rumba crowd, Mexican dancers and Cuban singers. She was an heiress cut adrift from the family and out for a hell of a toot. She tipped freely and if change was in anything less than twenty-dollar bills, she waved it off with a keep the change, dearie. While she often gave publicized gifts to her men friends, there were also those who reciprocated with an occasional unpublicized trinket like a mink coat or a sable wrap.

Although some of her spending was wild, it never reached the fantastic amounts manufactured by some columnists. Take the publicized $60,000 Hurricane investment. Joe only sent her $6,000, but one of the owners swears that she only put in $3,000 and quickly borrowed back one thousand of it to pay another bill. During this period she lived in the Savoy-Plaza Hotel in a room that cost fifteen dollars a day. Later she retrenched by moving into a room that cost only thirteen dollars.

Virginia set out for broader pastures with one bit of pungent advice. "Remember the Uncle," Joe told her. "With him you must always play straight." It is a bit of advice she never forgot. To him she told the truth. And so for those who have wondered about the size of her "legal" income—it is fifteen thousand dollars a year. That is what she writes on a sworn piece of paper called the income tax report. The Uncle has carefully scrutinized it and found it satisfactory. This document shows Virginia to be possessed of one of the most remarkable traits extant. It is called controlled luck. Her source of income is listed as "wagers" and this amazing woman has been able to win the same amount each year.

For years the source of Virginia's money intrigued newspapermen. One of them questioned her younger brother, Chick. The latter naïvely explained: "My sister told me that she doesn't really know where it comes from, but her lawyer tells me it is pouring in so fast she can't begin to spend it all." Lee Mortimer wrote in the *New York Daily Mirror* that "Her original gold mine was Brooklyn's top gang chieftain, a man supposed to be happily wed and with children, who preferred to keep Virginia as far away from New York as possible."

Some strange feeling of delicacy kept Mortimer from naming the man. He is Joe Adonis, better known as Joey A to the mob. In all fairness to him, it should be noted that he was never more than a casual love of Virginia's and there is no reason to question his veracity when he told intimates that he never gave her a dime. Aside from these minor divergences from fact, Mortimer came reasonably close. Not so close was a later story of his which scooped the world on Virginia Hill. It reported her and her two children embarked on a secret mission to Italy where, as the representative

197   **Virginia Hill**

of the "Syndicate," she was to confer with Lucky Luciano. The only woman even vaguely resembling the written report was the wife of a Washington, D.C., doctor, traveling to see her mother-in-law in Spain. When the ship docked in Barcelona, Franco's minions were all ready. The poor woman was hustled off to the pokey and kept there for two days before she could convince them of her true identity. At the time, Virginia was in Chicago fixing up an apartment for a long stay. The resultant publicity caused the management to cancel her lease.

The wonderful Mortimer beat which lacked only the inconsequential element of factuality puts me in mind of a second, even greater *Mirror* scoop, for which I was partly responsible. Although it does not deal with Virginia, it bears retelling if only to instruct the uninitiated in the almost insurmountable difficulties faced by our gallant cousins of this sprightly tabloid. It was at the height of the excitement brought on by Tom Dewey's forthright attack on vice in the person of Lucky Luciano. I was sitting in the office of the late Assistant District Attorney Charles Pilatsky in the old D.A.'s building at 137 Centre Street when, through the open door, I saw David Charnay, the *Mirror's* big gun, walking down the long corridor.

Now Dave had a manner peculiar to screen journalists in that he was brash and forward and simply rolled over anyone who stood in his way. So it seemed only natural for Walter Van Wagner, a special investigator for the D.A. who was in the room, to say, "Let's give Dave the foot." Nothing prearranged. Just those words. As the reporter stepped into the room, Pilatsky slammed a drawer shut, and looked innocently at the ceiling.

"What's up?" Dave asked me.

"The case isn't fully developed yet," I began and then pretended to change my mind. "It's too hot. If you want to know anything, you'll have to get it from Charlie."

Dave went into a tearful dissertation on what a pal he was of mine and I said that I was under oath not to repeat what I had just gotten in confidence, and so Dave said he would promise to respect the confidence and finally the prosecutor weakened. He extracted a solemn and sacred oath from the *Mirror* reporter; then he opened a drawer and pretended to read from a telegram supposedly sent by the Ohio State police that Mildred Davis, a small-time madam better known as Chinatown Millie, who had turned State's evidence in several vice cases, had been shot to death and her body dumped in a ditch outside of Canton, Ohio. Any premature break on the story would be very embarrassing to the investigation, might even permit the killers to escape, the D.A. warned.

Dave sat around for about five minutes like a man with a blow torch under his seat. Then, unable to stand the strain, he bolted for the door. Van Wagner yelled after him. "Come back, Dave. It's a phony!" But the *Mirror* man, whatever else he might have lacked, was possessed of tremendous speed. That night the first green edition carried this three-quarter page head:

VICE QUEEN

FOUND SLAIN

Under it was a one-quarter-page box in bold-face type telling how gangland vengeance had caught up with beautiful red-headed Mildred Davis, the madam whose testimony had convicted New York's vice barons. (I don't know why tabloids insist on turning all women connected with the sex-for-sale racket into beauties. Millie was a tall, bony, buck-toothed woman of about thirty-five.) It went on to describe in graphic fashion how the bullet-riddled body had been flung from a speeding car and then, realizing that the size of the headline was no substitute for skimpiness of fact, finished with the suggestion that readers see later editions for further details.

I remember receiving an anguished telephone call from mild-mannered Bob Shand, then city editor of the *New York Daily News*, asking me how come I missed the yarn and my telling him, offhandedly, to ignore it, it's phony, and he, as excited as I had ever heard him, telling me to go out and get a copy of the green edition and see for myself. Phony indeed! The front page was replated in the second edition of the *Mirror*. Neither in this edition, nor in any subsequent one, was there another mention of the murder. I ran into Millie on Mott Street shortly thereafter. She said that she had to give up her one-girl house in Harlem and go back to her Oriental trade because of all the bad publicity. Charnay suffered no such economic reverses. He went on to become an enormous success as a press agent.

Virginia Hill met Joey A and Frank Costello when Joe Epstein came East to discuss business with the leaders of what has been loosely called the "Syndicate." He took Virginia along to the Madison Bar and there made the formal presentation. Joey A took an immediate fancy to the girl and quickly pushed the relationship to a point that was not exactly novel for either of them. Joey A, however, couldn't keep up with the affair because of family obligations. Don't get the idea that a gangster whose very name strikes terror in the breasts of others doesn't get his ears pinned back by his own wife. So on a subsequent trip to Los Angeles where he was working out the details for the construction of a colossal gambling casino, he took her along and there, in turn, introduced her to Bugsy Siegel.

This meeting had a far-reaching effect upon Virginia. Because she fell madly in love with the Bug, she cut out her madcap night excursions and settled down to a life of tranquil cohabitation in the very center of a shadowy, though nonetheless real, empire called gangdom. I first met Virginia's true love, professionally, some fifteen years ago when I did a series of exposés on New York's racketeer kings. I found him a fascinating figure then. He was a hoodlum product of the East Side slums who started as a petty thief and rose to become a hired rod on alcohol truck convoys making the New York-Chicago run. He joined up with Meyer Lansky and for a time did well bashing skulls for both sides in labor disputes. In the thirties the team split to go with Costello's gambling combination, Lansky going down to Havana to run the National Gambling Casino and the Bug to Los Angeles. It was here that he experienced a deep yearning to become a gentleman. He hobnobbed with all the swells of Hollywood. Countess di Frasso invited him to Rome where, as Benjamin Siegel, noted American business-man, he was wined and dined by Italian aristocracy.

His taste for the finer things in life became so deep-seated that he even did time like a gentleman. In the Los Angeles County jail, while awaiting trial on the charge of having murdered Big Greenie, one of Lepke's torpedoes, he wore a tailor-made prison suit of soft denim which was pressed daily by an obliging keeper who served as his valet. During the lunch hour he was given his liberty so that he could take out Wendy Bar-rie, the British film player. All that ever came of this murder was a civil suit brought by Big Greenie's widow against Bugsy for $150,350. The $350 was for funeral expenses.

Taken by and large the Bug was a romantic figure, and the susceptible Virginia left her Adonis and went overboard for him. Shortly thereafter Bugsy moved into Virginia's imposing-looking mansion at 810 Linden Drive in Beverly Hills. This residence was taken to be another bit of evidence of her great wealth, but her patient boy friend in Chicago assured me that the landlord received no rental for the house. Even though the owner had, for a brief time, at least, lived under the same roof with his pretty tenant, his friends would be first to recognize how ridiculous it would be to assume that sex played any part in the bargain. Anyone who called Bugsy anything but Ben became her enemy for life. Virginia, living with gangland's hierarchy, yearned for respectability.

The ruling passion in Bugsy's and Virginia's lives was the six-million-dollar Flamingo Club in Las Vegas, Nevada, the most modern and ornate gambling house in America. The money for it was put up by such men as Frank Costello, Joe Adonis, Joey Batters, Phil Kastel and Abie Zwillman—the social register of the gambling world. The place was to be a monument to the greatness of men who were giants in the art of painlessly separating a citizen from his bankroll. Bugsy was named resident general manager.

The honor of being chosen to operate so important an enterprise was not lightly taken by him. The house opened on December 26, 1946, and came out $20,000 in the red. Opening night set the pace. The house never had a winning night. The townspeople hated the Bug, and they boycotted the place. Bugsy said he would bury them all before he got out. He gave $10,-000 to a local charity and raffled off a new car each week, but it didn't help. His own men crossed him. They robbed him at the wheel and ruined him in the kitchen. Knives that were purchased for six dollars apiece were heaved out with the garbage. Even more stuff was carried away, and an enormous amount of breakage was chalked up. Bugsy had his private police force, but they couldn't catch colds.

Virginia lived with Bugsy at the Flamingo. One of the bartenders told me that it was inspiring to see them together.

"They was like collitch kids—holding hands and everything," he said.

Virginia's favorite drink was a stinger, French brandy and white mint, and she would average fifteen in the course of an evening. She was considered a very good tipper, leaving the barman three dollars after each round while the cocktail girl who waited on her was good for a twenty note. It was the sort of conduct that prompted the hired hands to say that she was a real lady.

For one of such unsettled temperament, Virginia's idyll at Flamingo was calm. Only once did her temper flare up. An attractive blonde hat-check girl kept passing sotto-voce remarks about the "Duchess" and they got under her skin. The blow-up occurred in the chemin de fer room during the free midnight supper, an institution at the Flamingo. As the girl walked through the room, Virginia, no slouch as a fighter, yanked out a fistful of hair with her left, and threw a right cross that staggered the blonde. Bugsy was very angry about it because he really believed himself to be a high-class gentleman. What if people should say what can you expect in a joint run by a bum? When

Virginia tried to explain her actions, he angrily threw a couple of punches into her.

That's when life stopped having too much meaning for her and she took the first of the many overdoses of sleeping pills. But a constitution that can absorb fifteen stingers a night doesn't succumb to anything so mild as a drug. After she pulled through, she went to Paris for a little vacation away from the romantic Bug.

She was in Paris when on the night of June 20, 1947, an unknown person arrived at the Linden Drive home, carefully steadied an army carbine on the rose trellis and, when Bugsy seated himself on the living-room divan, fired nine shots through the window. Five slugs hit Bugsy in the face, one of them popping an eye out of his head. It was a very ordinary finish for a punk who thought himself good. Like all gang murders it would have ended there except for the existence of a very rich and supposedly glamorous redhead. The night Bugsy was hit, the Flamingo made $40,000, its first winning since it opened.

Virginia was in her suite at the Westminster Hotel in Paris at the time. A foreign correspondent visited her and told her that he had bad news for her.

"What is it?" Virginia asked.

"Ben Siegel was shot and killed last night."

Virginia's eyes narrowed shrewdly. "You're saying it to get a rise out of me, aren't you?"

The correspondent shook his head. "No, I'm afraid this is the McCoy." He took out a set of telephotos of the body and asked Virginia if she wanted to see for herself.

"No, I don't want to see them. All that blood and everything. How do you like my dress?" she said, forcing a smile. "I'm going to wear it to a ball tonight. Please get this straight. People are saying that I was his mistress and such stuff. That's nonsense. I never was. I never even spent much time with him. His only mistress was the Flamingo Club. The last time I saw him was about three weeks ago, in Las Vegas. He was working hard and I told him he could not come down to dinner with all those nice people while he was wearing a dirty sport shirt. He told me to mind my own business. I don't take that from anyone so I packed my things and left."

To a second correspondent she issued a formal communiqué from a barricaded hotel room. "The death of my friend Benjamin Siegel has caused me immense chagrin and I am seeking solitude because of my suffering. My plans for a vacation in Europe were made a long time before Mr. Siegel died, and it is pure fantasy to suggest that he made me leave." She later broke down and cried: "Ben was the only man I ever loved. I could kill myself."

She fled to the Hotel Reserve in Beaulieu-sur-Mer on the Riviera in the company of two young French gentlemen friends who were protecting her from the press, and there she took another overdose of sleeping pills. While recovering, one of the protectors brought her a huge bouquet of lilies which he laid across her chest. Then he photographed her, and one hour later was trying to peddle the picture to the reporters working on the story. Virginia got back to Paris where she took another overdose of sleeping pills.

While she was recovering from this jag, a friend visited her and revealed that the American Embassy, embarrassed by her presence in France, was going to request her to get out. Virginia got mad. She tore her passport to bits and flushed the pieces down the toilet.

"Now let them try to put me out," she announced triumphantly.

One wire-service dispatch quoted a high police source as saying that it was Lucky Luciano who had ordered the murder. I was in Rome at the time and easily traced the suspect to the lobby of the Albergo Savoia. I showed him the news item and his lip curled in a sneer.

"So they say I gave it to the Bug? Sure I did it. Why not? I'm the king of vice, the king of dope, and public enemy number one. And you read it in the American newspapers, eh? Anything you read there must be true. Now's there anything else you want me to confess to—any baby snatches, ax murders?"

When Virginia returned to the States there was a crowd waiting to meet her. There were the New York police, the immigration authorities, a district attorney from Los Angeles and several score of newspapermen. They all gave her a thorough going-over, and from then on she referred to the gentlemen of the fourth estate as those lousy heels of the press. Her brother,

Chick, drove her down to her palatial mansion at 1435 West 28th Street, Sunset Isle, Florida, where she encountered Bill Short, a two-fisted chief of police who had read enough headlines to know all about Virginia Hill. He told her to get out of town. If she was going to be rubbed out, let it happen to her in California, not in his city. Virginia went to Las Vegas, as a sort of final pilgrimage, and then checked into the Paradise Inn in Phoenix, Arizona, as Mrs. Norma Hall of Chicago. That night she swallowed another bottle of sleeping pills, but by this time she was so accustomed to them she could toss them off like stingers.

Joe Epstein, her patient, bespectacled bank roll, stepped in and hustled her off to a ranch in Kalispell, Montana. It was here that Virginia finally got the Bug out of her system. For a gag, one of her dear friends snapped a picture of her doing a take-off on Bonnie Parker, the gun moll, as she posed wearing a two-gun holster, a fat cigar in her mouth and one foot on the bumper of a car. Later that week this photograph was offered to me for sale for an exaggerated two thousand dollars. While she was in Kalispell, various newspapers reported her in South America, Florida, in New York night clubs and in Los Angeles where she was supposedly spending $50,000 to redecorate her Beverly Hills home.

It was during this period in my work on the story that I ran down Joe Epstein in Chicago. I found him in an uncommunicative mood. This was normal since he still had not been publicly connected with the girl.

By this time I had collected a fairly complete file, and I used it to overcome his natural reticence. I remember recounting many of the items in it that might easily be left out of a Hill story; stuff like a complete breakdown of both his and her income tax report; that on the West Coast she used the bank account of Coline Whitney; that Coline Whitney was the *nom de finance* of Mimi Capone. It would be far wiser, I pointed out, for him to receive me in a spirit of amicability. Joe countered with a concrete suggestion that there were three thousand reasons why it might be wiser for me not to write the story at all. I looked pityingly at him and said that this did not mark him as the intelligent person his friends said he was. Didn't he realize that the story was so big even President Truman couldn't kill it? It was time, I explained, for him to learn some ugly truths about my profession. No less an authority than the late Damon Runyon had this brief advice for the young hopefuls who came to him for a hint on how to get ahead in journalism. *"Nem,"* said Mr. Runyon in Yiddish. With this in mind, did he not see that by the end of the week he would need thirty thousand good reasons and that by the end of the month it would add up to three hundred thousand and even then some cub with a brownie camera would come along and knock him off? Joe felt that this was excellent advice and that I was truly a friend, and so he convinced Virginia that it was to their best interests to co-operate with me.

During our rounds of Chicago's hot spots, Joe told me that Virginia was a very much misunderstood girl.

Take the time she was living rent-free in the house of a handsome Latin man-about-town. Everybody was saying that she was his mistress. Joe was out there on a visit once and got somewhat plastered and wandered into the wrong bedroom where he saw the landlord sharing a bed with the gardener, so you can see how irresponsible such talk was. Virginia was a fine, independent girl. He was even willing to marry her, but he couldn't marry outside his faith because it would break his old mother's heart.

A few years later, on a trip back from Europe, I was in Chicago and I hunted up Joe Epstein. I found him at the Clover Bar with Barney Ross.

"I see by the papers that Virginia has married a ski instructor," I said.

"You know Virginia," Joe said. "She's a sucker for a sob story. This guy Hauser was facing deportation and the only way to keep him in the country was to marry him. There's nothing between them, though, if you know what I mean." (The Hauser baby was born five months later.)

"Did Virginia read my profile on her?" I asked.

"Yes."

"What did she think of it?"

"She didn't say much about it."

"What do you mean?" I pressed. "What did she say?"

"All she said to me," Joe said, "was 'You and your fucking friends.'"

It was as a witness before Senator Kefauver's crime-investigating committee that Virginia really scored. I don't know this of my own knowledge since I was in Europe at the time, but friends tell me that there has never been a public spectacle like it. Business in New York City was at a standstill. Workers literally poured out of offices to stand ten deep around television sets in bars. They saw a stoutish, though still attractive, woman of thirty-five, smartly dressed in a simple, expensive black suit, wide-brimmed black straw hat and silver-blue mink stole, step into the witness box immediately on the heels of Frank Costello.

For an hour the committee fired questions at her. Where did her income come from? "Oh," responded Virginia innocently, "it came from betting on horses. Friends would give me tips on sure winners. What is more, I paid my income tax every year." (I can almost hear Joe Epstein telling Virginia: "Honey, I don't care how you lie to me—but with the Uncle we gotta be honest. With him we are square. If you make any dough on the outside let me know so I can pay tax on it.") And about the Syndicate? "The big boys never talked when I was around." Who killed Bugsy Siegel? "I don't know. Ben was killed when I was in Paris." And how to account for the discrepancies between her declared income and her rate of spending? "Men liked my company and they gave me things. Not always money. Expensive gifts. Like Ben Siegel. He bought me the Florida house." This last must have handed the underworld a laugh. The truth is that it was Virginia who supported Ben, going so far as to make good some of his bum checks. Her testimony completed, she stepped down, walked through a throng of reporters, slapped one of them in the face and told the others that she hoped an atom bomb would fall on them. She had tossed off a Kefauver grilling with less difficulty than she would experience tossing off a dozen stingers. Those who viewed the proceedings were not so much surprised by her false and evasive answers, especially in regard to the source of her income, for this was no more than natural, as they were by the committee's apparent reluctance to press the witness on this score. The senators had been tigerish in their attacks on a long line of previous witnesses. Desperate criminals blanched before them. In what was the greatest televised spectacle to date, Virginia Hill turned the tables completely and had the maverick crime busters treating her with a delicacy and restraint that was touching.

Virginia used a stiletto-like perception to intimidate her questioners. She unsheathed her weapon during a private hearing a short time before the televised proceedings. The committee counsel had asked her bluntly, "Where does your money come from?"

"I win bets," she had responded.

"But that is only $15,000. Where does the rest of your money come from?"

"Men give it to me."

"Why should these men give you such large sums of money?"

"I would rather not say," Virginia said mildly.

"You've got to answer," Counsel pressed.

"I'd rather remain silent on that." Whereupon Counsel pointed out that this could be construed as contempt, the penalty for which might be up to three years' imprisonment.

"All right, then," Virginia said with feeling, "it's because I'm the best goddamn lay in the country!"

Mr. Calouste Sarkis Gulbenkian is a man who hates
to see his name in print, and he has gone to a good
deal of trouble trying to keep it out. In this, as in most
things in his life, he has been resoundingly successful;
so much so that chances were, when this profile was
penned at the turn of 'fifty, that you never had
heard of him. Being one of if not the richest individuals in the world today, it is not an unreasonable as-
sumption that newspapers and magazines should have
devoted considerable space to him. That they haven't
is another triumph for the pint-sized potentate with
the king-sized bankroll.

He never talks to the press and has never, knowingly, posed for a newspaper photographer. On one occasion, some years ago, as he was hurrying out of a London hotel, a quick-acting cameraman managed to sneak a full-face photo.

"Are you from the press?" Gulbenkian inquired politely.

The newspaper photographer said that he was.

"How wonderful!" beamed Gulbenkian. "You better take my card so that you spell my name correctly." He produced the business card of an Egyptian dealer in gold coins. The photographer looked at the card in surprise. "Aren't you Gulbenkian?" he asked.

"Who?" Gulbenkian responded.

"Gulbenkian. The oil tycoon."

Gulbenkian's manner indicated that he had never heard the name before. "If you could see your way clear to using the photograph and"—here his voice became confidential—"and saying a few good words about our business, I am sure that I could convince my partner that five pounds would not be too much . . ." The disgusted photographer had already departed.

On another occasion, in France, Gulbenkian, in a towering rage, smashed the camera out of a photographer's hand and the next morning had his secretary send a check to cover the damage.

The result of all this is that Gulbenkian has managed to keep his life private. Compared to him, Sir Basil Zaharoff, Europe's mystery man, was as public a figure as Roberto Rossellini.

Mr. Gulbenkian's feelings on other subjects are inclined to be strong, too. For example, his idea of a happy married life is to live in a suite in the Hotel Aviz in Lisbon while his wife lives in a villa in neighboring Estoril. She often eats in the Aviz dining room but not until Alberto, the Genoese who is the maître d'hôtel, has informed her that her husband has finished his meal. It is not an unusual sight for her arrival to signal his departure. Gulbenkian never fails to nod affectionately in passing. Hotel employees say that Gulbenkian's marriage is totally free from domestic friction.

At one time he had a great fondness for pets. One was an evil-tempered Pekinese that was his inseparable travel companion. The Gulbenkian entourage included a special cook who prepared its menu. Gulbenkian thought this the most natural thing in the world.

"Fifi had a weak stomach," he explained to an intimate.

Gulbenkian has pursued wealth with single-minded intensity. Yet despite the fact that he is a cold, methodical practitioner of international business who is as devoid of sentiment as a Burroughs adding machine, it was a beautiful Russian dancer who brought about his most serious business clash, one which resulted in a fight with Sir Henry Deterding, the oil tycoon head of Royal Dutch Shell. The Russian dancer made the mistake of marrying Sir Henry. In the battle of the Titans, Sir Henry, the world-famous oil figure, was beaten to a frazzle by little Gulbenkian, who forced him out of Shell, a company he and Gulbenkian had founded. The unsentimental Gulbenkian, by way of explaining why he risked so much for a woman, said only: "It was good business."

Business, for Gulbenkian, has always been good. As early as 1923 he was rated as being worth four hundred million dollars. Today, with a five-percent ownership of the eight-billion-barrel oil wealth in Iraq, another six hundred million dollars can be added to his fortune, making him the world's first authentic billionaire. A few years before the war, operating on the London Exchange, he cornered the world's pepper market, and this also added to his bank account.

While his wealth is solidly conservative, Gulbenkian, himself, is most unorthodox. Take the matter of health, for example. It closely rivals his interest in business. His approach to it may be regarded as unusual unless you happen to be Chinese. He has a contract with Dr. Fernando de Fonseca, noted Lisbon physician, to whom he pays a flat $25,000 a year. The only stipulation is that Dr. de Fonseca repay the sum of $250 for every day Gulbenkian is ill.

Gulbenkian, who has already passed his eightieth birthday, has not had a sick day in the last ten years. Those earth-bound mortals who still have to worry about getting up the scratch to cover Form 1040 of the Internal Revenue Bureau are apt to find a quarter of a million dollars a rather steep price to pay for the privilege of not seeing your doctor once a year. Longevity runs in the Gulbenkian family, his father having died at one hundred and ten and his grandfather at ninety-five. The octogenarian, a man not given to idle boasts, swears he will outlive both of them.

Whether all this makes him a rugged individualist or just plain eccentric probably depends on which side of the fence you sit on. From this side he is as queer as only those brought up in the habitual presence of an over-abundance of wealth get to be. Even his appearance stamps him as someone out of the ordinary. He is barely over five feet tall and bitterly resents being called short. He is very skinny and completely bald, the head resembling an over-sized pink billiard ball. He has long ears, a biggish nose, a pair of bushy white eyebrows that stick out like awnings, and a close-cropped gray mustache. His shoes are a pair of steamboats attached to pipe-stem ankles. In dress he prefers dark, conservative suits and a wing collar.

Because he has so strong-looking a face he appears far younger than his years. His age doesn't become apparent until he gets to his feet; then his body stoops over, but despite the stoop he has an amazing spring in his walk. More likely than not, he will take two steps at a time as he bounces up the stairs of the Aviz dining room. It is his way of thumbing his nose at those who think he is old.

"There isn't anything a man of fifty can do that I can't," he leered at an intimate recently.

Gulbenkian is a true internationalist. He is an Armenian who was born in Turkey, makes his official home in the enormous villa at Avenue d'Iéna in Paris, is a British subject, earns most of his money in the Middle Eastern Arab states and has not set foot out of Lisbon in the last ten years.

Several stories are told about his beginnings, but the one given greatest currency was printed, with more color than accuracy, in a news weekly which discussed "that wily Armenian, Gulbenkian, who learned to bargain in the rug bazaars of Constantinople." It left the impression that old Gulbenkian had to battle his way up from the Turkish gutter. Nothing could be further from the truth, for actually, Gulbenkian, born in Erzerum, Turkey on March 1, 1869, comes from a family of great wealth and power. His Armenian father, Sarkis, owned a huge import business which furnished the capital to found Turkey's leading private bank. By the time Calouste came of age, the old man was already looked upon as the Morgan of the Middle East. The banking house had strong branches in Berlin, Paris and London and was able to perform the miraculous political feat of being pro-German, pro-French and pro-British all at the same time. While young Calouste was supposedly sharpening his wits in the rug bazaars, he was attending a swank public school in England and later the University of Paris.

In spite of an overwhelming absorption with business, he has found time to take up some hobbies. In this, too, he has made a fabulous success. For example, he is the owner of the world's largest collection of gold coins, and it takes a huge vault to store it. These coins are not only the envy of experts but also of amateurs who cannot distinguish between a Napoleon and a sovereign.

One of these coins caused a flurry of excitement in the Hotel Aviz. It was a rare before-Christ gold coin valued at 300,000 escudos, roughly about $12,000. Gulbenkian reported it stolen from his room. The directors of the Aviz, a very fine and proper hostelry which is proud of its reputation, were mortified by the charge. They told the oil man they were certain that he was wrong since thefts in the Aviz were unknown. Their investigation strengthened the belief. They pointed out that Gulbenkian did not report the theft until many days after the coin had left his possession and that an informant had told them that the coin had been mailed, counter to currency regulations, to an address in England and that if the coin had been stolen, then quite evidently it happened in the post office, not in the Hotel Aviz. Now would Gulbenkian please remove the stain from the hotel's escutcheon? Gulbenkian let the matter drop.

He also collects art and has the most extensive grouping of Egyptian artistic activity dating from 2800 B.C. to the Macedonian conquest. He has permitted the British Museum in London and the National Museum in Washington to place these collections on exhibit without charge and this is noted as part of his charitable activity. His art collection, however, is probably better known to the man in the street because it contains the painting "September Morn" by Paul Chabas. It was the heated objection of the Comstock Anti-Vice League that first brought a measure of notoriety—if not fame— to the canvas of the daring nude of a chesty blonde that once decorated the men's bar of an old hotel. It was responsible for the classic crack that convulsed café society of the gay nineties. An annoyed bartender, whose name has gone down in anonymity, growled at a group of gaping patrons of the arts crowding around the painting to step back, gents, or get a bust in the mouth.

This painting was believed destroyed by the Germans during the occupation of Paris but the American forces found it intact in the Avenue d'Iéna villa. It led to one of Gulbenkian's rare communiqués to the public: "Since you have found out where the painting is," he announced in the third person, "be kind enough to tell the world that Gulbenkian has no intention of selling it and does not wish to be bothered by prospective purchasers."

The Avenue d'Iéna villa holds a richer collection of art than will be found in most state galleries. As Gulbenkian is a man of catholic taste, it contains paintings by Rubens, Rembrandt, Franz Hals, Van Dyck, Degas, Manet, Corot, Lancret, Fragonard and Romney. Aside from paintings he has priceless collections of Persian carpets, Egyptian sculpture, tapestries, jewels and dozens of other miscellaneous categories. Art experts say it is the greatest collection ever owned by a single person.

Gulbenkian's money comes from oil. Every time you step on your gas pedal, his cash register rings merrily. He was pushed into the business by the Standard Oil people who have spent a fortune trying to push him out again. Back about the time of his birth, the Rockefeller

Standard Oil interests wishing to buy petroleum in Turkey asked their agent in London to indicate the name of a shrewd merchant in Constantinople to represent their company. The choice was Sarkis Gulbenkian, the noted merchant-banker. By the time Calouste was twenty, he was completely sold on the profitable future of petroleum. Before the turn of the century, he drew up a paper which he submitted to the French navy. In it he wrote: "Petrol must be employed not only to warm the stove but to furnish the power for motivating the piston."

Brushing up on his knowledge of this comparatively new product, he took a trip with the son of Alfred Nobel, munitions czar famous for his Peace Prize, to the Caucasian oil fields. After long study, he summed up his findings (that Russian oil is far superior to American or English) in an article printed in the May, 1891, issue of the *Revue des Deux Mondes*.

When his father retired, the banking empire was divided into three parts, with his brother, Karnig, taking the Constantinople office, Calouste the London one and his younger brother, Vahan, who was supposed to take Berlin, selling out and retiring to enjoy the fruits of his father's labor. Years later came sad days for brother Karnig who found himself backed to the wall financially. He received no help from his dedicated brother in London and he went under. Still later, Gulbenkian ran afoul of his own son, in a business way, that is. Nubar Gulbenkian sued him for ten million. The case was later settled out of court, and today father and son are on good terms once more.

The international intrigue involved in collecting one of the world's greatest individual fortunes would make E. Phillips Oppenheim at his most lurid sound like Louisa May Alcott. Here is a bare outline of how he did it. And you better hang onto your hat because you'll be skidding around some slippery financial corners. It began just after the turn of the century when Gulbenkian, living at 27 Quai d'Orsay in Paris, though operating largely out of London, was much sought after by the big financial interests which wanted to exploit the wealth of the Middle East. It was common knowledge at the time that he was the pal of Sultan Abdul-Hamid of Turkey. During this period the Imperial Ottoman Bank, jointly owned by British and French capital, was the basis for British and French influence in this part of the world. The bank was run from the French capital by a shadowy group called the Parisian Committee in whose council the Gulbenkian figure loomed large.

But the big boys soon got tired of this happy arrangement and the French crowd began edging their English cousins out of the game. They got control of the Parisian Committee, and almost immediately the English boys began feeling cleats in their faces. The French team seemed to have the ball game sewed up, especially since Abdul-Hamid was booted off the throne by a new gang called the Young Turks who were great pals of the French.

The British, however, are no slouches when it comes

to playing rough. Their Minister of Foreign Affairs, Sir Edward Grey, gave the green light to a private financier named Sir Edward Cassel and told him to get in and fight. Cassel went into partnership with a man named Calouste Sarkis Gulbenkian. As a pal of the Sultan, Gulbenkian should, by all rights, also have gotten the heave-ho. But it turned out that the young fox, like so many American businessmen who give campaign contributions to both the Democratic and Republican parties, had, while being pally with the Sultan, been slipping money to the Young Turks. In gratitude, this new crowd named him financial adviser to the Turkish Ambassador in London. Gulbenkian and Cassel founded the National Turkish Bank, and pretty soon the Imperial Ottoman Bank discovered that someone had taken the play away from them. For some reason or other all their deals began floundering.

The reason was not hard to find. Monsieur Boppé, commercial attaché of the French Embassy in Constantinople, sent an angry letter to Monsieur Poincaré, the Minister of Foreign Affairs, in which he charged that an individual named Gulbenkian was single-handedly nullifying the Triple Entente; that while England and France were united by the strongest political ties, in the field of finance Gulbenkian was captaining a British-German team that was tackling France high, around the pockets, where it hurt the most.

The French government didn't fight back because it was already known that in Middle Eastern affairs you didn't fight Gulbenkian; you joined him. It was thought wiser to appeal to his higher senses, which are on a very high financial level indeed, and he was prevailed upon to work out a deal whereby the Parisian Committee became fifty percent British again, and the Imperial Ottoman Bank went back into the running. For this he earned the gratitude of England and France as well as a profit—an irresistible combination. It also reaffirmed the fact that if you wanted to make a deal in Turkey you made it with Gulbenkian first.

At this time there were two commodities in Turkey for which there was a concerted international grab. The first was petroleum and the second railroad concessions. In both of these Gulbenkian had the inside track. In the matter of oil, he brought the British, French, German and Dutch together and pointed out that the business about competition being the life-blood of trade was something you read in schoolbooks. In this case it was guilty of the awful sin of being unprofitable. His logic left them no alternative, and he was named representative for the oil interests of the four powers.

He held a meeting with the heads of the new Turkish republic. A large map of the Ottoman Empire was produced and Gulbenkian, with a red crayon, drew a line splitting the country in half. Gulbenkian took for himself and the group he represented the exclusive concession for the exploitation of oil reserves in all the territory to the right of the red line. This area is, roughly, all of the Middle Eastern Arab states and contains the world's richest supply of oil. This deal is the famous Red Line agreement. It provided for all the signatories to share alike in all future exploitation. It further added that Gulbenkian receive a five-percent ownership for his part in setting up the deal.

Since its signing in 1911, old governments have fallen, new ones have been created, wars have been fought, with Turkey once on Germany's side of the fence and once on the other. There have been fires, famines, and reorganizations. Through it all Gulbenkian, like a snappy broken field runner, swerving, pivoting, stiff-arming, but with the five percent tucked firmly under his arm, has raced safely into 1953.

The original corporation set up by Gulbenkian was called Turkish Petroleum, and its direction was in the hands of the Turkish National Bank. Through a long line of changes it has today become Iraq Petroleum.

In working out these deals he has earned the gratitude of England, France, Belgium, Germany, Holland and Turkey. It wasn't until it came time to pick up the chips and go home that it was discovered that Gulbenkian wasn't working for any of them. He was in business for himself. Standard Oil of New Jersey and Socony-Vacuum found it out, too. Gulbenkian is into them for that little five percent on their Middle Eastern holdings. Now the American oil boys can also play rough, but in trying to shake the five-foot, five-percenter, they discovered after a stiff joust in a London law court that they had met their match.

Today, when they speak of him, it is with respect. A vice-president of Socony-Vacuum, in a recent speech, pointed out that the Company's postwar crude-oil production in the Middle East had risen from 526,000 barrels per day to 1,328,000 per day and that by 1952 this figure would be doubled.

"Socony-Vacuum's production from this area dates from the middle twenties," he said, "when we acquired interest in the Iraq Petroleum Company. Although this company is incorporated under British law, it has a distinct international complexion, being owned by an individual, Mr. C. S. Gulbenkian, and four companies having French, British, British-Dutch and American nationality. The American interest is held equally by ourselves and Standard Oil of New Jersey."

Gulbenkian is the first to admit that none of his money-making talent was learned at school. Some university might conceivably profit by the wily Armenian's example and offer a course in manipulation of nations. As one of the great living practitioners of the art (or is it science?) he has amply proved its value. His handling of the railroad situation in Turkey at the turn of the century serves as a fine illustration. There existed at the time a German imperialist venture known as the Berlin-to-Bagdad Railroad, and history books list it as one of the causes of World War I. The German Bank—a private institution in the same sense that the Turkish National Bank was a private institution—was given the concession to build the line. This was done notwithstanding the fact that Turkey had already handed the concession to build a Homs-to-Bagdad railway to the D'Arcy-Anglo-Persian Oil Company.

Now along came Gulbenkian who procured a third

concession for a railway for the Royal Dutch Shell Company. For England this was more than just business rivalry because, in the words of the military analysts, the Berlin-to-Bagdad Railway was a dagger pointed at the heart of India. In the end it was Gulbenkian who straightened out the mess, and the side that showed the biggest profit, much to the surprise of nobody, was Gulbenkian. The Germans dropped fifty percent of their interests in Turkish Petroleum, and the British interests laid off on the railroad deal. Thus British capital made a profit, and the British Foreign Office a loss. German capital lost but its Foreign Office won. After the First World War, the Germans were completely frozen out of Turkey, and the Americans moved in.

Gulbenkian was married at a fairly early age to an Armenian girl named Nervatte. They have two children, Nubar Sarkis, who is forty-seven, and a daughter, Madame Rita Essayan, now in her fifties, who presented him with a grandson, Michael. During the last war Michael was an officer in the British army stationed in Palestine. Nubar is a chip off the old block and is considered a natural to carry on the family traditions. He bears an uncanny resemblance to his father. He has a coal-black beard and a pair of eyebrows that stick out as far as the old man's awnings. After an auspicious record at Harrow he entered business with his father. Friends point out that he inherited a strong dose of the family's wily Oriental traits. He also has developed certain peculiarities of taste. At the moment he has a passion for orchids and has a special variety flown in daily from London.

On one occasion in England he attended a very swank fox hunt, garbed very properly in red coat and wearing, in addition, a lovely orchid. The master of the hunt hinted delicately: "See here, old chap, one doesn't usually see an orchid at a fox hunt."

Nubar fixed the hunt's master with the Gulbenkian glare. "One doesn't usually see an Armenian at a fox hunt, either," he said frigidly.

A search through the morgue of a large metropolitan daily showed how remarkably few times the Gulbenkian name has appeared in print. The first mention was twenty-five years ago when the *New York Sun* headlined a piece: NEW MYSTERY MAN IN EUROPEAN FIELD. It stated that Gulbenkian shunned the social and financial spotlight, that he possessed a striking face, bushy black eyebrows, was bald as an egg and had deep intense eyes which were said to be hypnotic. In dress he was somewhat of a dandy and was noted for his extravagance in footwear. The next mention was fourteen years later when the *New York Daily News* headlined a piece: JILTED, OILMAN PUTS IRAN WITH NAZIS. It told the story of Gulbenkian's affection for Lydia Pavlovna Kudjaroff, a gay White Russian who dropped him for Sir Henry Deterding. It went on to say that Gulbenkian was a great friend of the Shah of Iran who gave him diplomatic status as Minister Plenipotentiary in France. Before the war, the British accused him of furthering the Nazi cause among the Arabs. The basis for this was the report that he persuaded General Bekr Sidky, chief of the Iranian army, to revolt and force King Ghezi to fire Premier Jassin who was friendly to England and replace him with Hikmel Suleiman who was a friend of Gulbenkian.

A more recent newspaper article noted that, with Oriental distrust, he never accepts the first dish put before him, but shouts, "Bah! Take it away!" even though the dish is prepared by his own chef whom he imported from Paris. Such stories, more legend than fact, never fail to anger him, and he usually blames the personnel in the hotel for having given out the information. This keeps the help in a highly nervous state—which is the way he likes it.

This writer saw Gulbenkian in Lisbon recently and became an expert on his eating habits. When it comes time for him to enter the Hotel Aviz dining room where he eats all his meals, tension among the help mounts. As his gnomelike figure comes down the carpeted stairs, Alberto hurries to his side while three waiters converge on the corner table reserved exclusively for him. He is always alone. The meal may consist of as many as ten dishes. He will take a few mouthfuls, eat them with great gusto, and send the rest of the food away. A favorite dish is strawberries. Two waiters, working in unison, prepare them. The berries are washed twice in sparkling mineral water. Then one waiter carefully picks up each berry individually and places it in a cradled napkin while the second waiter rolls it gently. Then they are placed in a dish, covered with orange juice and sugar and served. He hunches over his food, eats swiftly and methodically and doesn't straighten up until the last mouthful has been swallowed. Then he leans back like a runner taking a well-earned rest. We were together in the Aviz for a week—at different tables, of course, separated by a narrow, carpeted no-man's land. One day Gulbenkian crooked his finger at Alberto and whispered to him. Alberto nodded, came to my table and said: "Monsieur desires that you do not stare at him." I looked up at Gulbenkian who glared at me. I glared at him. He picked up his fork. I picked up my fork. His fork slipped, probably for the first time in half a century of consecrated trencherman activity.

Behind his back the hotel employees call him Old Mr. Five Percent, but in his presence they are so terrified they are tongue-tied. He occupies a five-room suite on the first floor of the hotel which serves as both his living quarters and office. His staff consists of a valet, a chambermaid and three secretaries. He tips the personnel of the hotel twice a year and then he takes care of everyone. The waiters get a hundred dollars. Alberto, who is his only confidant, gets considerably more.

His spendings for charity, while unpublicized, have been something less than sensational. He helps support the American University in Beirut and the Armenian Catholic Church in London. A cynical friend pointed out that he spends where it will do the giver rather than the receiver the most good.

Gulbenkian puts in a full ten hours of work each day. What it is he is working toward is sometimes hard to fathom. Certainly not security, since he has so much money it would take several lifetimes of the most dissolute living to run through it. And even if he did, there is always a good job waiting. His neighbor, ex-King Umberto of Italy, while examining Gulbenkian's coin collection, one day looked up at the old Armenian, and said: "I can use a Finance Minister like you."

Countess Dorothy Di Frasso

8

Some years ago, a dyspeptic critic wrote: "We have never owned a recipe for bouillabaisse or a home of tropical fish. We have never been on a treasure hunt with Elsa Maxwell or on a ski train with Francesca Braggiotti. We have never had our picture taken by Cecil Beaton or our horoscope read by Myra Kingsley. We have never been to Hoboken to see the *Black Crook*. We've never read anything by Queen Marie of Rumania, Grand Duke Alexander, Beverly Nichols or G. Selmer Faugner. We have never subscribed to *Vogue*, *Town and Country* or *Spur*. We have never even met Valentina Schlee or the Countess di Frasso. We claim

235

that this performance really means something. For anyone not a leper to ignore so much of the contemporary social scene has called for persistent concentration. We don't regret a minute of it."

This is a rather harsh judgment, particularly as it falls on poor Countess Dorothy di Frasso, a nice old lady who has dedicated a substantial portion of her adult life to the performance of good deeds. What is more, many of these have been performed on behalf of persons who occupy positions far below her socially aristocratic and financially solvent one.

One such object of her altruism was William McCoy, an exceedingly handsome model who posed for collar advertisements. Countess di Frasso, some twenty-five years senior to the plebeian McCoy, felt that it would further the career of the young Adonis no end if he joined her in Paris for the summer. Appreciating the fact that Mr. McCoy's financial means might be somewhat limited, she made out a check for two thousand dollars to cover the expenses of the voyage. The Countess, however, was not willing that the object of her good deed take the money and use it for his self-advancement in Hollywood, so she took the precaution of making the check payable in New York only. Now this lack of confidence on her part was somewhat hard on Mr. McCoy since he lacked the funds with which to travel to New York. He managed to borrow an automobile and one hundred dollars and set out for the golden pot at the end of the rainbow. His first stop was Nevada where he tried to run the hundred into a bankroll, but luck was against him and he dropped ninety of it at the gaming tables. In some way he managed to reach his destination on the remaining ten. Here he cashed the check, picked up his lovely wife, Eleanor, a buxom blonde hat-check girl, and drove back to Hollywood.

That the collar-ad man should prefer such narrow, mundane pleasure to the brilliant life she had planned for him infuriated the Countess. She hurried home from Europe and wrathfully demanded the return of the two thousand dollars. Mr. McCoy found this most embarrassing, in view of the fact that half of it had already been spent, and the other half deposited in a joint account that Bill McCoy had with Willard Parker, a young contract player for Warner Brothers who had been his roommate. At first, McCoy resisted Countess di Frasso's efforts at collection, whereupon the titled lady warned that she had powerful social connections in Hollywood, like Jack Warner, last of the old-style Hollywood tycoons, and that she would make it hot for the entire ménage. As a matter of fact, the next day a representative of the Warner Brothers studios telephoned the McCoy-Parker household and pointedly advised that it would be wise for them to repay any money owing the Countess di Frasso. In view of the fact that Mr. Parker was receiving $125 per week from the studio, this made him very nervous, since he did not desire to be separated from the payroll. There appeared to be only one solution to the matter. Repay the money. So the lovely Eleanor hustled around and managed to borrow

Countess Dorothy Di Frasso

a thousand dollars and this, added to what was in the bank, satisfied the claim of the lady in question.

Countess di Frasso has always been grateful to her good friend Jack Warner for his help. Hence, when Mr. Warner was in need of a favor several years later, he found her just as anxious to reciprocate. The reason the film magnate needed her support was because the fun-loving Dorothy was just about the first citizen of Rome's foreign colony, and therefore she could perform feats in this city that the ordinary plebeian was not capable of. This goes for Hollywood, New York and Mexico City, all urban centers she has graced with her charm and social leadership. Mr. Warner's request to the Roman expert was that she buy for him the American rights to a Polish film called *Welka Draga,* or *The Long Road,* whose merits had been pointed out to Mr. Warner by his titled friend and which, by a not so strange coincidence, had been directed by her then current protégé. It so happened that Mr. Warner was arranging this deal for his friend, Jimmy Coston, Greek film exhibitor who owns several theaters in Chicago's Polish district. Jimmy Coston is notoriously fond of the American dollar and it is a real strain on him to be separated from it, even for brief periods, so he begged Mr. Warner to get the picture for him as cheaply, but really cheaply, as he possibly could and these instructions were passed on to the Countess.

At that time the American rights to *Welka Draga* had a value of up to two thousand dollars, with no buyers in view. Dorothy went about her task in businesslike fashion. She called in the Polish producer and said, in effect, "I am bringing you prosperity. Your picture is worth very little without me. With me it's worth twenty thousand dollars. Therefore, we shall sell it to Mr. Jack Warner for twenty thousand dollars and we shall split the proceeds fifty-fifty." But even the ten thousand was an unexpected bonanza for the producer and he hastily agreed.

It so happened that a friend of Coston's, looking into the deal, had occasion to talk with the Polish producer and the latter, learning that the little Greek exhibitor was the eventual purchaser, got greedy notions. "Would it not be better," he said with fine European foresight, "for Mr. Coston to pay me directly the sum of fifteen thousand dollars? In that way he will save five thousand and I will make five thousand dollars extra." The Rome friend of Mr. Coston faithfully reported the situation, and this so filled the movie exhibitor with anguish that he hurried to Jack Warner, only to learn that the deal had already been consummated. Mr. Coston's laments over the unnecessary loss to his beloved bank roll were so loud—and who is there amongst us who can blame him?—that movie tycoon Warner whipped out his checkbook and dashed off a check for twenty thousand dollars which he gave to Coston, becoming, in turn, the proud proprietor of *Welka Draga*, a film still gathering dust in the Warner vaults.

Countess di Frasso along with Elsa Maxwell, Freddie McEvoy, while he lived, and Prince Mike Romanoff were the authentic social arbiters of the day. Dorothy's position as a society queen, aside from wealth and breeding, stems from her party-giving proclivities. To be excluded from a di Frasso shindig is, to a considerable section of what has been euphemistically termed international society, tantamount to being publicly drummed out of the elite corps. One object of her helpful attention in the field of society was Gary Cooper, the movie actor. Gary, she felt, was a natural for society, just as she believed society would be a natural for him. Her efforts in this direction were so successful that the long-legged cowboy actor became the darling of the international set. This was so outstanding an achievement that she set herself the task of helping him with his movie career. She could think of no better way to accomplish this than by becoming his business manager. At this Gary balked and a certain coldness developed between them. The chill turned more frigid when Cooper, launched in society by the Countess, fell in love with social registerite Veronica Balfe and, what is more, married her. The change in temperature was reported under a headline reading: EX-FIANCEE COUNTESS ICES GARY COOPER PARTY. It was a first-hand report by a society writer who noted breathlessly that Dorothy walked into the Colony Club where, unexpectedly, she ran into Gary Cooper playing host at a party for his wife. Icicles clung to their glances as they cut each other cold.

The writer pointed out that since her strong interest in Gary, she had lived more or less permanently in the environs of Hollywood with her father, Bertrand L. Taylor. She seemed to have lost interest in the famous

Villa Madama, her home in Rome, on which she spent nearly a million dollars in restoration work. Perhaps she now will return to Italy and the royal and semi-royal set in which she moved so gracefully before Gary happened on her horizon, the eyewitness to this terribly important event stated. He went on to say that there was much to be said on both sides in the dispute that finally split them. It was through Dorothy that Gary got to know all the notables of Europe, was entertained by Italian royalty and English titles and saw a side of life he never would have known. On the other hand, Gary, beyond doubt, resented Dorothy's interference with his various motion-picture plans. She made the mistake of attempting to be his love interest and business manager at the same time. As a sort of minor afterthought, he wrote that the Countess was some sixteen years older than the movie actor.

Another personage, though strictly of local importance, on whom Countess di Frasso lavished her great social talent was Bugsy Siegel, a gentleman who is treated at greater length in another chapter, of New York and Hollywood. She toasted Bugsy in every capital in which she reigned as social queen. Her invitation brought him to the Holy City immediately before the outbreak of war. She introduced him to Roman aristocracy at one of the famous soirées at the Villa Madama. The West Coast representative of that group of Eastern playboys nicknamed by the press "Murder, Inc.," was introduced as Mr. Benjamin Siegel, noted American businessman. He was presented to ex-King Umberto, then the Crown Prince, and to Benito Mussolini. Since Bugsy was one who liked to improve each shining hour, he wound up trying to sell the Italian dictator a patented silencer for a machine gun.

It was as easy for Bugsy to hide his background as it was for a zebra to disguise its stripes, and Roman society, which is encrusted with centuries of tradition, gave him a wide berth. But this only goes to show their lack of judgment. If they had not been so prejudiced, they would have realized that the Bug was just as much a leader in his own social group as they were in theirs. Perhaps more so. "After all," Bugsy said before his untimely demise, "how stuffy can you get?"

When an unknown gentleman, highly efficient as a marksman, used rifle slugs to splatter the body of Bugsy over the living-room divan of Virginia Hill's Hollywood home, an enterprising reporter felt that it might be useful to get Countess di Frasso's reaction to this tragic event. She was in Rome at the time. He called her by transatlantic phone and informed her that Bugsy had been wiped out.

"Bugsy?" she asked. "Why, I don't know any Bugsy."

The reporter explained, and Countess di Frasso said, "Could you possibly mean Mr. Benjamin Siegel?"

The Countess was informed that she had correctly identified the gentleman in question.

"I'm very sorry to hear it," she said calmly. "How did it happen?"

The reporter explained that an unknown gunman,

using an army carbine, had pumped six or seven bullets through his head.

"Where?" the Countess asked.

"At the home of Virginia Hill."

"So far as my feelings toward Mr. Siegel were concerned," Dorothy said, "you can say that I was very fond of him, but it is utterly ridiculous to say I was in love with him."

Did the Countess have any money invested in Bugsy's American Monte Carlo?

"That is just too utterly ridiculous," said Dorothy, who loves the word ridiculous. "Why, I couldn't even furnish a casino for a doghouse, thanks to your government. As far as my giving Benny money, that's a joke. He needed money like he needed those holes in his head."

Had Bugsy ever advanced any money to her?

"Oh no, it was just the other way around. Not that I ever borrowed any money from him, you understand. But if I had asked him for it, I am sure he would have given it to me gladly. You see, I knew him quite some time. He was a good friend of my late husband, the Count."

For several decades the irrepressible Dorothy had been the darling of society-page editors. With her they were able to liven up otherwise dull columns. To them she was just a high-spirited gal who was the envy of the American working girl. A faithful review of the clippings in the morgue of a large New York daily revealed that she had inherited fifteen million dollars from her father and that she used more than a million of this inheritance to renovate her husband's palace in Rome. It revealed, too, that despite this great wealth she felt that she had to do something useful with her life, and as a result of this she has kept on the go for almost half a century. Although good deeds have occupied a large part of her time, the society writers point out, this has in no way interfered with her penchant for romance and they feel certain that even at eighty, romance will be more than just a word to the spirited Countess di Frasso. Within a brief span, Louella Parsons pointed out that, "Her big moment is Reggie Gardiner, and vice versa," and that "her new boy friend is Jon Hall," and a little later that "her favorite escort these evenings is Willis Goldbeck." Other chroniclers pointed out that she was down in Mexico to be near her latest flame, a famous matador and "that she might become Mrs. Cary Grant, for the affair was more serious than most folks thought."

Friends of the Countess say that she is far more successful in her relations with men than she is with women. The men admire her for her honest views and direct way of life whereas women, for the most part, fear her. She is highly devoted to her friends and is always trying to help them, yet she makes a bitter enemy. Constance Bennett was once her close friend, and the friendship led to partnership in a cosmetic business. The business wound up in a fight between the partners. A few weeks after this row, Dorothy played poker with Tallulah Bankhead and Olive Taylor. Tallulah won two hundred and eighty dollars. Tallulah, who has a flair for these things, picked up her winnings, tossed them contemptuously onto the center of the table, saying, "This is tainted money. Give it to charity."

The little girl who was to acquire a title and make a big splash in society was born in the very middle-class town of Watertown, New York, on February 13, 1888. Her brother, Bert, was born four years later. Her father was Bertrand Leroy Taylor, Senior, who had married the well-to-do Nelly Cadwell. Mr. Taylor operated a leather-goods business which prospered handsomely. At the turn of the century the family moved to New York and Mr. Taylor purchased a seat on the New York Stock Exchange on whose Board of Governors he later served.

In her early youth Dorothy was on the plump and ungainly side, so that it was considered quite a catch when she married dashing Claude Graham-White, the British flyer who was the idol of his day. The wedding was performed in Windford Parish Church, Chelmsford, Essex. It was so important an event that the *Daily Express* in London covered the wedding by sending its reporter in an airplane flown specially from France (none was available in England). The paper reported in amazement that the forty-seven miles were covered in the fast time of forty minutes. The marriage failed principally because White's two interests kept him away from his wife. One was his strong attachment to anything that flew and the other, even stronger attachment, was to other women. Although she left him in 1914 and returned to America, she wrote a letter in a last attempt to patch up their marriage:

> "Dear Whitie, just writing a few lines to ask you to make a home for me and restore me my full rights as a wife. I am ready and willing to blot out the memory of all that's happened in the past to mar our happiness during our short matrimonial life. I've done my best to break off your attachment from the woman who so far has made our lives unbearable and I do hope it's not too late for you to give her up and return to me."

But by this time White felt that it had all been a mistake and he turned her down. In June, 1916, Dorothy sued for divorce on the grounds of adultery and produced evidence that Claude Graham-White had stayed at a hotel with another woman. The divorce was granted. Sometime later the British flyer married Ethel Levy Cohan, the widow of the American actor-producer.

A few years of freedom and a few trips to the continent brought her in contact with Count Carlo Dentice di Frasso, of an old Italian family whose previous brush with American womanhood had resulted in a brief marriage with Georgine Wilde. Count di Frasso was forty-seven at the time, a member of the Italian parliament and the owner of a huge marble palace badly in need of repair. Dorothy's mother died three months after her daughter's wedding, leaving an inheritance of $1,533,-204.38. Bert, Senior, received $133,333.33 and a life interest in four-tenths of the residuary estate. The son received one hundred thousand dollars outright and a life interest in two-tenths of the residuary estate while Dorothy was given a life interest in three-tenths of the residuary estate, having already received one hundred thousand dollars as a gift from her mother shortly before her death.

Her father died ten years later, leaving $1,250,000. There was a clash of interests over the will brought on by Geraldine Otts, a thirty-five-year-old dancer who had had a quiet romance with Dorothy's father and who, dissatisfied with the ten thousand dollars left her in the will, was now claiming one-third of the estate as his common-law widow. Dorothy and her brother, Bert, won the case and as a result, Dorothy collected approximately half a million dollars from the estate.

Brother Taylor was just as great a hand for romance as his father and sister. After being divorced by his wife, Mary Bovine, in Paris, he became the great friend of Gertrude Lawrence and many thought, including Gertrude, that a marriage would result from this friendship. Sometime later, the actress explained her financial difficulties by saying that she had to entertain considerably during the period in which she expected to become Taylor's bride. Instead, Taylor married Olive McClure, beautiful model and dancer.

After her marriage to Count di Frasso, Dorothy moved into Villa Madama. This house had been built in the sixteenth century after a design by Raphael for Cardinal Giulio de Medici on Monte Mario, the lovely hilltop overlooking the city of Rome, making her a close neighbor of mine, since the Villa Spiga, in which I live, is just a little farther up the hillside. The Villa Madama was badly in need of repair when Dorothy moved in, and she fixed it very nicely, although on an inherited fortune of three-quarters of a million it is somewhat over-enthusiastic to say that she lavished a million dollars on it. During the dictatorship of Il Duce, she sold the palace to the Italian government which turned it into a residence for such visiting state dignitaries as Hermann Goering. She maintained for her own use the small servant's house and a small part of the grounds on which Villa Madama stands. After the war, when Tyrone Power came to Italy to make films, she kindly offered him the use of her house for six hundred dollars per month. For this price she threw in her social talent and helped him with his parties.

By the time Power moved out relations with his land-lady were strained. His wife, Linda, refers to Dorothy as "that woman." When Robert Taylor showed up to star in Metro-Goldwyn-Mayer's epic *Quo Vadis*, the asking price for the cottage went up to a thousand dollars a month. Taylor was only too happy to turn her down, whereupon Dorothy offered it to the production manager. The latter thought the price was excessive by about 300 percent and very frankly told her so. The Countess became so angry that she warned him that he had better accept or begin looking around for a new job. The present tenant in little Villa Madama is Michel Olian, a passportless Russian man of mystery who has profited mightily from deals with the Russians and with gentry in enemy-occupied China and France. A leading figure in the film life of Italy, Mr. Olian is also a convicted black marketeer with a two-year sentence of imprisonment hanging over his head in France.

Fun-loving Dorothy is a gal who kicked over the traces of convention long ago. Stuffy people bore her. Because she proceeds on each task with determination, she likes people who get things done. In the difficult tasks she has undertaken, she has displayed real courage in carrying them to a conclusion. One such incident was her hunt for the stolen treasures of Peru. Dorothy got her first clue to the whereabouts of the treasure from a seventy-two-year-old Canadian who had a map drawn in lipstick on a speakeasy tablecloth. The story told by the bearded Canadian had just enough element of truth in it to make it intriguing. His story was that about one hundred years ago when a revolt was threatening, a notorious British sea captain named Thompson had been engaged by the fleeing government of Peru to take the state's wealth, as well as certain officials and church dignitaries, to saftey across the sea. One of the principal objects of this wealth, which totaled three hundred million dollars, was a six-foot, solid-gold statue of the Madonna encrusted with gems. While at sea, Captain Thompson killed the passengers and confiscated the treasure. He beached his schooner on one of the Cocos Islands off the coast of Ecuador and buried the treasure. He died before he could come back for it.

Now Dorothy just loves glamorous adventures of all sorts, especially when parlayed with a profit, and so she set about organizing an expedition. She asked Mario Bello, the late Jean Harlow's stepfather, to search for a likely craft to carry the exploration to the Cocos Islands. Bello found the *Metha Nelson,* a schooner that was part of the holdings of the sedate Detroit Trust Company. The cautious bankers were willing to charter the ship to the treasure hunters but insisted on naming their own captain. The man was a tough German named Robert Hoffman. The crew that was collected to make this voyage was evidently picked up from the beach at Hollywood and Vine. Not until the vessel had weighed anchor was it discovered that only three members of the equipage had ever been to sea before. One of them, much to the surprise of nobody, turned out to be Bugsy Siegel. Captain Hoffman complained peevishly that Bugsy acted as though he ran the ship. Two of the men broke into the liquor chest and distributed free drinks to everybody. Mario Bello fell in love with the nurse, Evelyn Husby, and on the third day out, married her. A pair of Broadway beachcombers whose only previous experience with seamanship was limited to pulling a rowboat in Central Park, ran amok and had to be clapped into irons. Other crew members made life difficult for the Countess. When she tried to take a sunbath in the nude, they suddenly discovered chores that set them to climbing the mast for gallery seats. At Costa Rica a colonel and five soldiers came aboard to join the expedition on the last leg of its journey and their direct notions about romance enlivened matters no end.

The expedition eventually reached the Cocos Islands and for three weeks they tunneled through enough earth to build a medium-sized subway without discovering anything more important than red ants, of which there were untold billions. On the return trip the inexpert crew ruined the ship's auxiliary motor. A storm came up and battered the helpless craft so that she had to be taken in tow by the Italian motor ship *Cellini* and brought into port at Acapulco, Mexico. The remainder of the trip was completed on the *Cellini*. When it put into Los Angeles, Captain Hoffman charged two of his Central Park seamen with mutiny. Some of the members countercharged that his punishments were excessive, and that he had kept some of them in chains for periods as long as a week. The FBI looked into the matter, although they weren't particularly interested in the charges and countercharges. They found the story of the treasure hunt one that stretched their powers of credence, and they had the idea, because of Bugsy's presence in the expedition, that it was an effort on the part of the Lepke mob to bring succor to their boss who at that time was the object of a world-wide search. In the end all the heat generated by the unsuccessful treasure hunt dissipated and left as its residue a small burlap sack which the Detroit Trust Company was left holding representing fifty thousand dollars' worth of damages to the *Metha Nelson*.

Dorothy has managed to leave her mark, socially, on every world capital in which she has lived. In the early nineteen-forties she decided to give up her Hollywood crown and move to Mexico City. She learned that here she was considered a commoner by Mrs. Wallace Payne Moats, local queen by right of prior domain. In fact, Mrs. Moats did not invite Dorothy to one of her important parties. This was tantamount to a declaration of war. The battleground was the salon, and the key heights contested by the opposing titans were the very royal figures of ex-King Carol and Magda Lupescu of Rumania. Dorothy went into battle with a preponderance of force on her side since this latter pair had been befriended in Rome by her and, in spite of it, had remained on good terms. She won the first round in this epic struggle by capturing the royal pair. To keep them won, she set about helping them. She tried to clear the way for them to emigrate to America. Having met Secretary of State Cordell Hull socially, she flew up to Washington to put the request to him personally. It was then that she received the rude shock of discovering that cordiality at a dinner party was quite another affair from an office reception. She never did get to speak to the Secretary of State personally, but a very young assistant told her it would prove too embarrassing for the United States government to permit so unconventional a couple to be given asylum in our puritanical States.

So, instead of helping her royal friends move across the border, Dorothy set about helping them find a home in Mexico. Finally they found one that was perfect. It is reported that Carol liked it because there was enough wall space for the priceless art collection he had smuggled out of Rumania and because it had floodlights which illuminated the grounds at the touch of a button so that a man could tell whether he was looking at a palm frond or a rifle. Magda liked it because it had loose tiles in the courtyard under which she could bury the pots of gold that she had dug up from her yard in Bucharest.

What Countess Dorothy Taylor di Frasso has accomplished as a society leader and international gadabout must have had a degree of merit. This judgment is based on the goodly amount of newsprint—a very expensive commodity today—that is consumed in bringing intelligence of her affairs to interested readers.

A society columnist aptly says that the Countess has forgotten more celebrities than most of us will ever meet in a lifetime. For some, this in itself is enough to make her a woman with Meaning. To them it will be obvious that the unjust critic who said that he had had to exercise persistent concentration in ignoring her must have been plain jealous.

The Gazelle Boy

9

Probably the most fascinating figure to sweep, meteor-like, across the international horizon was a supposedly human entity known only as the "Gazelle Boy." For a very brief space of time he was one of the biggest and, certainly, the most colorful personalities in the foreign news. The full-page, heroic-sized photo of him in *Life* set many a circus impresario's pulse beating faster. The brevity of the Gazelle Boy's appearance in the news columns can, I suspect, be directly traced to me.

My first inkling as to his existence came in the form of a cable which asked me to make every effort to become acquainted with this human phenomenon. The message reached me in the bar of the Stampa Estera, the Foreign Press building in Rome. There was no indication in it as to where this creature might be at the moment. So I set out to collect a clipping file, and then from later personal contact to reconstruct the events leading to the discovery. Here is the way it went.

Robert Cottam Noble, the waggish news editor of the Arab News Agency, noted with satisfaction that the atmosphere in his office at 26 Sharia Pasha in Cairo was easy and jovial once more. The tension in the Middle East in 1947 which had brought in a flood of newsmen had succumbed to the mid-summer desert heat. For the past twenty-four hours there had been no bomb outrages in Jerusalem, no tribal uprisings in Trans-Jordan, no bloody riots in Syria. Noble was contemplating the marvel of history, taking time out for the heat, when his eye lit on an insignificant paragraph buried in a welter of Arabic scrawl in the newspaper *Falestine*. He read through it carefully and gave the piece a few minutes' thought. He couldn't quite decide whether to laugh at it, become excited about it, or just play it as he read it.

He decided on the latter course and, having made this momentous decision, stuck his tongue in his cheek, a sheet of paper in the typewriter and banged out the following:

"A Tarzan Among the Gazelles of Trans-Jordan?

"*Jaffa, July 17 (ANA)*—According to a report published in the newspaper *Falestine,* some hunters have captured in the desert of Trans-Jordan a 'man-deer' aged about fifteen years and whose body is completely covered with long hair. The boy was seen among a herd of deer which the hunters were chasing aboard a motor car. After nearly an hour's chase he fell to the ground exhausted. He was taken to the Iraqi Oil Company hospital in the desert where Dr. Galbrout revived him. The 'man-deer' cannot speak, but simply utters grunts. He refused any food but grass and is very thin in figure. It seems probable that he was abandoned by his mother at a very early age and was then taken care of by a gazelle, who brought him up in the desert as her own child."

The story went out over the wires modestly, much in the manner of the one-paragraph birth announcement which touched off the Dionne quintuplet yarn. Robert Cottam Noble and his prankish British associates, now that the job was done, sat back and enjoyed the remainder of a very tranquil day in the happy precinct of the Arab News Agency.

They should have known what sort of response their blandly innnocent item would draw. Editors in America and Britain perked up their ears. Not only was it Kipling's Mowgli and Edgar Rice Burrough's Tarzan rolled up in one, but it was the greatest sports announcement of the age. Hadn't the article said that the boy kept pace with the gazelles and that the hunters chased them for an hour in a car before the boy

The Gazelle Boy

fell exhausted? And wasn't it a known fact that gazelles run at a speed of fifty miles an hour?

Here, then, was the world's fastest human. While grown men argued hotly about the possibility of a four-minute mile, a mere boy not only ran it in approximately one minute and thirty seconds, but rolled off this time mile after mile for an hour. The world's greatest miler, Gunder Haegg, set the record with 4:01.4 minutes. If Haegg could keep up that speed for an hour then he would be doing only 14.9 miles an hour.

Hurried queries from harried editors sped back to the parched Middle East desert and routed correspondents out of such oases as the Long Bar at Shepheard's and sent them on the quest for the miraculous Gazelle Boy. The correspondent from the London *Sunday Express* came through from fabled Bagdad with a story rivaling those told in the *Arabian Nights*. According to the *Express*, Prince "Lawrence" el Shaalan, while hunting gazelles, ran across a herd somewhere near the Damascus-Bagdad caravan route. He fired at them and was astonished to see what appeared to be a boy racing with a half-human, half-animal gait. The Prince dropped his gun in amazement and gave chase in his car. Although he was traveling at fifty miles an hour the boy stayed well out in front of him until, at the end of a fifty-mile chase, the boy tripped over a boulder and fell.

Then came a quote from the Prince: "He looked up at us with fear staring from his luminous eyes and shrank from our touch, emitting the sounds of a wounded gazelle." Doctors who examined the boy placed his age at about fifteen years. They recalled the famous case of Kamala, the Indian wolf-girl, who sometimes howled at night, and spoke only forty-five words seven years after capture.

This piece was followed by the clincher, an article that was accompanied by the first photographs of the Gazelle Boy. These showed a nude, lithe, handsome boy of about twelve, bound hand and foot, holding some drooping weeds, supposedly his dinner, and looking wistfully off into the distance. The photo was obtained by an enterprising free-lance Arab reporter, Hussein Hosny, who sent the photo and story to *Akhbar el Yom* (*News of the Day*), large Arab news weekly run by Mustapha Amin Youssef Bey and his twin brother Ali, the Peck's bad boys of Egyptian journalism.

The story stated that nine hunters went out in two cars and came to a place roughly four hundred kilometers north of Amman, capital of Trans-Jordan. They saw a large herd of gazelles running at full speed and they gave chase in their cars for almost an hour when suddenly the Gazelle Boy, who had been running in their midst, collapsed from exhaustion. Each hunter had a different interpretation of how the boy happened to be there, but the most logical was that he was the unwanted bastard offspring of a prostitute who had cast him off and that he had been adopted by the herd, a maternal act they were known to perform, according to *Akhbar el Yom*. This was a most interesting bit of information for Westerners who, in fact and fiction, had heard about a wide variety of beasts who have adopted humans, but were learning for the first time that gazelles could be included in the list.

The writer then detailed how he set off from Jerusalem and how he went to the town of Kamar on the Syrian-Iraq frontier where he found the boy living under the patronage of the El Tamar tribe, and its chief, Haj Mohammed Ayack (Haj is an honorary title placed before the name of a Moslem who has made the pilgrimage to Mecca). Here the boy was under the constant guard of a tribesman armed with a carbine. According to the guard, whom the writer says he interviewed, the boy would not sleep normally, but rather on his feet. He would not utter a single word. He was temperamental and hated strangers. The tribe tried to make him put on clothing, but did not succeed because he preferred to stay in the nude. He was handsome with big eyes, clean-cut features, a fair, thin body that was very strong and blond hair, unusual in an Arab. When first captured he refused to eat what was offered him, preferring grass. Gradually he began to eat bread and fruit, but even these he wouldn't eat unless he was down on his hands and knees.

The people of this tribe are in constant motion, never settling in any one place because they realize that the governments of Trans-Jordan, Syria and Iraq all claim the boy. In fact, the chief of the tribe has refused one thousand pounds from the Syrian government because the chief wants the boy to help him hunt gazelles. Also, says Hussein Hosny, it will be quite useless for anyone to try to seek out this boy because, aside from his natural hostility toward the press, the tribe will have lost itself in the vast trackless desert. And, to discourage the press further, Hosny points out that the armed guard could be counted upon to use his weapon.

"Did you ever show him (the Gazelle Boy) to a doctor?" Hosny asked.

"Never," said Haj Mohammed. "And I don't intend to."

Not to be outdone by their British and Arabian rivals, an American news agency of repute—the United Press, to be precise—launched its "gazelle editor" on a long and searching inquiry into whether the fabulous Gazelle Boy was fact or fantasy, and he, after a safari through Cairo's torrid streets, came up with a honey of a yarn. By-lined Ray Shohet and date-lined Cairo, September 12th, this is what the unerring G.E.'s typewriter knocked out:

"Prince Fawaz el Shaalan, leader of the famed tribe that co-operated with Lawrence of Arabia and who found the young savage, has given his version of the controversial affair. . . ."

According to Shohet, the Prince and his companions were hunting gazelles in the desert by car when they suddenly saw what appeared to be a human among the animals. It took the party two hours to overtake the boy who finally fell down, exhausted. The Prince took him to one of the stations of the Iraqi Oil Company and later he was sent to a Bagdad hospital.

The Prince was quoted as saying that in the desert the boy ate plants, but that the doctor in charge of his treatment doubted he could have survived much longer on such a diet, and that the youth had now learned to eat bread and butter.

From the Prince it was learned that while one doctor declared the Gazelle Boy an imbecile from birth, another attributed his dumbness to the fact that no one had ever spoken to him. According to the same source still another physician said that there was no doubt but that the boy had been brought up by gazelles, and was unquestionably the world's fastest runner. It was also stated that sports photographers had tried to prove or disprove the fifty-mile-per-hour clip at which the emaciated boy could allegedly run, but Shohet in his dispatch did not mention what the results were.

In addition to the story, Shohet was able to make a deal with Mustapha Amin Bey of *Akhbar el Yom* and secure from him the rights to the two photographs which the Arab newspaper had used to illustrate their piece. One showed a clear-featured youth of indeterminate sex with long hair and carefully trimmed bangs seated sidewise on the ground. The legs were so loosely tied that it would have been a simple matter to slip off the double strand of light cord. The hands likewise were bound and they held a mess of stiff-looking brush close to the face. The mouth was wide open in an attitude supposedly representing hunger in the

desert. It was so obviously posed that it was not published outside of *Akhbar el Yom.* But the second photograph, showing the same nude boy, bound hand and
foot, looking wistfully into the distant desert as though
seeking the vanished herd of gazelles which had nurtured and raised him, was sent to the Acme News
Photos which sent it broadcast around the world. The
caption that it accorded this picture scoop was far more
modest than the news article of the UP, its parent
organization.

It read: "NEA exclusive—Gazelle Boy, approximately fourteen years old, was found living with gazelles
in the Syrian desert. According to the Bedouins who
found the boy while hunting from a jeep, the boy runs
at a speed of fifty miles per hour. He was bound hand
and foot to prevent escape and, still clutching the desert roots he had been eating, taken to a Damascus
lunatic asylum."

Most of the world's press played it straight and
another miracle of the ages was born. *Time* magazine
played it safe by pointing out that the Gazelle Boy's
arms and face were well tanned while the rest of his
body was fairly white, evidence that the boy had been
accustomed to wearing clothing. But its sister magazine, *Life,* devoted a full page to the photograph of the
wistful boy, comparing him with Tarzan of the Apes
and Mowgli. Of the many world scoops it regularly
publishes, I distinctly recall one because it brought an
angry cable from my office. In common with the rest
of the foreign press, I had been caught flat-footed.

While this scoop does not deal with the Gazelle Boy, it does serve to illustrate the point I am making and might profitably be recounted here. Under the heading International Affairs, *Time*, February 12, 1951, there appeared a column-and-one-half article:

"The ladies liked Lieut. Gualtiero Gualtierotti, a handsome cavalryman with a toothbrush mustache and a roving eye. Behind his jingling spurs he left a trail of broken hearts. One day in 1936 a pair of black riding boots was delivered to his apartment in Rome. Said an accompanying note, written in a feminine hand: 'To Rome's best pair of legs, from an admirer.'

"In vain Gualtierotti tried to discover who had sent the boots. He was still puzzling three months later when he was promoted to captain and transferred to another regiment in Brescia, 275 miles away. There, for the first time, he pulled on his shiny new boots and marched off to report to his commanding officer. The interview was brief. Gualtierotti sprang to attention, clicked his heels, and was blown to bits.

"For fourteen years Italian police sought to discover who had sent Gualtierotti a pair of boots with nitroglycerin concealed in the hollowed-out heels. Last week police had their murderer— Gualtierotti's cousin, Pier Luigi Tamburlani. Tamburlani confessed after a Rome bootmaker, interviewed by police about another case, recalled making a pair of hollow-heeled boots for Tamburlani in late 1936. Tamburlani told the bootmaker that the heels had to be hollow because the boots were intended for an official who needed a hiding place for secret documents. Motive for the crime: revenge."

There was almost a column more explaining how the irresistible lieutenant stole his cousin's girl, how the killer plotted the crime and how, finally, the police solved the mystery. There was enough screwball element in it to render it dear to the heart of *True's* editor, Ken Purdy, and his editorial barbs stung me into action. I checked the file of Italian newspapers for a month before and a month after the explosive murder, but found nary a mention of the crime. So I went to the War Ministry and they checked through their records for Lieut. Gualtiero Gualtierotti. No such name exists in their files. This was mighty strange, so I checked the Ministry of Justice to see what fate they had in store for Pier Luigi Tamburlani, the hot-blooded killer. They informed me that there was no such person in their clutches. It was then that I understood *Time*, the news magazine, had whipped up the unbeatable scoop: they had reported an event that hadn't happened yet.

Throughout the furor occasioned by the miraculous discovery of the Gazelle Boy, only the Associated Press had remained silent. But it, too, was finally forced to send out something on the affair. The AP assigned its

Jerusalem correspondent, Carter Davidson, to do the stint. Now Davidson, a solid journalist who feels he can recognize a heat mirage as well as the next man, thought all along that this was the beery fantasy of a confirmed bar fly, but he had no way of proving it so he, too, played it safe and wrote that according to the various press accounts, the Gazelle Boy was: one, a mental deficient now lodged in an insane asylum; two, in a hospital in Trans-Jordan eating food, but not grass; three, being trained as a decoy for tracking down gazelles; four, in a Bagdad hospital where friends of the exploited working class claimed that a greedy oil company was training him to do a fifty-mile-an-hour pipeline patrol; five, was attending the American University in Beirut where professors were trying to teach him English in order that he might reveal valuable zoölogical details about his foster parents.

The foregoing press accounts will give a slight indication of the confused state of the Gazelle Boy yarn when the Stern safari jumped from Rome to Cairo on the first leg of a mission which included challenging this threat to American track supremacy in the fifty-yard dash. It happens that I fancy myself as a sprinter, having earned class numerals in 1928, running for the freshman team at Syracuse University. Lest the cynics claim that years of bar-sitting have dulled the temper of my leg muscles, let it be said for the record that during the late war in which I was a correspondent I earned a minor reputation for surprising bursts of speed, especially when the shell was an incoming one.

All investigations must have a starting point, and this one began in the Cairo oasis called Shepheard's. My immediate problem was to locate the Gazelle Boy. Quite obviously, if I didn't find him I couldn't race him, because the sport of racing, unlike chess, cannot be played by transatlantic cable. The information I picked up from the various members of the writing profession gathered here was most discouraging. The whole thing, they said, had started as a practical joke. It seemed that the previous February, an AP photographer named Tom Fitzsimmons had, while imbibing screwdrivers (equal parts of Vodka and orange juice) at the Ritz Bar in Teheran, invented the yarn in order to needle an opposition cameraman.

Being an old friend of Fitz, I checked directly with him. The locale of the questioning was Hess's Bar, the Lindy's of Jerusalem. Fitz gave straight answers to the questions I asked. Yes, he had been in Teheran in February. Yes, he spent some time at the Ritz Bar. And yes, quite naturally, what would he be doing at the Ritz Bar but imbibing screwdrivers? But as for pulling the gag attributed to him, he had no recollection of it.

Back at the Arab News Agency, a well-informed organization on Middle Eastern affairs, Bob Noble triangulated the problem for me. The Gazelle Boy had been reported in three cities: Bagdad, Damascus and Beirut. Bagdad was ruled out by no less an authority than Robert Mason, press attaché at the British Embassy there who stated that it was a lot of nonsense about there being a Gazelle Boy in his city. My own

The Gazelle Boy

visit to Beirut ruled that city out. All that remained was the ancient city of Damascus. Not only did it stand out by a process of elimination as the logical place to look for the Gazelle Boy, but also ANA informed me that Prince Fawaz el Shaalan, the potent Arab sheik who was generally credited with the discovery, was encamped with his tribe on the outskirts of that city. Final confirmation came in a report from one of ANA's native correspondents, stating that the Gazelle Boy, far from being a figment of the imagination, was still in a hospital in Damascus.

Now that I had finally discovered the whereabouts of the Gazelle Boy, difficulties presented themselves. How was I going to interview him when I did find him? According to the newspaper accounts the boy spoke nothing but "gazelle talk." Then there was the matter of a Syrian visa. Procuring one was not as simple as it might sound. The Vice Consul at the Cairo Legation, after asking me for a mass of impertinent information, thrust an accusing forefinger in my face. "And what is your religion?" he demanded.

"What does religion have to do with journalism?" I asked.

"Plenty," he said severely. "We do not permit all faiths to enter Syria."

"Then put me down as an F.R.W."

"What is that?" the Vice Consul asked.

"That is the belief held by all Americans."

"I never heard of it."

I took up a pencil and wrote it out for him. Freedom of Religious Worship.

That satisfied him, and he very carefully noted it on my application. The interest taken in me by the Syrian government was quite touching. When I arrived in Damascus, for example, no sooner had I left my room at the Hotel Omayad than the Syrian secret political police were in it going through my effects. The interpreter whom I hired was brought down to their headquarters for a severe grilling, during which he was made to account for all my movements.

"And should Mr. Stern ask the reason for this questioning, you will explain that we have received a report that his camera was smashed by some Arabs during yesterday's riots against the government, and that we are concerned about his welfare."

In Damascus I went directly to the Public Health Hospital where Dr. Douglas Cruikshank, a Canadian physician of high repute, with many years of service in the Middle East, held forth as director, and it was from him that I received the first authentic information about the Gazelle Boy. According to Dr. Cruikshank, the boy had been a patient in the Coussier Hospital, an insane asylum in a little Arab village just north of Douma. The doctor's son, in Canada, had sent back some of the American press reports concerning the Gazelle Boy, and this had excited Dr. Cruikshank's interest to the point where he had gone out to the hospital and had examined the fabulous creature himself. He had found a youth of about twelve, dark-skinned, with a bullet-shaped head cropped closely. The boy had been circumcised and since this is done to Arab children when they are between the ages of six and eight, it made it evident that those newspaper accounts which depicted the boy as having been reared from birth by the gazelles were somewhat over-enthusiastic. There was a thin circular scar around the boy's head, denoting feeble-mindedness. Many of the Arab tribes in the Syrian desert still treat insanity with a branding iron, the pattern prescribed by the tribal medicine men being either a circular one or a large cross on the top of the skull. Cruikshank remembered noting carefully that neither the arm nor leg muscles of the boy were developed, nor were there calluses on the soles of the feet or the palms of the hands. In fact there were fewer calluses than on the normal Arab child, and this, he felt, could be accounted for by the fact that Arabs look upon feeble-mindedness with a sort of reverence and it was entirely likely that the boy had been brought up in a harem with the women. He regretted that he could give no further information, but he felt that at any rate I could get it all from Dr. Asad el Hakim, the medical director of the insane asylum where the boy had been treated.

It was Dr. Hakim, a short, stocky mental specialist wearing a black-tasseled red tarboosh, who had the complete dossier on the Gazelle Boy. He told me the story through an interpreter. In the early part of July a caravan of the Kalmoun tribe, coming from Bagdad to Damascus, had headed toward a water hole in the vast

Syrian desert, and there they saw a herd of gazelles which took off at great speed at their approach. The tribesmen saw with surprise that when the animals fled they left behind a young boy who had quite obviously been in their midst. The boy, dressed in the normal, dirty fashion of a desert Arab, made no attempt to escape.

When the tribesmen questioned him about the strange phenomenon of a boy actually living with gazelles, they received no other reply than a grunt. The caravan left the boy with the Mudir of the Dmeir tribe, and the Kalmouns went on their way. The Mudir, when he failed to establish the boy's identity, turned him over to Rais (Captain) Mahmoud Binyan of the military patrol, and it was Rais Mahmoud who brought the boy to Prince Fawaz el Shaalan, sheik of the next tribe along the Bagdad-Damascus caravan route. Prince Fawaz looked the lad over and said that he was just a crazy boy who was not a member of his tribe. Rais Mahmoud then brought the boy to the Coussier Hospital where he was admitted on July 9, 1946. The admittance card listed the boy as "unknown Arab."

Dr. Hakim happened to be in his office when the boy was brought in and, intrigued by the gazelle part of the story, made a series of tests. He asked for verbal responses to his questions and, receiving none, said in a matter-of-fact tone of voice: "Your hands and face are dirty. There is a washroom at my back. I want you to go in there, clean yourself and return to me."

The boy dutifully went to the washroom, opened the

The Gazelle Boy

tap, took down a piece of soap and cleaned his hands, washed his face and dried himself on a towel that hung on a rack. Then he walked back to Dr. Hakim's desk.

The doctor said: "You have been a good boy. Here is a piece of chocolate."

The boy reached out his hand, selected a piece of candy from the box, carefully unwrapped the tinfoil and popped the chocolate into his mouth. A pipe was handed to him and he correctly placed the stem in his mouth. This, along with several other tests, proved to Dr. Hakim that if the boy actually had been raised by gazelles, then it was an uncommonly intelligent herd, well-versed in such acts as turning faucets, peeling tinfoil from chocolates and a dozen other small actions which we call civilized.

One week after the boy's admission to the hospital the Arab News Agency sent out the original item. Three weeks later the boy's father arrived at the hospital to claim him. And, also, to fill in the missing details. The boy's name was Toumie Ibn Barakat. He was a member of the Arab el Youmlan tribe and his tent was located near the village of Nachabich, about eighty kilometers east of Damascus on the Damascus-Bagdad caravan route. Up to the time of his discovery by the caravan, little Toumie Ibn had been missing from the parental tent for a total of eight days. How many of these the boy had actually spent in the company of the gazelles, no one could say, least of all the boy, who was not only a mute, but also a mental defective. The insane-asylum officials explained the boy's presence in the midst of the gazelles by saying that he was so meek and helpless that they treated him as they would any animal they did not fear and which they might encounter at a waterhole.

The good doctor hadn't thought of testing the boy's running ability until Dr. Cruikshank showed up with American press clippings detailing the marvelous fifty-mile-an-hour running feat. So far as the results of the test were concerned, Hakim felt that it would be far more interesting for me to learn them for myself. He assigned Moussa Bittar, the asylum supervisor, to accompany me to the Gazelle Boy's desert home.

The final leg of the safari was made in a rickety 1926 Chevrolet. Every time it hit a bump, the Arab driver, who spoke no other English, would shout angrily: "This costs you more." And, by God, it did. We crawled for hours over the bumpy sand of the ancient caravan route until we reached Nachabich. We parked the car and bribed an old Bedouin with the offer of a Syrian pound (roughly forty cents), and he led us afoot toward a distant hill behind which were the tents of the Arab el Youmlan tribe. The hill up which we climbed was pitted with holes and I asked my interpreter to question the guide about it. The old boy said that there was a buried city here and that whenever a tribesman needed money and was ambitious enough he dug down and got himself some sort of relic which he sold on his next trip to Bagdad or Damascus. When we crossed the crest of the hill we saw, stretched out in the arid desert valley, the sixteen Bedouin tents which called themselves the village of Uslania.

The sheik of the tribe came forward to greet us and Moussa Bittar explained our mission. It sounded screwy to the head man, but being a perfect host he obliged. By the time we had exchanged greetings the whole village had surrounded us. The father of the Gazelle Boy took the visit as a great personal triumph, and he tidied up the two long braids of hair that hung down each side of his face and grinned vacuously at everybody. The children gawked at us, alternately shy, curious and afraid. Only the Gazelle Boy was absent and, finally, his father had to go to the harem and lead him to us.

He was a very skinny, bony boy of about twelve— that's the age the interpreter got out of the father— barefoot and still wearing the rough cotton hospital gown. His hair was closely cropped from its last asylum clip. The eyes were large and moist and the mouth wide and foolish-looking. In no respect did he look anything like the heroic photo of the wistful athlete to whom *Life* had devoted a full page. But then, what *Life*'s picture lacked in authenticity it made up for in artistry.

Far from being a Tarzan or a young savage, the boy was so meek he lacked all initiative, standing around like a clod and moving only when he was specifically directed. I hated to take advantage of anyone so helpless-looking, but then I'd traveled hundreds of rough miles for this moment so I paced off fifty yards, cheat-

ing on the paces because I didn't think I could nego-
tiate the legitimate distance, while the interpreter
carefully explained what was wanted. In order to
make it easier for the Gazelle Boy to comprehend,
Poppa went down to the finish line to call his son to
him. Also, a third entry, an eight-year-old, was an
added starter.

The results are not to be taken as a desire to boast
of athletic prowess, but candor forces me to state that
I won the race going away. The eight-year-old was
second. Toumie "Gazelle Boy" Barakat was a poor
third, but he didn't seem to mind.

Never having roughed it with the other boys, his
muscles were under-developed and any contest which
required physical exertion would have found him a
loser.

Toumie took off for the harem as soon as his father
gave the word. He paid no attention to us as he
shuffled back to the calm spot in the troubled world
out of which an irresponsible press had routed him.

Vincenzo Moscatelli

10

Senator Vincenzo Moscatelli is a highly respected political figure who represents the industrial north in the Italian parliament. He is married to Maria Leoni of Borgosesia and is the father of two children, one born in 1938 and the other in 1942. The Senator's rise to success is a Horatio Alger story—with a twist. His father was a poor railroad employee who lived in the city of Novara where Vincenzo was born on February 13, 1908. His formal schooling, like that of the Alger hero, was meager. After finishing the fourth grade of elementary school, he was forced to go to work as an apprentice mechanic to help support the family. He studied at night to educate himself.

277

At this point Moscatelli veered away from the Horatio Alger precepts. He became a member of the Communist Party. He went to Moscow in 1927 and for the following three years was indoctrinated with the belief that communism is a world crusade that must be carried to the corners of the earth and that political infidels must be either coerced or educated into the faith. Those who would not be educated or coerced had to be struck down ruthlessly. The young Moscatelli returned to Italy filled with fervor for this cause. For twenty years he fought valiantly, becoming so successful that he rose to be inspector general of the Communist Party in Italy, co-ordinating the activities of all the regional units; to be, also, the head of the Red underground military forces, a member of the senate and one of the triumvirate ruling the party in Italy today.

He rose to these heights because he followed communism with rare single-mindedness and because he let no obstacles stay in his path. One of those who was in his way was Major William V. Holohan who, because he represented a threat to the party and as such stood in Senator Moscatelli's way, was cold-bloodedly murdered. As one who has dedicated a fair amount of effort to the unraveling of the Holohan mystery, I presume to speak as an authority on the subject. Holohan refused to be educated or coerced. Therefore he was murdered. In order to grasp this fully, it is necessary, in the recital of the Holohan story, to go back to the summer of 1944. At that time the belief was widespread that the war in Europe was at an end. While

Patton's and Bradley's armies sped almost unopposed toward the Rhine, the War Department gave the order for the diversion of supplies and replacements from Europe to the Pacific. Denuding the European front, especially in Italy, meant that the army would have to rely to an even greater extent on partisan forces. It meant, also, that these isolated bands scattered behind German lines in north Italy would have to be furnished larger quantities of arms since it was axiomatic that the better armed they were, the more effective their work against the Germans would be.

But there was a rub. If this aid were given exclusively to the communist partisans, it would insure for them control of the nation's most important industrial region when the fighting was over.

This was the situation that faced us when General William Donovan, head of the Office of Strategic Services, set up the Chrysler Mission. Because the job called for a diplomat, as well as a soldier, he selected Major Holohan, a tough six-footer, who had found time between army hitches to graduate from Harvard Law School, and to serve as an attorney for the Securities and Exchange Commission. General Donovan's instructions were three-fold: secure accurate intelligence on the political faith of the partisan groups; keep the communists from building an army with our weapons; and, finally, build the strength of non-communist resistance forces.

The Chrysler Mission, loaded in a pair of C-47s, took off from the Maison Blanche Airport, Algiers, on September 26, 1944, and headed north across the Mediterranean Sea. It was almost midnight when the four passengers in the lead plane, huddled together in the radio operator's cabin for warmth, looked down and saw pinpoints of flame pierce the darkness. These were the front lines. Beyond was the abysmal darkness of the strict blackout maintained by the Germans. The passengers were Major Holohan; Lieutenant Aldo Icardi, dark, wiry-built, balding, tough, an American of Italian parentage who had been a law student in his native Pittsburgh; Tullio Lussi, sandy-haired, about thirty-two, looking like a mild-mannered teacher of high-school economics—which he was—and who, under the name Captain Landi, was one of the brave leaders of Italian resistance; Gelindo Bartoluzzi, his Italian radio operator. In the second plane flew young, high-strung Sergeant Carl Lo Dolce, a radio technician from Rochester, New York.

The noise of the motors made conversation difficult and the members of the mission were silent as the planes flew deeper into enemy territory. When they passed over the waters of Lake Orta, reflected in the moonlight, the radio operator flashed a series of Y's, the prearranged recognition signal. From below three lights set in triangular fashion flashed on and off twice.

Captain Landi shouted: "I should like the honor of being first to drop on my native soil."

Lieutenant Icardi cut in. "No, the honor should go to the liberator. As the only American who speaks fluent Italian, it touches me."

Holohan closed the argument. "I'm the commanding officer. I will go first." He dug into his musette bag and pulled out an estimated one hundred thousand dollars' worth of lire and French gold pieces. These funds he divided with his men. The soldiers seated themselves around the circular opening in the plane's belly. The pilots swung their planes back across Lake Orta and deadlined for the rendezvous point.

The lead pilot yelled, "Go!" and Holohan dropped into the night. Icardi counted ten and went, followed by Landi and Bartoluzzi. The second plane discharged Lo Dolce and parachute-loads of guns and supplies. The white silk gleamed in the moonlight like giant flowers, giving the dangling men a feeling of nakedness. No gunfire greeted the descent.

Holohan dragged along the ground for a few feet before pulling in his 'chute. A group of men slipped out of a dark wood about two hundred yards up the slope and hurried toward him. As they drew closer, he saw that there were about ten of them dressed in a hodgepodge of American, English, German and Italian uniforms. Some carried machine-pistols, others rifles and revolvers. Most had hand grenades dangling from their belts. Their leader, a young, handsome man in his middle twenties, dressed in an Italian officer's uniform with a red-white-green partisan kerchief about his neck, saluted smartly.

"I am Lieutenant Belli, commanding officer of the Stefanoni Brigade of the Valtoce Division. I welcome you in the name of General Cadorna."

Vincenzo Moscatelli

Holohan returned the salute. "I would like to present you with this parachute as a memento of my visit," he said gravely. Belli led the way up the hill to a shepherd's hut where, soon after, the rest of the members of the Chrysler Mission were brought in. The Major collected the mission's money from them, then listened as Belli gave him a brief intelligence fill-in. The drop had been effected just west of the town of Coiromonte, on the south slope of Mt. Mottarone, a 6,000-foot mountain peak whose base separates Lake Orta from Lake Maggiore. At the moment it was a very hot spot to be in. About a month earlier, General Mark Clark had made a radio appeal to the Italian resistance forces to rise up. The Di Dio group of partisans in this area did. In fact, they went so far as to set up the independent republic of Ossola, printed their own stamps, even sent an ambassador to Switzerland. German reaction to this was swift. They sent twenty thousand SS and fascist troops, armed with tank and cannon, into the region to clean out the partisans. In a pitched battle, Di Dio was killed and most of his forces destroyed.

"It's because we lack arms," Lieutenant Belli said bitterly.

"My job is to get the arms to you," Holohan responded.

A partisan from the Garibaldi Brigade laughed cynically. "You're about the tenth one that's dropped in on us. Up to now we've only received promises."

A band of forty partisans, led by a pair of priests,

came up to the hut. Captain Landi walked out and greeted one of them, a slim sharp-featured man of about thirty. "This is Captain Giorgio, head of S.I.M.N.I., our military intelligence service," he told Holohan. "It will be his duty to plan for your security and to serve as liaison between us. I'm going to try to get through to Milan before dawn." He shook hands with Holohan, wished him luck and walked off into the darkness.

Captain Giorgio said, "I would like to say that your effectiveness here will depend wholly on the number of arms drops that reach us." In civilian life Giorgio had been an architect. His real name is Aminta Migliari.

The bitterness and disappointment of the resistance forces over the lack of arms came as a surprise to Holohan. He dug into one of the packs that had been parachuted with him, and pulled out four 12.7 mm. machine guns of a mile and a half range. He gave two of them to Belli and the other two to Giorgio. None of the partisans had ever seen this type before, and they murmured in approval.

"Once we set up a base, I'll fill the skies with them," Holohan promised.

Belli took off with most of the men to rejoin the forces battling the oncoming SS troops. Giorgio, the priest and three partisans remained behind. Giorgio, speaking rapidly in Italian to Lieutenant Aldo Icardi, who served as translator, said that the entire region was buzzing with news of the parachute arrival. There was nothing the Germans could do about it at the moment because Mottarone was still in partisan hands.

Vincenzo Moscatelli

But the enemy forces were sweeping swiftly down the Ossola Valley and Mottarone would be overrun in thirty-six hours. It was, therefore, urgent that they move out at once so as to reach Lake Orta before dawn.

The Chrysler Mission left the hut shortly past 2 A.M. Don Sisto, the partisan priest, and Giorgio, who wore the religious habit as a disguise and who, incongruously, carried a machine pistol in the crook of his arm, were in the lead. Strung out behind them were Holohan, Icardi, Sergeant Lo Dolce, and the three partisan porters loaded down with the mission's gear. The resistance men knew every rock in the fields. Swiftly and silently they made their way through the night, slipping into the little village of Pettenasco just before dawn. They holed up in the local church on the succeeding day and, when night fell, stole down to the lake front where Giorgio had a pair of rowboats waiting. The gear was piled in, the men took their places, and the partisans rowed across Orta to the Villa Nina, a large, unoccupied shore-front summer residence, surrounded by tall cypress trees. This became headquarters for the Chrysler Mission.

The Major set up a revolving system of guards and this caused some grumbling because the immediate area was considered safe. But Holohan was a stickler for detail and insisted on correct military behavior. Icardi was ordered to be in uniform except on rare daylight assignments, when civilian clothes were permitted. Lo Dolce, who set up the transmitters in the basement, was warned to keep them running only when absolutely necessary so as to avoid German radio detection teams. His assistant was to be Giuseppe Manini, a stolid thirty-eight-year-old factory worker whose resistance name was Manin. The cook was Gualtiero Tozzini, resistance name Pupo, a powerfully built peasant with ham-like hands. The mission's courier—they were known as *staffette*—was twenty-two-year-old Marina Duelli, a beautiful girl of rare courage who was already under sentence of death for partisan activities. Many years later, when I was working on the case, I ran down Marina in Geneva, Switzerland. I took her to dinner in a small Italian restaurant and listened to her recount her bitter experiences. When the war was over the communists and ex-fascists ostracized her. The funds set aside for her by the U.S. army were never handed to her, and other American promises were never kept. The only bright spot in her memories is Holohan. "He was a truly wonderful person," she said.

By his personal rigidity and uprightness, Holohan won the respect of all the partisans with whom he dealt. But it was Icardi, a colorful, daring figure, speaking perfect Italian, who won their friendship. Icardi's first act was to write a bulky letter to an uncle who lived near Milan telling him that his American nephew was now operating behind German lines and that it would give him great pleasure to meet with his relatives and bring them up to date concerning the developments in the American branch of the Icardi family.

He gave the letter to Marina for delivery. As the *staffetta* mounted her bicycle, Giorgio stopped her and took the letter away. He recopied it in fine script on a piece of thin paper and ordered her to sew it into the shoulder pad of her coat. "These Americans do not seem to understand that here the game is for keeps," he said sadly.

Major Holohan finally completed his list of partisan bands and, for the most part, was able to determine their political sympathies. He learned that the resistance groups fell, roughly, into three classes. There were General Cadorna's men, who were rightists; the Di Dio group which was, more or less, center, being composed of men of no particular belief; and, finally, the Garibaldi Brigades which were composed of all the communist resistance elements as well as an even larger segment of workers and peasants whose only political belief was that they were violently anti-fascist. At that moment the Garibaldi Brigades were by far the strongest. The reason for this, Captain Giorgio pointed out, was that their leader had forbidden his men to assist the Di Dio group in the Ossola Valley battles and thus, while the Di Dio group was decimated, his own strength remained constant.

"Who is the leader of the Garibaldini here?"

"His resistance name is Captain Ciro, but his real name is Vincenzo Moscatelli."

"Who is he?"

Giorgio had a complete dossier on him. Moscatelli was a Moscow-trained communist whose only job was to build Red strength in north Italy. Only when fighting the Germans happened to fit into this pattern would any fighting be done. In 1930, at the end of three years of Comintern instruction, he had returned to Italy to organize cells in factories and in the Italian army. Since the party was illegal, the police arrested him and put him through what is euphemistically called a vigorous interrogation in an effort to uncover the identities of those in the armed forces who were working with him. At first Moscatelli denied that he was a communist but the vigor of the questioning was such that blood poured from an ear. Moscatelli, being a man of great personal courage, would have laid down his own life for the cause he served. But the cause, he reasoned, would be best served if he, the leader, remained alive. So he sold out his followers in the army. Moscatelli was convicted before a special tribunal and sentenced to serve ten years' imprisonment. He was released in 1935 by a special amnesty after swearing that he had renounced communism and was now a believer in fascism. Despite police surveillance, he managed to build enough of a following so that when war broke out, he was able to take to the hills with one of the first partisan units.

"You know quite a bit about him," Major Holohan commented.

"I ought to," Giorgio said with a smile. "He tried to buy me into the Communist Party and when I refused, he had me sentenced to death. Claims that I sawed through the bars of his steering wheel. The real reason, though, is that I handed in a report to the Committee of National Liberation, charging him and his men with being personally responsible for ambushing Lieutenant Belli's men when they were transporting the gold from the Pastorene mine to Switzerland where it was to serve all partisan units. The communists added nine hundred pounds of gold to their party treasure on that one."

Major Holohan found himself facing one of the basic problems of those who dealt with partisans. It was a matter that could not be referred to Headquarters. The decision had to be made by him. He knew that he had to bring arms to the partisans quickly. He knew, also, that to give any to the powerful Garibaldi Brigades would strengthen communism. On the other hand, to deny them aid would certainly alienate their non-communist anti-fascist members and make it easier for them to succumb to Red blandishments. He was still wrestling with the problem when Manin came racing down the path that cut through the heavily wooded villa grounds from the village of Egro, shouting that the Germans had begun a roundup.

"On what side of the lake?" Giorgio asked.

"From both sides," Manin spluttered. "They're going up from Gozzano and down from Omegna." Giorgio's thin face went white. There could be no doubt that the entire operation had been called to smoke out the Chrysler Mission, and that a considerable force was being used to do the job, because German troops traveling in small groups after dark ran the very considerable risk of never arriving at their destination. Holohan told the men to get their arms ready; that in the event of conflict there was to be no surrender. Pupo and Manin began packing gear for burial on the villa grounds. Icardi went up to the cupola above the attic where, with field glasses, he kept watch on the surrounding countryside. Lo Dolce went on the air with an urgent message to OSS headquarters in Siena. Icardi spotted German troops climbing into three boats on the other side of the lake. There were about sixty soldiers in all.

Holohan went down to the radio and put through a request for an air mission. At three o'clock that afternoon a pair of fighter planes swooped low over Lake Orta and dropped a string of small fragmentation bombs across the path of the three boats. It was like shooting fish in a barrel. Those who weren't killed or wounded in the first blast dived wildly over the sides. Giorgio and Holohan, armed with machine guns, ran out of the villa, hurried along the shore to a point of concealment and opened fire on the one boat that had not been sunk in the air attack. Their fire sank the craft and they hurried back to the villa. The planes, after the bombing, strafed German road transport.

At 3:45 P.M., after the gear had been disposed of, the men filed quietly out of the house. The escape plan called for the mission to take off for the surrounding hills, hoping that in the confusion they would be able to get through undetected. They marched Indian file parallel with the lake through the heavy underbrush to a point where the road swings widest from the shore.

Vincenzo Moscatelli

Here they turned eastward, crawling on their stomachs toward the main road. From their place of concealment they could see German patrols racing by on motorcycles. At dusk a heavy mist descended, and Major Holohan signaled for the men to cross. They regrouped on the opposite side, then began climbing the steep, rocky fields toward the little village of Grassone.

Giorgio suddenly dropped to the ground, and the rest of the mission followed suit. Clumping down the hill a squad of booted Germans passed within fifteen feet and, miraculously, did not see them. Giorgio crawled back to Major Holohan, whispered that the presence of German troops on the hillside meant that they must have placed a garrison here and that this avenue of escape was cut off. He suggested sending Manin across the lake to Pettenasco to see if it was any safer there. Holohan agreed and Manin crawled off in the darkness. The men spent the remainder of the night on the side of the hill, hidden only by a small clump of bushes, knowing that by morning they would stick out like a sore thumb. It was almost 4 A.M. when the miserable group heard a rustling noise. Giorgio and Icardi silently unsheathed their knives, wiggled toward the sound. Before them loomed the figure of a man. It was Manin. He reported that the opposite side of the lake was just as heavily patrolled. For Holohan it meant that they were hopelessly trapped and he laid plans for defending themselves to the last.

Giorgio cut him short. "That's suicide," he said. "It's

not that I am afraid to die, I wouldn't be in this work if I were, but we've got to save the mission."

"What do you suggest?"

"That we try to reach Grassone, anyway."

The Chrysler Mission took off once more across wet fields, now crawling, now walking, now running. It was still dark when they reached the outskirts of the town. Giorgio led them around the back of the church, jimmied open a window and they crawled in. He wakened Father Carlo Murzillo, the local priest, who was a sturdy partisan, and the latter hid them in the bell tower.

For five days the Chrysler Mission was holed up in the tiny tower. They subsisted on K-rations and apples. The shattering noise of the bells almost deafened them each time they tolled. But it was here, while the German forces, augmented by the victorious combat troops which had just swept the Ossola Valley, fine-combed the region for them, that Holohan worked out the details for Operation Pineapple. This was the first drop arranged by the Chrysler Mission. In order to demonstrate a lack of prejudice, he decided that the arms would be divided equally between the Di Dio and the Garibaldi brigades.

The prolonged use of so many men against a handful of Americans proved to be uneconomic and the Germans finally pulled out, leaving to the lax fascists the job of smoking them out. That night the Chrysler Mission, stiff and weary, crawled down from the bell tower and headed back toward the shore of Lake Orta. Gior-

Vincenzo Moscatelli

gio took them to the Villa Castelnuovo, an imposing summer residence of twenty-two rooms, set on the summit of a series of wooded terraces that stepped back from the shore. The gear that had been buried in the Villa Nina was found intact and carried to the new base. Marina had returned to the Orta district while the SS were in the midst of their search, and she stayed around until they left. Then, learning from the local priest that Villa Castelnuovo was the new base, she rejoined her command.

She told Holohan of the close call she had while delivering Icardi's message. It happened at the Casal Monferrato bridge where the SS maintained a traffic control post. Noticing that the bridge at this moment was deserted she began pedaling across. What she didn't know was that an air-raid alarm had sounded and that the German troops were in shelters. A German soldier ran after her, carried her to safety just as Allied bombs came raining down. After the planes left she was subjected to close questioning as to who she was, where she was going and why. All her effects were searched carefully but they didn't find the note which was sewn into the padding of her coat.

"What message was that?"

"It was the letter that Lieutenant Icardi wrote to his uncle in Castiglione d'Asti."

Holohan's eyes blazed with fury. He upbraided Icardi for endangering the mission with his personal affairs. He also found fault with his lieutenant for appearing in a neighboring town in broad daylight both in his U.S.

army uniform and in civilian clothes, while courting local lovelies. Icardi's companion on these outings—in fact, it was Holohan's opinion that they were set up by him—was Captain Leto, a free-lance partisan who had attached himself to the mission after his radio man and *staffetta* had been captured and executed by the Germans. Holohan distrusted Leto and issued a direct order that he be barred from the Chrysler Mission territory. Icardi was charged with carrying this out. Instead, Icardi installed Leto in a village near the Villa Castelnuovo and warned Giorgio to say nothing more about it.

There were other points of contrasting opinion between the Major and his lieutenant. Icardi wanted aid given on a system of independently operating bands while the Major worked toward creating a unified command with control firmly out of communist hands. Also, Icardi was angry with what he considered Holohan's stinginess with OSS funds which Holohan kept firmly in his own possession. These were to be used for the purchase of information, payroll for partisan units and maintenance of the mission. Icardi felt that it wasn't being spent fast enough and he grumbled over Holohan's insistence on wanting to know to whom the money went, for what precise reason and in what precise amount. Icardi felt this to be most unreasonable, and in his opinion he was supported by many partisans, because this was war and the funds were expendable, anyhow.

Sergeant Lo Dolce heard Icardi's frequent mutterings

and the tension within him grew. Of all the people in the mission Lo Dolce was most concerned with his own safety, and the days he spent behind German lines were for him a never-ending torture. He spent hours staring at the photograph of Ruby Lee Clark, a Rochester, New York, girl to whom he was engaged. On one occasion, Icardi took Lo Dolce aside and pointed out that the manner in which the Major was running the mission would result in death for all of them.

"It's not the Germans we have to worry about," he said. "It's the communists. You know that as well as I do. They don't even have to have a good reason for sending you to Switzerland without shoes, and here the Major beefs about a few lousy bucks that don't even belong to him." Being sent to Switzerland without shoes was partisan slang for murder. Lo Dolce knew just how cheaply both Germans and partisans held human life and the conversation filled him with dread.

Operation Pineapple started smoothly. An announcer, during a BBC musical show, broadcast the key words, "When it rains," meaning that the drop would be effected that night. Icardi, Giorgio and thirty partisans left for Madonna di Sasso. The first intimation of any trouble came when they arrived at the contact point soon after dark. Captain Leto was there with a group of about one hundred Garibaldini. Two of them stepped forward and grabbed Giorgio, declaring that he was under arrest. Icardi spoke sharply to the communists, telling them that if they persisted in this nonsense there would be no supplies for them. Giorgio was released.

A pair of C-47's flew overhead shortly after 11 P.M., flashing their identification signal. The ground radio answered with a series of Y's. Twenty parachutes mushroomed in the sky and floated down to earth. The packages that were attached to them were filled with machine guns, ammunition, wireless sets, food and clothing. Icardi supervised the division of the material between the Di Dio and the communist groups.

Because it was very late by the time the work was over, Giorgio ordered that the Di Dio arms be hidden in burial vaults in the cemetery near Boletto. The next day Moscatelli laid claim to these weapons on the grounds that they were hidden in his area. Captain Leto inserted himself as referee in the argument and he ruled that the disputed arms be split between Di Dio and Moscatelli. The net result was that Moscatelli received three-quarters of the arms.

The amount of supplies that were furnished by Operation Pineapple made a tremendous impression on Moscatelli. Up to this point he had almost ignored the Americans. But now, through Captain Leto and Lieutenant Icardi, he pressed for an appointment with Major Holohan. The meeting was held the first week of November at the Alzo-San Maurizio-Pogno crossroad. Holohan was somewhat surprised by Moscatelli's appearance. He saw a pleasant-looking, mild-appearing man of about thirty-six, with dark hair and dreamy eyes. It was a fateful meeting. Holohan, with American directness, laid his cards on the table. It was our declared policy, he said, that we would not impose any

295   Vincenzo Moscatelli

political system on a liberated nation. It was not our intention to replace fascism with communism. Even De Gaulle, the French patriot, received assistance only by adhering to this formula. If Moscatelli wanted arms, and in prodigious quantities, let him demonstrate to Holohan's satisfaction a command set-up that was honestly non-political. What guarantees did the Major desire? Moscatelli asked. A key group of non-communist officers to be attached to Moscatelli's forces to insure that the arms and other supplies be used to fight Germans and not to intimidate other partisan units.

Moscatelli asked, "Suppose I do not agree?"

"Then there will be no further arms for you."

"Very well," Moscatelli said quietly. "I do not agree."

The situation that faced Moscatelli as a result of Major Holohan's blunt declaration was an impossible one—if he sat back and did nothing about it. For Holohan was saying very plainly that he was going to arm to the teeth all the anti-communist partisans. It was an act that would render the Communist Party impotent, that would nullify fifteen years of arduous toil in which Moscatelli had daily risked torture and death. It is too naïve to think that Moscatelli would have permitted his life's work to be ruined. What he did was to hold several conferences with Icardi. Soon after the meeting in which Holohan laid down the law, Holohan was dead and was replaced by his second in command, Lieutenant Icardi. Lieutenant Icardi called in drops for a total of six hundred tons of arms. All these arms were given to Moscatelli.

In the course of my investigations into the Holohan case, I had occasion to visit Rochester, New York, where I questioned Sergeant Lo Dolce. How, I asked, was Icardi able to get OSS completely to reverse General Donovan's orders in the matter of arms to the communists?

"We didn't tell OSS headquarters about it," Lo Dolce said. "The requests for drops were made in the names of anti-communist units, even though we knew that all of it was going to Moscatelli. What I want you to know is that I had no responsibility in this. Icardi wrote out the requests and I merely coded and transmitted them. He was my commanding officer and I obeyed orders."

I asked about the conferences held by Icardi and Moscatelli in the period preceding the Major's death, but Lo Dolce swore that he was not present at any of them.

Immediately after the abortive meeting between Moscatelli and the Major, the participants took off in opposite directions. Giorgio, persona non grata with the Reds, was waiting two hundred yards from the road and hurried up to the Americans. He spoke rapidly to Icardi in Italian. "What happened?"

"There will be no more drops for the communists."

"How about us?"

"There'll be no drops for anybody unless we get rid of the bastard," Icardi spat angrily. "If we could send him to Switzerland without shoes, there would be arms for everybody."

"You're fooling."

"Maybe I am, but think how nice it would be if we dressed a couple of our boys in fascist uniforms and pulled a phony arrest on him. Or supposing we got him sick and he had to be sent back. Then there would be enough for all of us."

Major Holohan requested no further drops, concentrated instead on the information branch of his service. He located the factory in Sesto Calende where the two-man collapsible submarine, which played such havoc with the British fleet in the Mediterranean, was being manufactured. He dug up the German plans for the defense of the Val Padana area, gateway to what was supposed to be Hitler's southern redoubt. These were so important that Marina personally ran the Swiss border blockade in order to deliver the documents to Mr. Jones, officially the American vice-consul in Lugano but actually the OSS liaison officer.

Although the mission had made a clean break with the communists, Icardi kept up a close contact with Moscatelli but was careful that Holohan knew nothing about it. On December 3rd, a unit of Di Dio partisans captured a three-man team of German radio detectors, dressed in civilian clothes, on the road between Pella and Boletto, less than half a mile from the mission's command post. The prisoners were hustled into the hills behind Grassone to await Lieutenant Icardi's interrogation. Here they were stripped and their radio detection equipment was found strapped around their waists. One member of the team was a Swiss technician who was working for the Germans. Icardi questioned the latter closely but was unable to gain any information, so he turned him over to the partisan guards. The Swiss prisoner was taken to the rear of the hut and a shovel was thrown at his feet. When he had dug down three feet the pair of guards let him have a short burst with a machine pistol. Through an interpreter, Icardi asked the Germans what they knew about the location of the Chrysler Mission. The German soldiers retorted that they were required only to give their names and unit identification.

"You boys need a priest more than you do a lawyer," Icardi said flatly. "Now how close did you get to our headquarters?"

When the Germans still refused to answer, Icardi turned to the partisans and told them to go to work. Although tortured for the better part of the afternoon, they still refused to speak. Partisan Falchiro who served as Icardi's German interpreter and who later was captured and executed by the Germans, asked, "What do we do with them now?"

"Hold on to them," Icardi answered. "I just got a message from Captain Landi that the Germans have arrested Renzo Boeri. He's coming here to arrange a swap." Boeri was the brother of one of the leaders in the Di Dio group.

Icardi returned to Villa Castelnuovo, told Holohan about the capture and said that, in his opinion, it might be wise for the mission to move into new headquarters. Giorgio suggested the home of Signora Angela Rizzoli whose villa was farther down the lake front. On the night of December 6th, Captain Landi came to the house of Signora Rizzoli and found Marina and Giorgio. Giorgio told him that the mission would move either tonight or the next day.

"I sent *staffetta* Bruno there half an hour ago. If the move is tonight, he'll flash a light, and I'll go and personally guide them here."

The description of the events that transpired in the next few hours is culled from the sworn confessions of three of the four men who took part in the murder, and by double-checking the confessions to the extent of finding the man who furnished the poison, discovering the location of the murder gun and finding the body of the missing Major.

At Villa Castelnuovo that night the atmosphere was taut. Lieutenant Icardi confronted Manin and said, grimly, "It's got to be tonight."

"*Si, signor tenente,*" Manin nodded impassively.

"Have you got it?"

Manin patted his pocket where he had a small envelope containing 0.60 grams of cyanide.

"In the soup. And make sure you mix it well."

At seven o'clock Major Holohan came down to the kitchen from his room and seated himself at the head of the table. His back was to the stove. On his left sat Lieutenant Icardi and Sergeant Lo Dolce. On his right sat Manin and Pupo. Major Holohan said grace, and Manin went to the stove to ladle out the soup. As he did, Icardi drew Holohan's attention to himself. Then the soup was served. The Major tasted his, complained that it was sour but finished it all. When the meat and potatoes were served, he said that he felt ill and went to the toilet.

No sooner had he left the table when Pupo stiffened. "There is somebody outside," he whispered hoarsely. Icardi grabbed up his machine pistol and flattened himself against the wall just inside the door. The others jumped out of the room. A figure muffled in a dark cape came through the door, and Icardi jammed the machine pistol into his side.

"Put the gun away," the newcomer said brushing the muzzle aside. "I'm Bruno. Giorgio wants to know if you are moving tonight."

"Tell him we'll make the move tomorrow night."

"In that case, Signora Rizzoli says for Major Holohan to come to dinner tonight."

"He can't do it. He has too much packing to do." Bruno looked longingly at the table set with food, but Icardi hustled him out of the house. None of the men felt very hungry after that and Pupo cleared the table. Manin produced a deck of cards. When Holohan returned to the kitchen, the table had already been cleared and the four men were playing *scopone,* a game similar to rummy. He watched for a while but, feeling worse, went up to his room. After the third game, Pupo asked, "Is he still alive?"

"I don't know," Icardi said.

Pupo went to the foot of the stairs and listened. He could hear Holohan groaning in agony. He came back to the table and said, "He is still alive."

301   **Vincenzo Moscatelli**

"Does poison leave traces in a body for years?" Icardi asked thoughtfully.

"It sure does," Lo Dolce responded.

"Then we have to shoot him, anyway."

"Yeah, but who?"

Icardi jerked his thumb at Manin. "Not me," the partisan said decisively.

"All right, if you're yellow," Icardi sneered. "I'll toss Lo Dolce." He took a coin from his pocket and flipped it into the air. "Heads," Lo Dolce cried. The coin dropped to the floor, heads up.

Lo Dolce shivered nervously but tried not to show it. "Always winning at the wrong time," he said in an attempt at humor. Nobody laughed.

"Pupo, let him have your gun," Icardi said. The sergeant took the 9 mm. Beretta automatic that was handed to him and walked shakily up the steps. As he entered Holohan's bedroom, the Major sat up in bed. "Who is it?" he asked. Lo Dolce shot him twice through the head.

Icardi sprang into the room with a towel to stop the flow of blood. While Manin helped roll the body into a sleeping bag, Pupo fingered the Major's gold wristwatch. "Let it alone, you fool," Icardi said sharply. "The CID looks for little things like that."

Now that the murder was committed, the killers worked surely and swiftly. The Mission's money was carefully collected and given to Icardi. Lo Dolce returned the Beretta to Pupo, told him to drop it in the lake. Manin and Pupo carried the body down to the shore front and dumped it into a rowboat. They tied a strong cord around it and looped the other end around a heavy stone. About one hundred yards out they threw the body over the side. Pupo pulled the murder gun out of his pocket, thought a moment, came to the conclusion that it would be a criminal waste to throw it away and put it back in his pocket.

With the mission's gear stowed in the rowboat, the men got together for a final conference. "Remember, we were attacked by either the Germans or the fascists. It was too dark for us to see. If anyone says one word about it, even to his mother or to his wife, I'll sentence him to death," Icardi said. Manin ran back into the house for his bicycle, loaded it on top of the other stuff in the boat, and then pulled out his gun and fired toward the house. Lo Dolce fired south with his Colt .45. Icardi, his machine pistol held at his hip, fired a whole clip toward the Grecian columns in the back of the villa. Then the killers scattered.

Later that evening Icardi burst into the Rizzoli house and announced that the mission had been attacked. "Don't be ridiculous," Giorgio said sharply. "There isn't a fascist or German squad within miles."

"Where is Major Holohan?" Captain Landi asked.

"I don't know. We all fled in different directions."

Next morning Pupo and Sergeant Lo Dolce arrived. They repeated Lieutenant Icardi's story. They said that after the fire-fight they went north to the Villa Maria where they spent the night. They didn't know what happened to the Major. They saw him jumping down the

Vincenzo Moscatelli

terraces toward the lake and then he disappeared. Later in the day Father Murzillo brought in a message from Manin. It read: "We have been attacked. I am at Pettenasco. I have the radio. The Major is not with me."

Knowing that the disappearance of Holohan, the highest-ranking American officer operating behind German lines, would be regarded as a serious matter by the OSS, Captain Landi made an intensive investigation on the scene. He found no sign of enemy action, neither discharged shells nor footprints. It was evident, also, that the villa itself had not been subjected to a search. The mission's funds were missing but because Holohan kept them with him at all times, it was assumed that they were with him now. The only explanation was that the Americans were seized by panic and had raced out of the house firing blindly. But if there had been no real fight, then what happened to the Major? To Captain Landi's mind it was a physical impossibility for a hulking figure like Holohan, dressed in an American uniform, speaking not a word of Italian, to disappear without a trace.

Holohan was a deeply religious Catholic and priests in the partisan movement used to hold services at the command post every Sunday. Because he was a great favorite with all of them, Captain Landi asked them to launch a search for the missing man. They scoured the countryside and, on one pretext or another, questioned all their parishioners. They also came up with a total blank. At the end of the week, with the Major still missing, Landi wrote a long report which he handed to a *staffetta* for delivery to Switzerland. In it was his frank admission that he lacked the experience necessary to get to the bottom of the mystery and that it was urgently necessary for the OSS to send down a trained investigator. The courier who was carrying this report, while running the blockade, was captured and executed by the Germans.

Captain Landi radioed the following message to the OSS base in Siena asking them to advise Icardi:

"ONE X GERMANS CAPTURED LIEUTENANT IKE'S COURIER X COURIER KILLED AND PAPERS IN HIS POSSESSION INDICATING POSITIONS AND COUNTERSIGNS X PLEASE IMMEDIATELY ADVISE IKE REPEAT IKE TO TAKE NECESSARY MEASURES X TWO X TRANSMIT URGENT INFORMATION AND VERY SECRET OUR BASE IN SWITZERLAND IS ADVISABLE FOR SAFETY TRANSMIT TO US AND WE SHALL TRANSMIT SWITZERLAND X THREE X KEEP US INFORMED MEASURES TAKEN"

As its new commanding officer, Ike Icardi moved the Chrysler Mission into the Villa Peverelli. Under him fifty-one drops of arms and ammunitions were made to the partisans. Of these, fifty-one drops in their entirety went to Moscatelli whose collaboration with Lieutenant Icardi was now an open one. Giorgio made no complaint, at the time, about this. Icardi gave him $16,000 to invest in a toy factory in which Giorgio and Icardi would be partners. Icardi claims that he came into possession of the $16,000 by pocketing the difference between the legal and black market price of gold coins

Vincenzo Moscatelli

that he exchanged for Major Holohan. The toy factory failed.

In the middle of January the mission moved to the mountain village of Quarna. Here Lo Dolce's mind snapped. One night he tied bedsheets together, climbed over the balcony and ran barefoot through the snow screaming that the partisans wanted to kill him. Pupo heard the commotion and chased after him. He calmed the Sergeant, told him to stay put while he went back to the villa for shoes and clothing. When he returned, Lo Dolce was gone. A woman with partisan sympathies found him the next morning lying in a heap of chestnut burrs suffering from exposure. He was taken back to the villa and Icardi waited until he recovered, then shipped him to Switzerland.

At the end of the war Moscatelli emerged as the most powerful single military figure in north Italy. His forces effectively filled the void left by fascism's collapse. The Allied Control Commission, acting on the recommendation of the OSS, named Moscatelli mayor of the city of Novara. He served in this capacity from April, 1945, to June 2, 1946, when he resigned to devote himself entirely to Party affairs. Shortly thereafter he was nominated for senator on the communist ticket and was elected.

As a hero of the liberation he was nominated for the post of Minister of War in the new Italian republic. When forthright General Charles Dasher, U.S., head of the Rome Allied Area Command, heard about it, he sent word to the Premier that if Moscatelli got the job, there wouldn't be a government, and the nomination was withdrawn. As a footnote, Captain Leto, distrusted by Holohan and the secret liaison between Icardi and Moscatelli, two years later was charged by Italy with being a spy for Russia.

The fate of Major Holohan was one of the real mysteries of the war. Time and again General Donovan, who felt a personal responsibility in the matter, sent in teams of investigators without result. Even Icardi felt called upon to make some sort of explanation and he wrote the following letter to Joseph Holahan, a New York stockbroker:

"What happened to your brother I will not venture to even surmise for we above all others who were accustomed to seeing dead bodies lying beside the road and hardly taking the time to see who it might be, can appreciate how cheap life was in the situation we found ourselves. One's life could be taken away at any time, by friend or foe, or even by a disinterested party, perhaps just for the joy of killing, or even for no reason at all.

"I feel this, that perhaps some day something may come to light concerning the disappearance of your brother and I for one hope that this should be soon, for until something does come up, even we, who were his officers and men, are subject to suspicion as to his fate."

But two things happened. The first occurred when Italian agents solved the mystery of communist Plan X. Throughout January and February, 1951, they swooped down on scores of factory buildings in north

Italy. They smashed through phony passages and bricked-up air-raid shelters, uncovered hidden caches of .50-caliber machine guns, hand grenades, rifles and cleverly disposed dynamite depots, ready for instant detonation.

The plan was an ingenious one. On X day—the day the Western powers would be at war with Russia— Red workers would seize control of the plants. These would become self-sustaining fortresses inside the large cities. Should a factory be threatened with recapture, a single flick of a switch and the plant would be neutralized for the duration. More than that, all Italy would be rendered economically helpless.

The weapons with which the plan was to be executed were in excellent condition. And they were of the highest quality, as well they might be, because most of them had been manufactured in the United States. Intelligence men who were called in to examine the rich haul stared bitterly at American arms ready to be used against Americans and their friends. Their bitterness was deepened by the knowledge that what they were looking at was part of the six hundred tons of arms that the Chrysler Mission had parachuted behind German lines during the war. They did not know then that these arms had all gone to Senator Moscatelli. They found that out when the second event happened.

This was the publication in September, 1951, of the Holohan story. This broke the case wide open. It showed the direct connection between the murder of Holohan and the arming of Moscatelli, between the arming of

Moscatelli and the arms employed in putting lethal teeth into Plan X.

The Senator, in his home in Turin, read about the disclosures in *L'Europeo,* leading Italian weekly which holds the exclusive reprint rights for my articles in Italy. His first reactions were cautious. He deplored the use of violence and then said that he found it impossible to believe that Icardi, whom he knew to be a fine, upstanding young man, could have had any part in such a horrible murder. Much later, when the Italian authorities showed that they intended to proceed vigorously in the matter, Moscatelli dumped his upstanding young friend. He found it easier to believe that he was involved in the murder. "They [Icardi and Lo Dolce] committed the murder," he said darkly, "on orders from the U.S. State Department because Holohan was endangering the safety of the mission." (In my recent visit to the United States to give testimony before the House Armed Services Committee, I heard this absolutely false and malicious statement made by people whose source of information was barroom gossip, high-class bars, if you please.)

The most immediate reaction to my story came from Clayton Fritchey, Assistant Secretary of the Defense Department. He was appalled at the prospect of a full-sized scandal in his department because it had tried to hush up the matter, and in order to blunt the impact of these disclosures, he hastened to issue that very day a lengthy statement on the case. Because speed was of the essence, there was no time to dig through his department's voluminous files. It was far simpler, and speedier, to use the printed article which had already digested the facts.

Mr. Fritchey prepared the article in that manner. Of course, there are certain disadvantages to working like that. One never knows when the author might not be in error over some of his facts. Should one reprint the errors faithfully, one would find oneself in the position of the pickpocket whose fingers are caught in a mousetrap concealed in the victim's pocket. In my original article I noted that the murder house was a twenty-two-room villa. I never did make an accurate count of the rooms when, in the course of my snooping, I investigated this structure in the company of Captain Giorgio. I merely guessed at it. Actually the Villa Castelnuovo might have eighteen rooms or twenty-four or twenty-five rooms. The chances are only one in a hundred that it will have twenty-two rooms. Mr. Fritchey's statement blithely reports that the murder took place in a twenty-two-room villa. In the original article I misspelled the name of Manini, one of the Italian killers. I spelled it with a double "n." Mr. Fritchey copied my spelling even though his Defense Department records had the correct spelling. I wrote, "The party carried with it radio-sending sets, arms, and an estimated one hundred thousand dollars in gold, American currency and Swiss francs." Mr. Fritchey's release gave it exactly that way even though the hundred-thousand-dollar figure was strictly my personal estimate and is not to be found in any official or unofficial report on the case. Also, I erred when I said that Holohan carried Swiss francs with him. Mr. Fritchey by coincidence erred in the same way. Such talent as was displayed by this public servant had to be rewarded and it was. Mr. Fritchey was promoted by Harry Truman to the post of presidential secretary.

Moscatelli's fine hand runs throughout the entire Holohan story. He had the most compelling reason for wanting the Major out of the way. He profited most from the murder. I must confess that in the course of my investigations of the case I tried desperately to come up with the evidence that would permit the Italian government to indict the Senator for murder. I lacked only one element to complete the chain of evidence and that was a statement from Aldo Icardi with whom he worked so closely. Sergeant Lo Dolce has already gone on record with the information that Icardi held his conferences with Moscatelli out of the presence of his subordinate and that he never once confided the nature of his relations with the communist leader nor what their individual conferences were about. Obviously, therefore, Icardi is a key figure in the investigation, not only because he, himself, is implicated in the murder, but because he holds the key to a possible trial for murder of the Italian political leader. It took an independent investigation put in motion by a pair of honest and forthright gentlemen—W. Sterling Cole, a New York State Republican and a distinct credit to the House of Representatives in which he sits, and John Courtney, a Minnesota Democrat, both of whom hold the old-fashioned notion that murderers should be made to answer for their crimes—to uncover the disquieting fact that since the time Mr. Fritchey's department became aware of Aldo Icardi's connection with the murder of Major Holohan, no attempt has been made by them or by any other official agency to question him. Soon after Cole and Courtney began taking testimony on this matter, the Italian government requested the extradition of Icardi and Lo Dolce, both of whom, along with Manini and Pupo Tozzini, are under indictment for murder. They have, therefore, suspended their hearings until such time as the United States courts come to a decision on this point.* Should the request be an adverse one, they will resume their work in getting to the bottom of the mystery, for they, too, seek the missing link that will transform the honorable Senator Vincenzo Moscatelli to simple Vincenzo Moscatelli—killer.

* In August, 1952, Federal Judge Knight, in the U.S. courthouse in the Western District of New York, ruled that the application of the Italian government for the extradition of Carl George Lo Dolce on charges of highly pluri-aggravated homicide and robbery be denied. Judge Knight's opinion stated: "The facts disclosed in the description of the crimes are so gruesome as to be almost unbelievable were they not supported by the oral and written confessions of Lo Dolce and numerous other testimony. . . . It is not disputed that the alleged crimes upon which this proceeding is based were committed December 6, 1944, at a place in northern Italy then occupied by the German armies, the common enemy of the United States and of Italy; nor that the demanding government was not then, with its armies or otherwise, physically in control of the place of the crimes . . . (therefore) the treaty between the United States and Republic of Italy is not applicable to the present matter."

Michael Stern comes close to being a legend in the field of foreign correspondence. From his headquarters in Rome, this colorful practitioner of a colorful craft travels the highways and byways of the world in search of the bizarre and the sensational. He writes his findings with such zest that they have won for him a wide following, not only in this country, but in Europe, especially Italy, where his reputation is as great as it is at home. During the past decade he has broken some of the most outstanding scoops of our time.

Stern was born in New York City forty-two years ago, attended local schools and studied at Syracuse University School of Journalism. His first newspaper job was as a sports writer for Hearst's Syracuse *Journal*. While a reporter on the Middletown (N.Y.) *Times-Herald* in 1932, Stern's first story involved Joseph Quinn, a hard-boiled citizen who was awaiting transfer to the Rawlings, Wyoming, penitentiary from which he had escaped. The author's series of articles so angered the criminal he had labeled a "love racketeer," that he broke out of jail and, armed with a cop's revolver, went gunning for the young newspaperman. He killed two special policemen and was later captured behind the plant of the *Times-Herald* where he had been hiding, waiting to kill Stern when he came to work. Later Stern became a leading crime reporter in New York City during the Thirties, scoring solid scoops on such thrillers as the armored car robbery in Brooklyn, the Parsons kidnapping, the Ronnie Gedeon murder, and the Nancy Titterton bathtub slaying.

Stern was a war correspondent covering the European front during World War II. Two of his articles, the "Memphis Belle," the story of a B-17, and his first-hand report on the gallant stand by General Tony McAuliffe and his 101st Airborne Division at Bastogne, rank with the finest coverage of the war. Since then Stern's editors have dreamed up for him some of the weirdest assignments on record. *No Innocence Abroad* covers some of the most spectacular. A recent exposé on the operations of Lucky Luciano in Italy brought from the gangster this sinister retort. "I hope nothing happens to Mike Stern. People will blame me."